Praise for Rage to Riches

"For anyone who's ever wanted the underdog to win, *Rage to Riches* is a raw, relatable, and often hilarious page-turning memoir that charts the course of an unlikely entrepreneur's journey, leveraging his emotions derived from childhood experiences to create a new life of freedom, grace, and prosperity."

—Chase Jarvis, professional photographer, entrepreneur, and creative innovator

"Stories are journeys that entertain, inspire, and reveal truths about the storyteller and the world. In *Rage to Riches*, PJ Ohashi vulnerably delivers on all these and more."

—Dr. Arthur Sherwood, Cole professor of entrepreneurship and founding director, entrepreneurship and innovation programs, Western Washington University College of Business and Economics

"Authentic, candid, vulnerable, and humble, PJ has written a wonderfully entertaining story. His humanness is fully relatable while his perseverance and grit in overcoming his setbacks, fears, and insecurities will inspire and motivate aspiring entrepreneurs."

—Pierre Gallant, serial entrepreneur and coach for business owners

"With raw emotions, admirable candor, and heightening suspense, PJ takes us on the ride of his life. From growing up envisioning how his life would be, through deeply revealing aspects of his personal travails, and on to traveling the often cutthroat road of business, PJ is a self-effacing and bold storyteller. The twists and turns are entertaining and well worth your time to read—especially the satisfying ending."

—**Gina Harris, fractional chief information officer**

Rage to Riches

Rage to Riches

An Entrepreneur's Story of Anger, Ambition, and Achievement

PJ Ohashi

Rage to Riches: An Entrepreneur's Story of Anger, Ambition, and Achievement

Copyright 2024, PJ Ohashi

All rights reserved. No part of this publication may be reproduced or transmitted in any form or by any means, mechanical or electronic, including photocopying and recording, or by any information storage and retrieval system, without permission in writing from the author (except by a reviewer, who may quote brief passages and/or show brief video clips in a review).

Disclaimer: Some details have been modified and fictionalized. Other events were omitted, compressed, or fabricated, and dialogue has been recreated.

ISBN (hardcover): 979-8-9914927-0-6
ISBN (paperback): 979-8-9914927-1-3
ISBN (audiobook): 979-8-9914927-2-0
ISBN (e-book): 979-8-9914927-3-7

Library of Congress Control Number: 2024919772

Edited by: Jocelyn Carbonara, Spiritus Books
Cover design by: George Stevens
Interior design by: Jenny Lisk

Published by 6th Man Publishing, Seattle, Washington, USA

*For my wife, Sherry,
and for my parents.*

Contents

Preface	xi
1. Fuel	1
2. Money and Me	11
3. Building a Network and a Professional Toolkit	37
4. Stars Aligned	69
5. Starting the Business	87
6. The Business Evolves	107
7. A Time for Change	133
8. From Five to Three to Four	161
9. #WeAreTeamSociety	175
10. Growth and Growing Pains	191
11. Divestiture	209
12. Project Seahawk	219
13. Calm Before the Storm	243
14. #WeAreEY-Society	273
Epilogue	297
Acknowledgments	303
About the Author	315

Preface

I'm forty-eight years old and sitting on a beach. Not a literal beach, just an expression of sorts. In fact, right now I'm sitting in my office writing this book roughly 147 miles from the nearest beach. I'm retired and wondering, *What the fuck am I going to do with the rest of my life?* My original plan was to take six months off work, recharge the batteries, do some much-needed deep thinking about my true passions, and search out a new professional endeavor. I had just left (or more accurately was asked to leave) my position as a principal within Ernst & Young's (EY) Advisory Services Group. My partners and I had sold our digital analytics consulting company to them a couple years prior and had since been fully integrated into their vast depths.

To be frank, I struggled with this integration, and in a short time found myself lacking motivation and care in general. I was lost, and all the opportunities for success within EY just didn't seem to match my skill set. I tried for a while; I really did. But the futility of my jack-of-all-trades, master-of-none professional identity left me without a natural fit. Maybe because of my short attention span. Or maybe because I came to realize I just wasn't built for that environment.

My intention had been to stay at EY for the long run, as they were a major global brand with some serious market clout. An employer to be proud of. A stable organization where I no longer needed to worry about things like making payroll, but could focus instead on revenue-driving activities near and dear to my heart. And I cared deeply about the people there, including those who came to EY from our previous company and some I'd been building relationships with in the new role. Additionally, financial incentives—for each of my first three years there—delivered significant motivation to remain committed.

However, after only two and a half years, both parties concluded that it was best for everyone if we just called it what it was: not a good fit. So, I "resigned." It was a welcome exit for me, as I was disenfranchised by all the corporate bureaucracy, relatively stagnant culture, and general bullshit one is forced to deal with in any massive global company. My confidence waned as I struggled to get traction. Further, I was earning a seven-figure salary—money EY would've been much happier investing in something besides me, which didn't sit well with me. I had no children counting on me. No responsibilities that stood in the way. From my perspective, the timing was ideal to call it quits.

That was five years ago when I was forty-three. What have I been doing all that time since, you ask? Fucking around. Not in any unfaithful, unethical, or immoral sense of the expression. No, I've been fucking around by traveling the world, playing golf, mentoring young entrepreneurs, exploring new recipes to expand my culinary outlets, pondering new business opportunities, developing new friendships, keeping up with old friendships, running half marathons, fine-tuning my pickleball skills, working on home projects, reading, and living my best life with my wife, Sherry.

Oh, there was also a pandemic that derailed normal life for a period. So sprinkle in a little social distancing, lots of hikes, stashing away rolls of toilet paper, and catching up on the latest Netflix series to boot.

Perhaps to some this might not fall in the realm of fucking around. But after hustling for ten years, building a company from scratch in one of the hardest economies, and then selling it for enough money to set me up for the rest of my days, I just wanted to be *done*. No more meetings. No more conference calls. No more employee issues. No more transcontinental flights to see clients. Done.

But is there really such a thing as *done*? Answering that begs another question: what next? For the first time ever, I was blessed with options that I'd only dreamed about. Lots of options. I could find a normal job and be an employee. (That sounded boring and uninspiring.) I could start another company. (It would certainly have been easier this time around given my experience.) I could continue living a life doing nothing profound. (That would have also been just fine.) I could volunteer my time and resources to a worthy cause in hopes of helping others. (I definitely added that option to the docket.) Or I could stretch my mind, look deep into my soul, unearth every ounce of creativity within me ... and write a book.

I blame my wife for this. More appropriately, I credit my wife for this. Sherry and I had talked about me writing a book for years, and despite my best efforts to procrastinate with every excuse known to man, I was forced to concede when she hired me a writing coach.

I think she just felt that writing a book would be a positive addition to my fucking around. And she was right. I needed a new challenge. A new goal. A new dimension that would be both therapeutic in nature and test my overall mental fortitude. A way to prove to myself that I did have some creativity deep down in my gut.

So let's kick this story off first by setting appropriate expectations for you, the reader. This is my first—and if I was a betting man, my last—attempt at writing a book. And I say this for many reasons. The writing process for me was filled with hesitation, epic levels of consternation, and a bit of self-loathing. It was also a walk down memory lane, reliving a series of stories filled with a wide array of emotions. Although this book is about a company that I was extremely privileged to be a cofounder of, it also represents my inner demons, self-deprecating nature, Japanese American values, and a healthy dose of some proverbial blood, sweat, and tears. It embodies pride, disappointment, and plenty of self-reflection.

This book represents my truth with regard to the reason I started a company in the first place.

Everyone asks about *the why* to better understand some deeply held motivation or justification. Every person has a why to motivate them. Some whys are complex and deeply cerebral. Others involve a desire to discover one's true self. Some whys involve educating others. And some whys cannot be articulated—at least not at first.

My why was very simple: I wanted to change my life trajectory by creating options for a lifestyle I only dreamed about. Essentially, money became the measuring stick—an effective motivational tool—that hid all my insecurities, fears, and belief that I had something to prove to this world.

I believe this started in my adolescence, when I was filled with impressionable ideas that countered how I was raised. I was obsessed with checking out the latest consumer electronics magazines and luxury automobile TV advertising, and traveling to distant foreign lands. My developed affinity for what can only be described as a refined way of life—full of travel, good food and wine, exploring different cultures, spending time with interesting people, exciting life experiences, and of course, toys—was a slow yet significant evolution of my ethos.

This desire didn't come from my parents, as they raised us to be frugal, never show off, and live humbly. Nothing was ever extravagant. The house we lived in. The cars we drove. The clothes we wore. The food we ate. The vacations we took. Always penny-wise, with no overindulgence. Maybe I just surrendered to the vast world of the superficial. Maybe I just wanted more out of life than succumbing to the ranks of mediocrity. What was certain was a compilation of events that shaped my perspectives like a glacier slowly carving out a valley between two mountains.

When I was a teenager, maybe thirteen years old, my uncle and aunt came to visit our family. They drove up from the San Francisco Bay Area to our house about thirty miles south of Seattle. At the time, my uncle, an attorney, was a partner at a legal firm. But beyond this success existed a level of sophistication and intellect that caught my attention. He talked about travel. He spoke multiple languages. He had adept knowledge of a wide spectrum of historical and current affairs. He enjoyed performing arts and had an appreciation for good food and wine. My uncle (and aunt, for that matter) represented a world full of culture, experience, and erudition.

When they pulled into our driveway, we all came out to greet them. I stood there awestruck, mesmerized by the lines of his brand new 5 Series BMW. I'd never experienced this glorious vehicle up close. Then I ran and gave them a big hug, which they welcomed and compassionately returned. You could say the clouds parted and heaven beamed angelic rays of sun onto the shining Bavarian automobile. The gleaming exterior, a mix of polished steel and chrome. The smell of the brand-new leather interior. And the small details that were only to be found on a BMW. The angel-eye headlights. The kidney-bean front grill. The wood trim. Love at first sight. You could further say that at that moment, I saw my future.

My intention for writing this book was to entertain first and a distant second would be to inspire. That's it. This is not meant to be a how-to book in any way shape or form. I won't share lists of tactical or strategic methods, best practices, or playbooks. Rather, this book is a compilation of personal experiences and business anecdotes. It's a story reliving the ride of the many highs and lows of starting a business (Society Consulting in 2008), operating that business, and eventually selling it. I've tried not only to represent the truth as I remember it, but also a unique perspective that is intended to entertain at the least. At any given time throughout the company's existence, we encountered extraordinary highs and painful lows. On multiple occasions we could very well have imploded both due to poor execution and outside factors. Let's just say there was never a dull moment.

Why share this story now? I had considered capturing it for a long time.

"What did you do?" people would often ask me.

I'd answer with a macro-level synopsis, usually skipping over mundane details of how I got there: "I started a digital analytics firm with four other guys. We grew the company to about 250 employees and eventually sold it to a global consulting firm." How we got there was unimportant against the end result—selling out and deciding to just play.

Their response is usually, "That's a great story. You're young. You should capture and share it in a book someday."

Details matter. So in this story, I'll fill in that elevator speech with a few more details, so you can see how it all truly began—and ended.

But before you think this book is only about me, let me contradict myself a bit. Beyond the experiences I share, you'll notice a foundation of life principles that helped me succeed. So, incidentally, there might be some nuggets of information buried deep in the pages that could represent what someone might think of as help—small tidbits of lessons based on the values and convictions I was brought up on and applied accordingly.

My upbringing—especially the values passed on to me by my parents, family, friends, and mentors—influenced my unlikely journey as an entrepreneur. I unknowingly brought those principles to the office every day, as they helped me navigate a myriad of situations.

I looked back at my childhood—the years of adolescence, my professional career, and everything else that led me to this point in my life—and discovered hidden layers of complexity I never knew existed. Don't get me wrong, I'm not exactly saying my life has been all that profound or that I'm special. Consider it an epiphany of sorts, that I was finally able to connect the many dots of my past to where I am today. It didn't require years of therapy, any spiritual journeys, or self-help resources. All that was required was to write a book.

So here I am, doing my very best to squeeze every ounce of creativity I have in my gut, and share the many stories that make up my narrative.

For context, I'd like to offer a small peek into a few relevant events that stand out in my life to help you see why I think the way I think, but more importantly, why I do the things I do—opening a microscopic behavioral view of sorts into my half-developed brain. So, let's start with what ultimately drives me.

Chapter 1

Fuel

It's a beautiful sunny March day, and I'm struggling to find the energy to finish the final two miles of the Los Angeles Marathon. With each stride, I can feel my body's fatigue, the uncomfortable blister on my left foot that just erupted, and blood running down both arms from the chaffing of my sleeveless shirt against the inside of my biceps. I am in pain. The muscles in my legs twitch spasmodically and are on the verge of cramping. Forward motion is the only thing keeping them from completely locking up. But I quickly realize that most of what I'm feeling is emotional pain, not physical. It's all in my head, I tell myself. Dig deep. Search for fuel. I think about the disappointment I'd feel if I called it quits; I think about the failure. I pass mile marker twenty-five. One more to go. Then I think about how irrationally pissed off I would be to not finish, especially after all the training I've endured over the past few months. I am angry at the thought of it. I search for more. A fellow runner a few strides in front of me just slighted me, I imagine to myself. Fuck him. More rage reveals itself. Somehow my anger is converted into motivation. Fuel source located. I dig deeper and relinquish a burst of energy hidden within my soul. I cross the finish line, endorphins swimming around in my head, with feelings of pride, triumph, and satisfaction. I am physically and emotionally taxed, and all I can do is weep.

If I'm being honest with myself, I would have to admit that I'm an inherently lazy person. Self-motivation doesn't come naturally for me. Some people I know are just motivated to do stuff without any external push. That's not me. It's not like my life is about lying on the couch eating bon-bons all day, but if I get the opportunity for downtime, I capitalize, guilt-free. I say I'm lazy, since I generally must seek out motivation to get shit done. Small tasks. Big goals. Doesn't matter. So, since as long as I can remember, I've had to locate an artificial source to push me forward—a source of incentive, stimulus, and energy.

From an early age, I located that fuel, and it's been my driving force ever since. It's made from multiple, absolutely vital ingredients, fine-tuned over time, carefully measured with exact precision somewhere deep within my brain's limbic system. I'm certain this energy source originates from some sort of fight-or-flight primordial response to adversity. The primary components consist of outrage, conviction, self-preservation, self-righteous indignation, and attitude. Secondary ingredients include spite, loyalty, and a sprinkle of purpose. Over the years, I've learned to consciously evaluate any given scenario and activate this fuel accordingly.

The recipe has constantly changed as life's endeavors change. One scenario might require me to add in a little more purpose. Another might very well be all about anger.

Bobby Axelrod, the head protagonist in the hit show *Billions*, said it best, "Hate is nature's most perfect energy source ... it's endlessly renewable" (season two, episode three).

I couldn't agree more. For some deranged and inexplicable reason, I've learned to go out of my way to look for scenarios that force me to think about my fears, insecurities, and therefore anger. Some are created in my mind artificially, while others present themselves naturally through life's day-to-day dealings.

Even with nothing specific to be angry about, I've found myself dreaming up shit that makes me angry, thus creating the biproduct of motivation. Maybe it's someone I cared about being hurt. Or finding myself in a precarious position of danger. The fabricated *what if* situations become the basis for playing and working harder.

Essentially, I've discovered an indispensable need to emotionally conjure up bad things in order to do good things in life; this has become my most reliable energy source.

To be clear, I don't literally act upon these thoughts constructed in my mind. They simply exist, many times temporarily in the moment—providing the necessary motivational response before they disappear from my mind forever.

However, some I hold onto in perpetuity.

This all started with specific events, one after another, collectively contributing to my toolkit of motivation. This bunch of shit that I experienced became a bedrock of anger, which was foundational for me to leverage when even more shit was thrown my way.

My upbringing helped form my attitude that I had something to prove.

I grew up as the youngest of four children, with thirteen, eleven, and five years separating me from each sibling. You can think of me as an accident who changed the dynamic of our nuclear family structure. Being the baby of the family naturally gave me benefits that my older siblings weren't afforded. And a more relaxed disciplinary system and better economic situation for my parents created different opportunities for me than the others. Because of this, I was branded with words like spoiled, lazy, and over-nurtured.

Perhaps this was accurate when I was young and didn't know better, but over time, this shit started to piss me off to no end and push me to prove everyone around me wrong. I had no say in my birth order or the economic position of my parents at various stages in their kids' lives. People assuming that just because I was the youngest meant I never had to work for anything brought disdain that culminated into a vendetta to demonstrate otherwise. I took it upon myself to overcome the stigma of being the youngest.

This frustration and rage motivated me to start working to earn my keep at an early age. Janitorial work. Washing cars. Scooping dog shit for my neighbors (who happened to own two very large Doberman pinschers). Scraping gum off tennis courts. Working as a clerk in a video store. Teaching tennis. Selling shoes. I did anything I could to show I was willing to put in the time and effort. No one was ever going to ever say I didn't pay my way through life or that I was self-entitled. I'm more than gracious enough to recognize privilege when I see it, but no one was going to say I didn't earn what I had.

But besides my birth order and its implications, other significant events helped me come to terms with what I would eventually describe as a *chip on my shoulder*. Particularly one event.

I'd never been called any derogatory, racially driven insults up to that point in my life. To be honest, I didn't really understand what I was hearing.

At thirteen years old, I was a late bloomer of sorts, standing at a generous four-feet, ten-inches tall. The guy confronting me was at least eighteen years old, White, over six feet tall, and had a look of anger and hate that made me feel even shorter. Not only was I experiencing a barrage of verbal attacks aimed directly at me, but the young man also found it necessary to exhibit his obvious physical dominance over me. Animated and all up in my personal space, the stranger pushed and prodded me with an outstretched finger, threatening to take further action.

"What the fuck are you looking at, nip? Why don't you go back to your home, you gook?!"

The insults were relentless, making me fear for my physical well-being while deeply confusing me. *Why the unwarranted hostility?*

My friends Dan, Jay, Shannon, and I had been doing what thirteen-year-old boys do during a random summer day. They play outside. They ride bikes. This time, we were innocently playing basketball, minding our own business as we focused on what little athletic talent we could muster in this two-on-two battle. As the game continued, we were suddenly interrupted by four older, much bigger, high-school-age boys from around the corner. They were all White. So were Dan and Shannon. Jay was Filipino. I was Japanese.

Initially, I thought they wanted to come out and join us, perhaps to get a game of full court going. That notion immediately evaporated as two of the older boys became inhumanely hostile, spewing venom-like words meant for nothing but intimidation. They were all aimed at me, which was perplexing. I'm still not sure why they singled me out. Maybe because I was the smallest of the four of us. Maybe because I was Asian. Jay was ignored, as they focused all their fury on me.

"Fuck you, you little fucking chink! You don't belong

here, so why don't you go back where you came from?" one of the boys taunted.

After realizing I was scared out of my mind, confused, and on the verge of emotionally breaking down, the teen then proceeded to take out his apparent anger on my bike, which was lying next to the basketball hoop along with the three others belonging to my friends.

At first, he mistakenly grabbed Dan's bike. Just as he picked it up over his head ready to toss it, Dan shouted, "Hey, that's *my* bike." The guy put it down softly, even apologetically. He then grabbed my bike and heaved it across the blacktop into a concrete wall. It crashed down into a twisted mess. I couldn't do anything but stand there, physically shaking from the sheer display of anger mixed with physical hostility. Eventually, the bullies must have become satisfied with their show of dominance, so they went back to the covered basketball area from whence they came. The whole incident escalated out of nowhere and lasted about three minutes. But to me, it felt as though that time stood still, and its effects would last for years.

Once the situation deescalated, we left the playground —shaken, fighting back tears, still trying to understand what just happened, and occasionally looking over our shoulders. From afar, the insults kept coming. "Go back to your home, gook!"

I thought to myself, *What is a gook?* I'd never heard that word before. Obviously, it wasn't an endearing expression. I slowly walked across the street, pushing my bike—despite its wobbly, broken wheel—to my home, ensuring they didn't see where I lived.

Back home, I immediately went to my mother and shared what I had just experienced. I told her about the name-calling. I told her about the guy pushing me around. And I told her about the bike. You could see the emotion filling up her heart as she did her very best to show compassion toward me, manage her anger at the older boys, and remain pragmatic in turning the whole incident into some sort of learning experience. My mother could tell I was shaken and confused.

Soon, she started to walk across the street to the school. I'm not sure what her intentions were, as it's not like one could reason with such idiocy. If the guys were willing to pick on a ninety-pound boy, what would stop them from doing the same to my mom? When they saw her approach from a distance, they began shouting the same disrespectful insults her way. And she kept walking toward them.

"What the fuck are you looking at, chink?" one of the teenagers shouted as my mother crossed the road. "Go back to where you came from!"

I stood witnessing from afar, peeking out the front living room window, hoping the boys wouldn't see me.

Laughing and cajoling, they continued throwing foul language my mother's way, without the slightest hint of decency. Eventually my mother turned and walked home.

"There's nothing more to do," she told me. I could tell she was frustrated, even a bit disappointed, that there was little action she could take to make a difference. "Those guys are assholes, and people like them are not worth any amount of attention or care," she said calmly. The fact that my mother used an expletive meant the incident really touched a nerve. She never swore (at least in front of us). She then finished with, "You're going to run into people like that in life and there's not a lot you can do about it. You just can't let it bother you, as life's too short."

We never talked about the incident again. This wouldn't be the last time I was bullied in my younger years. But it would certainly be the most memorable.

On that day, a very small chip started to develop on my shoulder, and it's still there to this day. In fact, over the years, that chip has gotten larger. And instead of merely burdening me, it has been the foundation for many of the principles that drive me on the daily. Every time I was told I wasn't smart enough, tall enough, good enough, old enough, talented enough, or ambitious enough, that small, innocuous chip grew. It became my stimulus for action—an edge for proving all the haters of my past wrong. In time, I would apply it to pretty much every aspect of my life, big or small, significant or inconsequential.

To this day, the growing chip on my shoulder hasn't led me down a path of self-pity. And it's not necessarily about vengeance. There's no victim here. I haven't been wronged. And I don't want anyone to make any assumptions to the contrary. But I know I have a bone to pick with the rest of the world. Something to prove. And I harness that raw emotion into change and positivity. I use it for everything from finishing marathons to navigating the turbulent waters of entrepreneurship. Essentially, I use bad thoughts for good things.

But I must also admit the chip hasn't always served me well. In many cases, it's gotten the better of me. My ready-fire-aim attitude and compulsive reactions have resulted in plenty of embarrassments and failures. I've been fired (multiple times). I've lost tennis matches. And I've said things I'm deeply ashamed of to people I care about. The chip is also expensive, as I'm sure it correlates to my dysfunctional relationship with money. I've had to replace a great number of golf club shafts and pickleball paddles on account of my temper. So it's been, and will continue to be, a lifelong process to learn to how to harness this fuel for positivity and good.

My upbringing taught me humility, nonviolence, and

honor. But I'm a paradox. I thrive with some elements that can be described as overconfident, hateful, and even contemptuous. It's why I have an undying respect for humanity yet am fascinated by old-school gangster rap despite its violent, superficial, and demeaning lyrics. It's why I appreciate pacifism yet own more guns than I'd like to admit. It's why I'm innately introverted but created a career as a salesman. My parents despise foul language, yet four-letter words are a compulsory staple in my everyday vocabulary. This contradiction in life, I've come to realize, is intentional, bringing purpose and character.

My chip on my shoulder has ultimately become my fuel source. I hold onto that edge deep inside of me for ambition and conviction. That edge makes the difference between something I could not care less about, and something I'd be willing to wage war on.

Chapter 2

Money and Me

It's six o'clock in the evening, I'm eleven years old, and I'm sitting at the kitchen counter watching my mother finish up tonight's dinner. She's preparing one of my favorites—a cream of mushroom-based chicken served over white rice. Complete comfort food. The fragrant aroma of cooked chicken permeates my senses, and I can feel my hunger growing. I'm watching every step my mother takes in preparing the dish. I glance behind me and see my father sitting at the dining room table, paying the monthly bills. It's quiet, and he's seated at the end of the table, surrounded by envelopes, bills, his checkbook, a Casio calculator, and a half-consumed glass of inexpensive red wine. His face is beet red from just a few sips of wine, but also from the apparent stress that overwhelmed him. He has a constant look on his face that exudes anxiety, disappointment, and frustration. A screwed-up face, they call it. No smiles. A slight scowl. It doesn't look like a happy occasion, but one that my father reluctantly endures. I refocus my attention on my mother's cooking, but in the back of my head, I wonder: What is so bad about paying the bills? Why is it so stressful?

Money wasn't talked about much in my family. It wasn't explicitly taboo; it was simply understood that we shied away from the topic. And when the subject did come up, there was always an undercurrent of uneasiness, tension, and reluctance. The idea of money seemed shrouded in some mystery and restricted to an unsaid code of conduct. I'm not exactly sure how this came to be, but it existed from as long ago as I can remember. My siblings surely experienced the same—arguably to a much higher degree. This eventually led to very few discussions about money whether bills, allowances, or incomes.

Therefore, growing up, I never knew exactly how much money we had, or didn't have for that matter. My parents certainly didn't offer up any ideas, and it would have been out of line for any one of us to ask.

So, early on it became abundantly clear to me that paying bills equaled discomfort. I'm sure there isn't a soul on this planet who would admit to "enjoying" the idea of paying bills. Committing the time. Looking down at the stack of envelopes staring back at you. Wondering how you're going to stagger the payments to align with your next paycheck. It's not fun, but a necessary evil we all must deal with. An evil that can inflict consternation.

This was evident with my father, as we never attempted to talk to him during this time. My mother would quickly intercept any effort at disrupting his focus. She'd swoop in from nowhere and redirect one of us to a chore, tell us to go finish our homework, or send us off to bed. She knew the drill and played her own role in keeping any discussions about money to a minimum. No distractions. Leave him alone.

From an early age, I adopted a weird relationship with money, and despite my best efforts to manage it appropriately, there are still remnants that stay with me even today.

One would think that if I had a weird attachment to money, then I would hoard as much as I could in a scrooge-like fashion. But no, I never saved. I didn't know how to. I'm certain my parents told me to put the money in a piggy bank or checking account, but it was lost on me. As soon as I received my weekly or monthly allowance, consider it spent. The cool new action figure, candy, video games, you name it, I would buy it.

As I entered my teen years, the purchases kept coming, this time in the form of fast food and tapes or CDs. Later in life, my behavior was exacerbated by discovering that I could access lines of credit. *What?! Purchasing power without the need for cash?* I took advantage of it in the most unresponsible of ways, and it cost me dearly.

And as much pleasure as it gave me to buy frivolous purchases, I always seemed to have some sort of buyer's remorse afterward. I can only liken it to the constant emotional rollercoaster of drug use—an absolute high from a frivolous purchase followed by a low filled with shame. That regret never lasted very long, as I would continue making the same poor decisions about spending every dollar I came across in my name, plus more. It's as if what little money I had in my possession would spoil in time, and I didn't want it to go to waste.

As long as I can remember, when the topic of money did come up between my parents, more times than not, tension would fill the room to uncomfortable levels. I imagine several factors led them down the path of their own financial dysfunction. Values, experiences, and emotions all played key roles in how they individually thought about money. Times were different back then, forming a generation with a unique view of money.

My parents grew up in tough circumstances, each with five other siblings and limited resources. Both were born to first-generation Japanese immigrants just south of Seattle, back in the 1930s. My father grew up on a farm in Auburn, Washington. My mother grew up with greenhouses just north of there in Renton, Washington. Both of their parents came over from Japan to start new lives with little money but dreams of offering their children a better future.

In 1942, each family was dragged from their homes and businesses and placed in internment camps, a response to the US entering World War II with Japan. For the next three years, they would live behind guarded barbed-wire fences in contemptuous conditions, trying to make the best out of life. Their only possessions were what they could carry with them. Although their civil liberties were stripped from them unlawfully, my parents remained steadfast citizens with zero animosity or resentment toward the government.

When my father was old enough, he joined the Army's 10th Battalion Signal Core as a communications specialist during the Korean War. Although he never had to use his rifle, danger lurked all around him as he navigated darkness near enemy lines while setting up radio towers. My mother held various jobs from receptionist to clerical worker to homemaker.

Each of their experiences would eventually create distinct attitudes, perspectives, and emotions around money, which they brought to their marriage.

Although times were certainly different back then, conflict between two adults over money matters has been a constant since the dawn of time. Most relationships, at some point, experience some affliction in this area. How do we make financial decisions? How do we prioritize one thing over another? *Who* makes the decisions? You can imagine, thousands of years ago, a woman blasting her partner for spending the last of their seashells, shekels, or whatever currency of their time.

My parents were no exception. My father would say no to one thing but yes to others, using his own subjective justification. Although this probably wasn't done intentionally, this was his way of ensuring smart money decisions for the family. He probably felt he was doing the right thing.

Early in their marriage, my mother wanted to travel to another city to see her younger brother graduate from the Air Force Academy. She delicately broached the request, knowing very well they didn't have an abundance of extra cash. To my mother's dismay, my father said no, claiming times were hard and they didn't have the extra funds to expend regardless of the importance of the event. My mother's disappointment was palpable, but she did her best to understand and respect the decision.

However, a short time after the decision, my father felt justified in lending his family member some money. As you can imagine, this did not sit well with my mother and set the stage for a lifetime of resentment, feelings that would somehow manifest their way to the surface periodically. Despite my father's retrospective guilt, the wound was just too deep to ever heal.

Years later when I was ten or so, my parents got into an argument, and as an act of retribution, my mother went out and purchased a whole new bedroom furniture set. I'm not referring to just a bed and some nightstands. I'm talking dresser drawers, an armoire, and even that wooden stand you hang your trousers on, all made from solid cherry wood. At the time, my parents' financial position was more established, so the purchase didn't necessarily put them in harm's way. Maybe they were planning on it, but either way, my father was pretty upset about the purchase.

This example reflects exactly how money became a

conduit for physical and emotional control. On one side, you had years of pent-up guilt and remorse for being too controlling over the purse strings. On the other, you had resentment and aggravation, which inevitably would lead to one thing: spending money.

It took me years to understand the dynamics of how money was used between them as a form of control and to incite some emotional response. When my mom chose to spend money against his will, the act hurt him, or at least made him temporarily uncomfortable—the exact result she intended. Neither was proud of this ugly dynamic. Unfortunately, that exposure would somehow taint my own perspectives subconsciously as I grew up.

As far back as I can remember, my mother was addicted to QVC, the TV shopping network that was on 24-7. She'd sit in front of the TV for hours on end watching various hosts present a wide array of shit. Pots and pans. Jewelry. Exercise equipment. You name it, QVC sold it. And a bunch of that shit was sold to my mother who wouldn't hesitate to pick up the phone, dial the number, and place her order. It even got to the point where the fucking operators who took all the orders knew who she was.

"Hello Martha, so good to hear from you. It's been a while since we last spoke, maybe three days ago or so," she'd hear on the other end of the line. These purchases led to a consistent flow of packages arriving on our doorstep each and every day. Eventually my mother couldn't even keep up with everything that she had ordered. Stacks of unopened boxes filled every available spot in the house. This happened for decades. Even the UPS drivers got to know her on a first-name basis.

The ironic thing about all of this is my mother possessed strong ideas around protecting the environment. She recycled fucking everything. Aluminum cans, labels, a small piece of cellophane. She would go out of her way to wash a glass jar that was once filled with tomato sauce, using dish soap and hot water before placing it in the recycle bin. If I ever threw anything in the garbage that could be considered recyclable, she'd run over, pull it out, wash it, and recycle it.

On a random day much later in life while visiting my parents from college, I stated, "Mom, if you really cared about saving the planet from some pending climate apocalypse, perhaps you should just consider buying less shit from QVC." I continued to make my point. "Whatever carbon footprint you feel you're reducing by recycling a small piece of tin foil is drastically superseded by the manufacturing of the products, the packaging of the products, the transportation and delivery of those products, and the eventual disposal of those products."

My statement didn't make a difference. She just kept on buying. She accumulated so much useless shit in her house that she started giving it away to her kids. Random dish sets. Exercise equipment. The occasional casserole dish. Don't get me wrong, when I was just starting out, it was great. I needed all the help I could get. All my siblings also benefited in some form over the years from my mother's shopping addiction. But seriously, how many sets of Wolfgang Puck pots and pans can one person use? It became a family joke providing a little levity to everyday life. Even my mother poked fun at herself, knowing it was excess.

Years later, I asked her why she was so addicted to buying all this stuff. Her answer not only took me by complete surprise, but it left me stymied, unable to respond, even with some rational or witty retort. "When I was five, I pretty much lost everything. We were given little notice and had to pack up what we could carry. All my possessions left behind, I lost. The idea of being able to buy and own stuff is a privilege, and even though I know it's in excess, it satisfies something deep in my soul."

How do you respond to something like that? Who was I to question my mother's antics in the first place, especially given how her civil and constitutional rights had been snatched from her, along with three years of freedom as a US citizen? This shit ran deep, in ways I would never fully comprehend.

I want to be extremely clear that my parents did their very best to treat each other with respect and love. It's certainly not my intention to make it look like I grew up in a horrible environment, or that my parents couldn't properly communicate. We never questioned whether we were loved, nor did we ever question our parents' love for each other. We weren't the most affectionate family, but that just seemed normal. The scarcity of hugs and *I love you's* in my childhood didn't bother me.

Again, times were different back then, and their relationship with money was a product of how their parents managed it, and so on. Their attitudes, idiosyncrasies, and habits were formed both directly and indirectly by their previous generation's attitudes, idiosyncrasies, and habits. Whether we like it or not, plan for it or not, our respective relationship with money transcends each generation with its own distinctions.

They've been married now for over sixty-five years—an achievement very few can claim. All relationships have issues, and I'm simply pointing out how their handling of money played a key role in shaping my perspective.

A lot of good also came from them. Values that I will forever be grateful for. Values that would lay the foundation for all my professional and personal endeavors, relationships, and decisions. They taught me the principles of a work ethic that have stuck with me my whole life. If you show up on time, you're late. Always show up early. Stay late. Out-hustle the person next to you; it's the one thing you can control.

An undercurrent of Japanese values permeated my upbringing, principles that were reinforced through daily reminders and family stories. We never did anything that would tarnish the family name. Everything we did encompassed ideologies that were nonnegotiable. Integrity. Mindfulness. Honor. Humility. Hard work. My father certainly lived by these values.

Not only did he have a nine-to-five job with a two-way communications company for over forty years, but he also volunteered to earn extra income by doing janitorial work on the weekends at one of his employer's service shops. As long as I could remember, my siblings and I would pile into a car and drive over there first thing on Sunday mornings. I'd vacuum offices, sweep the floors, empty ashtrays, and throw out trash while my older brothers washed company vehicles. This was a responsibility my father held onto for years, beyond the time my older siblings grew up and left the house.

As a teenager, I would sometimes sleep in on the weekends, only to find out that my father had driven to the shop and done all the work alone. Despite the monumental amount he took on, he never complained.

Beyond that, my father also earned extra money by engraving custom placards for the company. There was no end to the sacrifices he made for his employer, and I'm sure I only witnessed a fraction of them.

My mother made her own sacrifices by raising four children and managing a home. She couldn't get a higher education, as she was too busy helping the family make ends meet. There was never a time she didn't provide us all with homecooked meals, a clean and well-organized home, or a car ride to our next soccer game or tennis match. My mother's work was never ending, and she took it in stride.

A Vicious Cycle Starting with Shoes

When I was young, I got into competitive tennis and entered various junior tournaments. Eventually I played for my high school and college. At the time, Andre Agassi was hot on the scene and had an image any young tennis player wanted to emulate. He carried himself as a bad-boy tennis player, disrupting the classic yet boring appearance of white tennis shoes, shirts, and very-short shorts. There he was, with his Nike acid-washed denim shorts with the neon spandex underneath; brightly colored, fluorescent graphic-accented shirts; and equally flamboyant shoes.

It was the very first time I paid any attention to clothes. Prior to that, brand names hadn't interested me, as they weren't important to my parents. But for some strange reason, the look struck a nerve, and I did my very best to beg and plead with my parents to hook me up.

At first, they resisted. Never in the history of my family did anyone spend anywhere close to $100 on a pair of sneakers, let alone sneakers that would be destroyed through the daily wear and tear of playing, or quickly grown out of. But I wouldn't back down and accept wearing the equivalent of the Pro-Wings brand. All of my tennis friends seem to be able to afford the shoes, and the whole outfit. One of my former doubles partners, Rob, had the whole shebang—all the way down to the color-coordinated headband. And if Rob had the fancy Nike shoes, I thought I better too.

I was fifteen years old when my mother took me shopping for tennis shoes. Up to this point, I pretty much wore the very basics—general athletic shoes that weren't specifically designed for any sport. They were all-purpose, meaning you ran in them, you participated in physical education in them, you played baseball and basketball in them, you played tennis in them. The pair of ordinary white sneakers didn't have a swoosh or three stripes down the sides. You get the picture.

We drove down to Olympic Sports, a Seattle-area retailer that carried everything from bikes, skis, rollerblades, to shoes. They had a large selection of various shoes for different sports displayed on a massive wall as long as the store itself. *What? You mean there are actual shoes made specifically for running? Or basketball? Or any other sport?* I continued perusing and finally made it over to the tennis section, enamored at the selection of brands, styles, and colors. I was nervous with excitement, as I knew choosing one wouldn't be easy. Prince. Nike. Adidas. Wilson. So many options. I began inspecting each one on the shelves, checking out the different styles and color patterns with attention to every detail.

And then I saw them. The clouds parted, and the heavens shined down on the most spectacular shoes on the entire wall: the Nike Air Tech Challenge. There they were, sitting there in all their glory—three-quarter height, white, with neon crimson and black accents. I stood in awe, admiring the intricate details of the gray plastic bits integrated into the laces and the bright neon swoosh across the side. *Magnificent.* I showed them to my mom and gave her the signal that these were *the ones*. The shoes were so cool, it didn't matter if they fit right, or even hurt my feet for that matter. I wanted them.

No, I *needed* them. I knew that if I wore these shoes, my tennis skills would skyrocket to new heights. I'd be unstoppable on the courts. I'd be one with Andre Agassi.

Then we looked at the price: an astounding $120. I

could immediately tell my mother was uncomfortable. The idea of spending that much on any type of shoes was unheard of, let alone a pair that I'd inevitably either destroy or grow out of. My heart sank, as I knew these were a little too aspirational for my parents' liking.

I knew my mother wanted to buy them for me. But she would need to rationalize the cost to my father. She was stuck in a no-win situation: either disappoint her son, or deal with the aftermath. As frustrating as it was, I suggested a compromise, as I knew my mother was in a tough spot.

"Mom, if you're good with it, I'd be more than happy to get the Nike Equalizer," I said with a tone of hope. "They're a bit cheaper, and I really like the way they look."

They were low-top, white, and had a bright red Nike swoosh on the side. Better yet, they were $75 dollars, a price that still superseded all other shoes my parents had bought over the years. My mother gave me the nod and a look that said, *I'll buy these for you, but you sure as hell better appreciate it.* I tried them on, and they fit like a glove. They also looked great. *They may not make me play like Agassi, but it's a fair compromise in my book,* I thought. I was appreciative of the purchase, and my mother could justify the cost within reason to my father.

The Nike Air Tech Challenge shoes were symbolic in my learning about money and life choices. I was angry that they were out of my reach, and this led me to vow that I wouldn't be in this position when I was older. I could feel the chip on my shoulder growing, which pushed me to think about how I could learn from the moment.

Now, granted, those learnings came in the unfortunate form of irresponsibility. If I wanted something, for a long time I would just go buy it—whether I could afford it or not. I made shitty choices throughout high school, college, and beyond. For some strange reason, I always felt like I needed the latest and greatest in superficial possessions, which were usually one notch above what I could afford. They call it champagne taste on a beer budget.

For instance, during my final year in college, I purchased a whole futon furniture set for a rental house, all on credit. It was so easy to apply—ignoring pertinent details like interest rates and terms—sign, and go! Done. I would worry about how to pay for the shit later. That four-piece furniture set probably ended up costing me three times as much as if I had simply paid cash up front—not that I had that much to my name.

I clearly represented both parents in this scenario. Spending money on a furniture set felt liberating and brought an immediate rush, similar to how my mother behaved. Shortly after, all I felt was frustration and anxiety, especially when I got my first statement showing me how much interest I would be paying. But this time, there was no one to disappoint or make unhappy, which gave me even more reason to spend freely.

Another example is a cell phone. We're not talking about the modern-day mobile phone that every adult, teenager, and most children possess. We're talking mid-1990s phone technology. My father seemed so cool, because given his work in the communications field, he was one of the first people to have a mobile phone in the early nineties. The gaudy piece of hardware is now referred to as "the brick," as it weighed at least two pounds. Nonetheless, I thought it was so cool to be on the leading edge of technology and communication. I was enamored by the status it represented.

My senior year of college, I went down to Circuit City and purchased my very own Motorola StarTAC flip phone. There I was, feeling like I was on top of the world with my new, black mobile phone, which was much smaller than my father's old brick. Very few people, especially students, had a phone back then. It was a luxury few could afford.

It was also a luxury I couldn't afford. There were no unlimited call plans back then. Not even SMS/texting was really a thing. I was rocking an analog phone with mediocre coverage and paying a ridiculous $30 for thirty minutes of use per month. But I had to have one, and I relished the glory by showing it off any time I could. I even bought the faux-leather case that had a belt clip for easy access—a look that made me feel like a grown up.

My parents just shook their heads when they saw me walk in the door with it on a weekend visit. "Why do you need a mobile phone?" my father reasonably asked.

I stood there for a minute and couldn't think of a good reason other than I wanted one. I began blabbering nonsensically.

"Well, I thought it would be good to have in case my car broke down again, or if you guys needed to get ahold of me or something."

They weren't convinced in the least and did their best to refrain from turning this into some sort of life lesson. Their look was enough: *It was excessive. It was beyond my means. I shouldn't be buying stupid shit like that.* But I didn't care.

I carried much of the same emotional money-baggage with me beyond college and into my adulthood. I bought cars I couldn't afford. I overreached on houses. I had shitty credit scores. I represented everything my parents raised me not to be—lots of debt and nothing to really show for it.

At the age of twenty-three, I got a part-time job working at a local wine retailer and bar, thus setting the stage for my adoration of fine wines—an experience I'll talk about a bit more as I explore my work history. The owners welcomed me as part of the family and shared their passion for all things wine. I was captivated by the vast selection of wines from around the world. The sophistication. The culture and history. The chemistry. The variation of color, smell, and taste. It opened me up to a whole new world I never knew existed. I worked there part-time for close to six years and was essentially paid in wine. Fine wines led to fine foods. Fine foods led to fine luxury clothing brands. And you can't have luxury apparel without fine shoes and watches to match. A vicious cycle, and I jumped full-on into the deep end.

Then, when I was twenty-five years old, I somehow managed to make enough money to eliminate all my debt. No more floating credit card balances from one month to the next. A clean slate. And what did I do the very next month? I rewarded myself by buying a fucking Volvo C70 sports coupe—and with a brand-new car loan, nevertheless. I blame Val Kilmer for pressuring me to do so. He just looked so damn cool driving one in the 1997 movie, *The Saint*.

Welcome back to normalcy, and $50,000 in debt. I never thought about the ramifications of silly purchases. My idea of planning for the future meant projecting out a month at most—a paycheck-to-paycheck lifestyle, that sometimes borrowed from future paychecks.

By the time I was well into my twenties, my emotional development relative to money had already reached irreparable levels. Shit that I did or didn't do built up over time, creating the overwhelming feeling of insecurity and uncertainty. This followed me like a dark cloud I couldn't outrun. Bill collector calls. Rock-bottom credit scores. Past-due notices. Scrounging to find the next month's rent. I was reliving my father's woes of doing the monthly bills, without the worry of providing for a wife and four children!

At twenty-five, I married a long-time friend, Lisa, with hopes that by settling down, my financial problems would all fade away. I was earning a good income as a professional headhunter for a large staffing firm. The thought of potentially adding a second income to the family looked promising, as Lisa held a manufacturing engineering degree and solid work experience. But in the end, it only led to one thing: more spending.

I purchased a $3,000 mountain bike with all the bells and whistles. I loved that bike, and beyond my car, it was really my only asset of value. One year later, I was forced to negotiate with my landlord, exchanging a month's worth of rent for my bike, which was easily worth twice that. He got a great deal, and I walked away with only temporary relief followed by disappointment in myself.

This was just another example of me doing everything I could to plug the many cracks in the dam. I would stop one leak, only to start another.

This ill-fated position came through factors under my direct control, as well as an incident that can only be described as un-fucking lucky.

A Best Friend, a Detective, and a District Attorney Walk into a Bar ...

Lisa had a former housemate and best friend, Tillie, someone she'd known for several years. Tillie was living in New York and working for Sephora, the large retailer of personal care and beauty products, as their marketing director. Although Tillie lived three thousand miles away, she and Lisa shared a genuine friendship, and we considered her family. Everything seemed great ... until we were contacted by some detective from New York City.

In the beginning, the district attorney and detective assumed that Lisa was a part of some illegal scheme involving Tillie. This prompted a full campaign of threatening calls and letters demanding my wife turn herself in. I recall the words, "felony," "grand jury," and "indictment" being used. This was a foreign language in our world as we simply tried to sustain a modest suburban lifestyle, like any couple in their mid-twenties.

We had to identify and retain a New York based criminal attorney to help us navigate what seemed like a nightmare come true. I borrowed some money from a friend. I liquidated what little I had in my 401(k) in order to afford the initial retainer required by the attorney.

We flew to New York to learn what exactly was going on. We met with the district attorney and detective spearheading the case. They didn't give us any information other than that Lisa was a suspect in a major felony case.

The whole scene felt like something straight out of *Law and Order*. I waited in a hallway while they grilled my wife for hours on everything from people she'd known while living in New York to personal finances, travel, and family. Then they asked me a barrage of questions.

"How long have you known your wife? What was her job back in New York? How much money did you make last year?" I'd answer a question only to be followed up by an even deeper question. Their relentless interrogation became mind-numbing. An hour sitting in the dimly lit office fielding the multitude of questions felt like an entire day. I was exhausted and my brain felt desensitized. To say the least, it was a complete clusterfuck. Helplessness flooded my heart when no answer seemed to offer any sign that the district attorney and detective were letting up.

We eventually learned everything that Tillie had done behind our backs. Using Lisa's identity, she had created a scheme to embezzle hundreds of thousands of dollars out of Sephora. She created a fictitious photography company in Lisa's name and wrote checks to this company based on the marketing budgets under her direct control. The two had similar physical features, allowing Tillie to use a driver's license she stole from Lisa for an old bank account she never closed. Given all the evidence, the detectives assumed Lisa was in on it.

This all came crashing down on us. The embezzlement. The photography company. Lisa's stolen identity. The bank accounts. The check cashing and laundering of money. The wire fraud. Most important, the betrayal. All of Tillie's nefarious deeds happened while she was "best friends" with Lisa—trips to New York to visit, being her maid of honor in our wedding, and so forth. I felt bad for my wife, thinking, *How do you ever trust anyone in the future?*

In an exhausting process, we tried to prove Lisa's innocence in all of this. We shared personal emails and correspondence. Receipts. Credit card and bank statements. Tax records. Anything we could think of to help prove she wasn't a knowing participant. We even went so far as to retain logs of our local health club visits. How the fuck could my wife be depositing a check in a bank on Long Island when she was working out at a local gym in Seattle?

The evidence that she was innocent was overwhelming, yet it took all our effort to prove this. For weeks, we navigated the ambiguous landscape, hoping for some resolution. It's as if the system presumed guilt before innocence, contrary to what we'd expected.

In time, the D.A. gave her absolution from any crimes associated with the case in exchange for her testimony in front of a federal grand jury against her once best friend. She testified, and Tillie was indicted and arrested. Eventually, Tillie was found guilty on multiple felony counts and spent the next few years in an upstate prison. Lisa never saw nor talked to her again.

I'm leaving out an obscene amount of detail to this story

in the spirit of brevity. I could easily write an entire book on the incident, no doubt. But our involvement left a trail of emotional scar tissue so deep and so long that I still get anxious thinking about it to this day. The whole experience was an emotional rollercoaster in itself. I mean, you read about shit like this in books or watch it in movies. But it's not supposed to happen in real life, right?

For me, the money factor associated with the incident is what fucked me up the most. The liquidation of all assets to hire an attorney. Knowing that I'd never get any sort of restitution from Tillie. The need to borrow cash from our attorney to pay for a cab ride back to the airport.

I will forever remember Lisa and I sitting in a Newark terminal, waiting for our plane. We were exhausted, broke, and emotionally taxed. We hadn't slept in days. We'd just experienced hours of grilling from the New York D.A. and detective. We had no answers. It was the darkest of times for us. We had about twenty dollars left to our name and used half of it on a bowl of clam chowder that we shared. In that moment, I looked down at my phone and saw that I had a voicemail. I had been fired from the job that I had only started a month prior, since I'd taken too much time off to deal with Lisa's predicament. I sheepishly shared the news with Lisa, and all we could do was laugh, as it became obvious that things just couldn't get any worse. Rock. Bottom. Located.

Overcoming the effects of this lawsuit took years, and even then, we found ourselves building walls to hide the imperfections in our lives. Lisa was embarrassed, and I was bitter. After the criminal case came the civil lawsuits. The insurance companies and banks didn't care how they were going to be made whole, so Lisa was named as a defendant.

Everything we'd put behind us came back to the surface. The ordeal was so overwhelming, so impossible to navigate, that Lisa completely gave in. She refused to acknowledge it, so I was forced to deal with it head-on. Instead of engaging with another attorney to help, I did the unthinkable and called the law firm that was suing Lisa. I explained what happened, directing them to the public records as evidence that Tillie was solely responsible for their loss. It might have been a bone-headed move on my part, but at that point, I had no other options. I couldn't afford another attorney, so I figured, *What do I have to lose?* After a few phone calls and time for them to research the truth, they pulled Lisa's name from the lawsuits.

But that experience only increased my resentment toward her. *This was her mess. Why is it all falling on me to resolve?*

Beyond all the frustration, desperation, and embarrassment, I felt angry. Angry that I was broke and had to borrow money. Angry with Lisa, as she also resented me for seeking support from my family members in navigating the elaborately challenging situation. Angry that I was fired and at the mercy of unemployment benefits. Angry that Tillie did what she did. Angry that I was failing as an independent adult who could support myself and significant other. The innocuous chip on my shoulder found new life.

One might think that dealing with a criminal investigation including my wife's stolen identity, a fictitious business, and embezzlement of lots of money—leading to grand jury testimonies, indictments, defense attorneys, and district attorney interrogations—would reasonably put me in the category of *victim of circumstances*. You might actually feel sorry for me. Call it what it is. A shit end of the stick. A raw deal. We were dealt a lousy hand. Insert metaphor here.

Just navigating all the emotions related to it would be enough to give anyone a healthy dose of some form of

PTSD. The betrayal. The fear. The feelings of helplessness. A distrust in the system. Knowing there never would be closure. The resentment between me and my wife. But it was the money component that made it all that much more significant for me.

To me, it exacerbated an already fucked-up situation. I knew I needed to change my ways and adopt a new perspective on how finances affected me emotionally. But now I had even more reason to take control, so something like this could never happen again.

At twenty-six years of age, however, I didn't yet possess the necessary tools to unpack such emotional baggage. So unfortunately, I continued down the path of least resistance.

In an effort to be my own man, I ventured into entrepreneurship with my very first staffing company. I thought, *Why give over half of my billable dollars to an employer? I can do it myself and keep all the cash.* This was 2001, and the internet bubble was well on its way to imploding. Businesses were folding daily, and people were getting laid off in droves. I was grinding on the daily, trying to find a client who would be willing to pay me a fee for recruiting talent to their organization.

I finally found one, a small startup called Viack, and after a month of recruiting, I successfully placed a software engineer. I immediately sent my contact an invoice to the tune of $21,000.

Holy shit, I thought. This was a serious windfall, and it came when my bank account was in the negative.

Then, about twenty or so days into the software engineer's placement, I received another call from him.

"I think I made a mistake in taking this job," he told me. "I'm seriously considering leaving, as the work isn't what I originally signed up for."

I immediately thought of the thirty-day guarantee in my contract with Viack. If for any reason the candidate didn't work out within thirty days, I would be obligated to refund the entire fee. My heart sank. I panicked. Desperation set in.

"Do you think you might have regrets moving on so soon without giving the company enough time?" I asked anxiously. "Maybe stick it out for another couple weeks."

"I don't think I can do that," he replied. "This job doesn't align with what I want to be doing, so there's no use in wasting anyone's time, including theirs."

My plan to talk him into staying failed miserably, and righteously so. I wasn't thinking of anyone but myself in that scenario. Three days later, the software engineer quit.

The internal recruiter called to let me know the engineer had left, and that they would be requesting a refund. Fuck me. A portion of the money was already spent on rent, getting current on my credit cards, and other living expenses. I probably only had about $15,000 of it left in my bank account, pretty much all of it spoken for given my level of debt.

These were stressful times. Times when you reflect and wonder how the hell you got to this place. Times when your self-worth has reached an all-time low.

I had one week to refund the entire fee, so I immediately began scheming up quick ways to get my hands on $21,000. I spent a few more hours working at the wine store and stashed away every dollar I received in tips. I maxed out the little still available on my credit cards with cash advances. I even sold some of my prized wines I'd collected over the years. After a week of scrounging for every nickel, dime, and quarter I could muster, I came up with the full amount. I hand-delivered the check to the client the next day—a painful experience that I will never forget.

My money woes never seemed to course-correct, perhaps in direct correlation to my childhood experiences with money. I recall irrational justifications for expenditures I was originally reluctant to move forward with, but did so eventually because my wife wanted them. I didn't want to be that husband who said no to everything. I don't know if I was weak-minded, or if she simply was that persuasive. Likely a bit of both.

But on the flip side, I probably said yes a little too often. Hubris overshadowed reason, and my ego eclipsed rational behavior. I wanted the finer things in life. I also didn't want to refuse one request only to be unable to indulge in something I wanted later. This created a battle between us at times, very reminiscent of the trigger for my parents' arguments. Oh, the irony and hypocrisy that transcends from one generation to the next!

I felt I needed to control the money, making our major purchasing decisions, as I had better visibility over our general finances. Historically, my wife didn't make great financial decisions, I thought. Consider the Tillie incident. Perhaps it wasn't preventable, but she certainly could have done a few things to make it harder to be taken advantage of. *Who leaves random checking accounts open? How did Tillie get ahold of her ID? Who could be so careless? I'm the more responsible and rational one*, I thought. *After all, it wasn't my best friend who fucked me over.*

It soon became clear that I wasn't; I was easily talked into spending money we didn't have on shit that she wanted. For example, I was later convinced to essentially level the entire yard and build an extravagant garden filled with exotic plants, herbs, flowers, and trees. We even had a vegetable garden with its own chicken coop. We didn't have the money to spend on such an endeavor, so we put it all on credit. I had a decent job and was making six-figures at the time, but every dollar seemed to be paying for something I'd bought in the past. Don't get me wrong, it was a fucking fabulous garden, and we certainly got enjoyment out of it. But it was a shit-ton of work to keep up, as well as expensive.

From there the list went on. Breast augmentations, elaborate gardens and lavender farms, larger homes, Volvo SUVs, and so on. Credit cards and credit lines. We spent. I stressed. I resented. Rinse and repeat.

You're likely thinking to yourself, *Why don't you just stop being a little bitch and change your lifestyle to align with your relative income? Everyone is forced to live within their means, so why didn't you? Don't pawn off blame for your juvenile antics on your parents. Shit happens to everyone, so just deal with it.* Insert any obscene, crass, and gender insensitive remark next. *Why don't you just grow a pair? Just man up. Stop being a pussy. Grow the fuck up and act like a responsible adult.* The list goes on, and I deserve every single statement. Seems very straightforward, right? No, I struggled constantly with balancing a life that I coveted with an underdeveloped emotional quotient, while navigating the realities of money.

These behaviors would lead me to eventually face my demons nearly eight years into my first marriage. I'd enabled a situation that was leading me down a path just like my parents. Despite my best efforts to "not be that same person," I somehow managed to create nearly the exact same scenario. Was it fate—something I couldn't have avoided? Was it essentially hard-wired into my brain, manifesting in reality via some unexplainable subconscious destiny?

For the most part, I don't feel my wife was to blame for how things turned out. She would be the first person to say she wasn't perfect, but looking back, it was *my* imperfections that led us down an ill-fated path.

First and foremost, I just couldn't say no, as I've shared. I lacked a thermostat for managing all of life's decisions. And what if I had said no? Would that have recreated emotionally filled drama similar to my parents? My guess is probably not, and things would have been just fine. In hindsight, I never gave it or her a chance.

Second, I just didn't possess the necessary tools to manage our relationship responsibly and with maturity. The best way to describe me back then was as a late bloomer in many areas—self-awareness, conflict resolution, bigger picture thinking, effective communication, and a great many others. My pride and ego eclipsed reason, and those shortcomings were unfortunately directed at my wife.

So, as it turns out, she was a victim of me, if that makes any sense. This was a product of my own doing, and as of today, I accept all the culpability.

Perhaps as one of life's great ironies, we grow up consciously trying to do our very best after viewing our parents' shortcomings—fine-tuning the evolution of humanity into a more refined generation, a constant pencil-sharpening in hopes of a better life than our parents. One with more sanity. More intention. Less baggage. Less drama. Yet despite those best efforts, we inevitably turn out, in some freakish capacity, to be exactly the same.

I could see where this was leading me: into a carbon-copy life filled with bitterness and frustration. As much as I loved and respected my parents, I didn't want to walk the same exact path in my relationships relative to money. The chip on my shoulder grew. I needed something to change.

Chapter 3

Building a Network and a Professional Toolkit

I park my car, not caring that I'm well over the line separating the next space, and race into the four-story building that houses Hall Kinion's Bellevue office. I'm late. Ten minutes late at that. Fuck me, this is not a good first impression, especially for a job interview. My gray pinstriped suit awkwardly hangs on me, as I don't quite fill out the chest and shoulders given my twenty-four-year-old frame. I tug at my collar. It's too tight, so I loosen my tie a little. I'm sweating. Disheveled. After deep breaths, I walk in and am greeted by Catherine, a tall redhead with a welcoming demeanor. "I'm here to see Maureen Kerber," I tell her as I look down at my watch to double-check exactly how late I am. Catherine eases some of my tension with a warm smile. I sit down in the lobby, nervous with excitement to hear more about the opportunity, but a bit frazzled by my tardiness. The tapping of my foot is a dead giveaway. I hate being late. No, I despise being late. I imagine my mom shaking her head in disappointment. Get your shit together. Compose yourself. Find your A-game. Get the job.

In an effort to best understand my road to entrepreneurship, one must first understand my past in relation to education and work. It's a confluence of people, successes, failures, modest effort, and a lot of luck—starting with my attendance at Western Washington University in the nineties, and including some early career endeavors and a plethora of learnings. Most important was the meeting of all my future business partners.

My time in university can be summed up using two words: Bare. Minimum. Okay, maybe three words if you add in disenchanted. Like I said before, I was a lazy person who looked at this monumental opportunity for higher education in all the wrong light. My attitude was poor, clearly reflected in my sheer lack of fucks to give. Attending college, in my mind, became a box to be checked. A means to an end. A line item for my resume. An example to a prospective employer that I was indeed capable of accomplishing a goal—in this case an undergraduate degree. Get in and out as fast as possible so you can move on to more important things in life, whatever that truly means.

University life for me, like pretty much everyone else in similar circumstances, was full of the usual happenings. A few hours of class each day. Navigating the intimacy of dormitory life with three perfect strangers who exhibited questionable hygiene practices. Mediocre chow at the food hall. Tennis practice for the university team. Very little studying. Socializing with neighbors and fellow classmates. Maybe a late-night run or hoops before going to bed. Tomorrow, rinse and repeat.

I took advantage of university life in the worst of ways. I'd skip classes to hang out with friends; playing tennis or basketball became a regular routine. I'd cram whatever content was needed for midterms into my brain and pull all-nighters during finals week. Somehow, I managed to squeak by my first year with a B average.

I was even less responsible my sophomore year, as turning nineteen gave me the license to legally drink just forty minutes north across the Canadian border. This led to weekly caravans to the great white north in search of cool bars and dance clubs. We hit them all. Go-Go's. The Ozone. The Roxy. Cheers. If there was house, hip-hop, or dance music playing, you could pretty much count on my roommates and I being there.

Academically, I miraculously was able to maintain decent grades. I can't explain it, as it certainly wasn't because I absorbed all the material. In fact, I was a terrible reader with a short attention span and even worse retention. By the end of my second year, I sat down with a guidance counselor and mapped out a path to graduate in four years. Economics became my major. I could see a light at the end of the tunnel. *Two more years,* I thought. *Maintain. Keep playing tennis. Get the fuck out of this place and figure out my path in life.*

I showed up the first day of my junior fall quarter ready to capitalize on my newly established plan, only to discover that sometime over the summer, the Western athletic department unfortunately decided to eliminate tennis as a team sport. They had absolutely no communication about this. No phone call explaining the situation. No letter of regret. Nothing.

Playing on the team didn't just mean we were part of something we were passionate about, there were also financial incentives, namely tuition waivers. Only covering a quarter's worth of tuition, the money still meant a ton to my parents and me. Losing tennis brought a larger financial burden. To say the least, we were furious.

One day, my roommate and teammate, Rich, and I

marched down to the athletic department. Then we verbally unloaded on the poor unexpecting athletic director.

"This is complete bullshit," I declared to her. "Where's the courtesy of informing us ahead of time, perhaps giving us the opportunity to transfer schools?"

"Times are tough right now and budget cuts are affecting all parts of this program," the AD responded. "Tennis doesn't bring in any money like some other sports. If things keep going the way they are, we're seriously thinking of eliminating our football program altogether."

There was some more back-and-forth quarrelling, as she didn't show any signs of remorse or guilt. In the end, that's all we had really wanted. An apology. Some sincere acknowledgements that they, in fact, screwed up. It never came, leaving me with a deeply sour taste in my mouth toward the university.

This was the day the chip on my shoulder reappeared larger than ever, and it led me toward absolute disdain for the school based on what I perceived as a betrayal. I contemplated leaving for another university but knew that credit transfers weren't always equal, and that could push out my graduation. That was a nonstarter, so I'd need to power through. So I channeled my fury into motivation and execution aimed at getting out as fast as possible. I'd grind through each quarter by doing just enough to pass, but not too much, as caring was of little concern.

Somehow, my nonchalant attitude and minimal effort paid off, and I earned a bachelor's degree in economics in exactly four years.

Looking back, I let negative thoughts taint my overall university experience. I regret not taking full advantage of that time in my life—including the opportunities to learn, lean into more connections and develop more friendships, and capitalize on the vast resources of the school. I focused solely on the end goal of graduation and not the means of getting there.

Don't get me wrong; I had lots of fun. Arguably too much fun. Partying. Frequent trips to Canada. Traveling and competing with the tennis team. Intramural sports. Even working at a local athletic shoe store brought me joy. And the small yet uber-close group of friends I developed over that time was life-changing. Enter two people: Josiah Johnson and Jesse Perbix.

Meeting Josiah

Josiah and I first met sometime during my junior year, when our paths crossed in several ways. He was behind me by around a year, but nonetheless, we would run into each other on campus, see each other at parties, and compete at intramural sports. Josiah was quite the athlete and a varsity letterman for Western's men's soccer team. Given we played different sports, we didn't exactly hang out in the same crowds, although fortuitously, we would nevertheless run into each other often.

I got to know Josiah's friends as well over the years—a group of highly loyal guys, many of whom would become long-term friends. Running into them during intramural basketball season was a regular occurrence. Josiah stands at a tall six-one (that's tall, as I'm five-foot-seven on a good day, with shoes on). But for some reason the organizers allowed him to play in the six-foot-and-under league, which was no fun, because at the time, the kid could leap out of the fucking gym and dunk on people with ease.

Another place Josiah and I got to know each other was Bellis Fair Mall, where we both worked to help pay our way through school. Josiah was employed at a small outdoor gear store called Track and Trail, where he sold walking and hiking boots as well as outdoor clothing. I worked just around the corner on the way to the food court at the Foot Zone, a local chain selling specialty running and other athletic footwear and apparel. When business was slow, we'd wander over to each other's stores and check out the latest gear while shooting the shit.

Our friendship at that point, if you could call it that, was cordial and respectful, yet it wasn't personal and brother-like. We ran in different circles and focused on different life priorities.

Even though we seemed to connect every so often around campus, or at work or parties, I don't think we ever had any classes together. And once I graduated in 1997, I moved on to live in the Greater Seattle area, where I scored a job at Boeing in their commercial airplane division. From there, we would inadvertently but naturally pause our relationship, unknowing that our paths would cross again (a great many times).

Roughly two years later, Josiah and I would run into each other and pick up as if no time had passed. The two of us ended up working together at two different companies over six or seven years before reuniting to start our new venture.

Meeting Jesse

Jesse and I were college roommates during our senior years at Western. Even though we lived in the same house (along with two other roommates), we rarely spent much time together beyond the occasional flag football game, intramural hoops, and late-night battles playing Mario Kart (the Nintendo 64 version, which I would argue was the best version). Jesse was a workaholic, even in those days. He ran operations for a student grocery store on campus, so while his days were spent in the classroom, his nights were spent managing all aspects of the store till late, or sleeping. He couldn't ever sit still for very long and filled his schedule to the brim, with commitments that perplexed me.

My other roommates and I would joke about the randomness of Jesse's presence. He'd goad us into going out on a particular evening to the bars, and within an hour, he'd be done. No notice. No, *I'm out of here, fellas*. He became infamous for what I like to call a French exit—leaving a gathering under the radar, without anyone noticing. His idiosyncrasies became normal to us, so we were never surprised when he'd show up unexpectedly or bail at the drop of a hat.

After one year, Jesse found his way down to California where he lived with his girlfriend, Heather, doing similar work managing large dining halls, except this time for University of California, Davis. A few of us drove down to visit him one weekend, but beyond a few emails and the occasional phone call, that was the extent of our interactions over the next couple of years.

Career Moves

Upon my graduation in 1997, a former college girlfriend referred me to a manager at Boeing who was hiring. I somehow navigated the lengthy interview process, passed all the necessary tests, relocated down to Everett, Washington, and jumped into my very first real job—as an industrial analyst for Boeing's 767 tooling division.

First off, Boeing is an extremely large company, and it's very easy to get lost in all the layers of employees, commercial airplane models, geographic locations, and organizational structure. My new office was then the largest building in the world, spanning 4.3 million square feet. I once heard you could put Disneyland inside of it—hard to fathom.

Within a short time, I knew this wasn't the place for me. This epiphany came at six in the morning as I dragged myself in to work after a late night of debauchery. Entering my office, I never saw the light of day, as my cramped cubical resided in a room with no windows, inside an even larger building with no windows. I attended pointless status meetings with middle management that would put the most hardened insomniac to sleep in no time. Care appeared to be absent throughout and beyond our group, except for management's constant reminders on *S5 methodologies*—a system whereby everything had to be in its designated and labeled place down to every hammer, stapler, and paperclip. Nobody hustled. There was no urgency. I think back and wonder, *How in the hell did planes ever get built?*

If it's not already clear, my role working for Boeing wasn't my dream job, nor was I all that excited about working for such a large organization. I felt lost, and every direction appeared meaningless and without virtue. I took the same attitude I'd possessed in college: *just deal with it, as it's simply a means to an end*. At the time, I thought this was what I was supposed to do to grow up and become independent. *Isn't that the case? I asked myself. Once you get your education, you get a job with a large company like Boeing and work there for the next forty-five years until you retire with a pension. With hope and hard work, you can work your way up the corporate ladder, and someday make upper management (where the big bucks are).*

Oh, was I naïve.

I slaved away at spreadsheets and PowerPoint presentations, and ran meaningless meetings with status reports on the building or repairing of tools. A tool, as it relates to building airplanes, doesn't mean a hammer or a drill. No, tools are massive steel structures that house airplane wings and fuselages while people work on them. I was the conduit between engineering and the manufacturing shops that did all of the fabrication and repairs. It certainly wasn't change-the-world-type-of-work, and perhaps my continued poor attitude didn't exactly help my future prospects at "Lazy B," a term frequently used throughout the company.

Picture the character Peter Gibbons from the movie *Office Space* as he attempted to fight boredom and frustration "working for the man" at a fictitious financial software company, Initech. That was me. Only this was for real. I was a very small cog in a gigantic machine that I perceived as having little actual relevance. And that machine placed monumental importance on its very own version of the infamous "TPS Reports."

If you haven't seen the movie, please, go watch it. You'll understand.

The silver lining for my Boeing days was that I got off work around three in the afternoon, which allowed me to work a second job.

One random Sunday, a twenty-three-year-old me walked into The Grape Choice, admired the enormous selection of wines from all around the world, and made a comment to the man standing behind the counter. "This is great! How cool would it be to someday own a store like this?" At the time, I knew nothing about wine. To me, a bottle with a real cork was a big deal, as the only thing I could afford was a screw-top.

Larry , the store owner, graciously agreed with me, and then proceeded to ask if I wanted a job. After a couple of days noodling on the idea, I came back to meet with Larry, and the rest is history. I'd work an additional three or four days a week, including weekends, to supplement the mediocre salary Boeing provided. To say the least, I was not happy at Boeing, but I got by through spending my off-hours selling, pouring, and learning about the world of wine.

Another saving grace came 360 days after my first day at Boeing when I was called into my manager's office. At this point, I had already been reorganized one time into a different division, and rumors of layoffs were circulating. Given my short tenure within the group, I knew that if changes were imminent, I would be the sacrificial lamb. I walked down the hall to the eight-by-ten cubicle he resided in and poked my head in.

"Hey Charles, you wanted to see me?" I inquired with a light knock on the outside of his cubicle wall.

"Hey PJ, yeah, come in and take a seat. As you probably are aware, Boeing is going through significant restructuring, and unfortunately, your role within my team is directly affected. I'm sorry to say that I'm forced to let you go at the end of the week. I know this came out of nowhere, so why don't you take the rest of the week to yourself. If there's anything you need, do not hesitate to ask."

I took a deep breath, let out a defeated sigh, and indignantly thought to myself, *What I need is another job. Can you help me with that?* After a little more dialogue, I walked back to my desk to pack up my belongings. *Let go*, I thought to myself. *Let me go where, exactly?* Oh, and because I hadn't been employed for a full year, I didn't receive any form of a severance package.

Just like that, I was out of there, exiting the massive manufacturing plant in Everett, Washington, box in hand, with mixed emotions including bitterness, relief, and panic. But it's the fear of what my future would look like that hit me the hardest. Fear of how to fund my rent, food, car payments, and everything else weighed me down. And with fear came anger, and the reappearance of the chip on my shoulder.

What to do now? I was twenty-four years old, possessed a bachelor's degree in economics from an average, public liberal arts university, and had debt hanging over my head from a lifestyle I lived but couldn't afford. Terrible decisions had led to multiple credit cards, auto loans, and a rock-bottom credit score that followed me around like a dark cloud. With over $40,000 in debt, it was time to start making some moves and getting my life on the right track.

I applied for a bunch of roles in sales, data analysis, and general business operations. I went on a few interviews, but nothing presented itself as an opportunity I could get excited about. I was lost and frustrated. All my work experience had involved some sort of sales, service, or analysis work. All those fields appealed to me, but I lacked direction on which one would resonate with me the most. I had no idea what I wanted to do, what I was good at, or how I could even apply my limited experience.

This uncertainty brought fear for my future. And if history had taught me anything, where there was fear, anger would not be too far behind. I needed to dig deep.

How do I get off the hamster wheel of financial purgatory? I asked myself. Then I remembered my uncle's BMW. I thought about the Nike Air Challenge shoes. I thought about all the really expensive wines I had on my wish list. The answer was simple: *Make some real money. Fuck the shitty salaries Boeing has to offer; go become rich.*

My First "Real" Job

One day, I got an interesting call.

"Hi, I'm Maureen Kerber, branch manager at Hall

Kinion," the voice announced. I'd never heard of her company, which wasn't really saying much given my complete lack of experience in the working world. "I found your resume on Monster.com and wanted to see if you had any interest in the technology recruiting industry."

I listened.

She shared a little about the company as well as the opportunity within her team, and it piqued my curiosity. Maureen led a team that provided full-time placement of technology professionals to local companies.

We set up an interview for two days later at their office in Bellevue, Washington. This was the first of a series of interviews I would endure—individual face-to-face meetings with each of their ten or so team members, a video conference with an executive named Jennifer down in Cupertino, California, and then a meeting with a couple of their senior staff.

The morning of my first interview started out badly. I couldn't find my favorite tie. I got lost based on the directions MapQuest provided. Back then, Google Maps or other GPS-based apps didn't exist. So I was late. For a second, I thought I might just cancel and come up with some reasonable excuse—something akin to my dog ate my homework. Then I thought about how disappointed my mother would be if I bailed. *Follow through with your commitments* is all I heard in the back of my mind.

I finally found the building in the large office complex, gathered my composure, and proceeded inside. The noisy space was filled with dozens of voices coming from the adjacent room. I then entered an office with a bullpen environment, with desks doubled up facing each other, creating two-person pods. I could immediately feel the energy as people were pacing around in front of their desks, having passionate conversations on their wired headsets.

A large gong sounded at the far end of the office. Someone apparently had closed a deal and rang it. Everyone in the office cheered loudly and clapped encouragingly. It was chaotic with sensory overload, but in a good way. The energy felt infectious. The sound of commerce. The bedlam of twenty or so simultaneous conversations without the slightest notion of conflict. The scene reminded me of the floor of the New York Stock Exchange —with a practical order to the chaos—and I could feel my curiosity growing.

One of the team members I met with was Stan Eng. He looked like he was eighteen years old but talked like he was thirty-five. I think he was actually around twenty-four. Picture a teenager wearing his father's business suit that didn't quite fit. Shoulders that didn't quite fill out the jacket. A shiny black head of hair with a side part and front that stood up perfectly, not quite the height of a pompadour. Regardless, his energy was unlike anyone else's I'd ever known, and confidence radiated from both his communication and body movements. I could tell right away he was someone I could learn from. Every word that came out of his mouth was full of conviction and sway. Stan had swagger. Real swagger. The type of swagger that I wanted to have.

He broke it down for me like this: "We're all individually motivated to be as successful as we can, yet we also work very well as a cohesive team." He explained that even though someone's title was "recruiter," or "senior recruiter," the reality is that they were a salesperson. And with sales came commission. Potentially big commissions.

Uh, yes, please. That was certainly something I could get excited about.

You could tell Stan was driven by money. I recall he moonlighted with some Amway-type business after hours, which brought in a steady income in addition to his Hall Kinion compensation.

"How much money would you like to make this year?" Stan asked directly.

I paused to think for a moment, even though I already had a well-prepared response. "Well, I'd love to make forty or fifty thousand." Given my most recent salary was a whopping $28,500 at Boeing, I felt like this showed I was aggressive but grounded in some reality, given my age and experience. This was the beginning of 1999, after all, when minimum wage was somewhere in the $5 range.

"That's too low," Stan sternly replied. "This job is too tough, the hours are too long, and the pressure to produce is too high for us to make fifty-thousand dollars a year. You might as well get a normal job without all the madness. I suggest you set your expectations much higher."

I was processing Stan's words when he took out a piece of paper and started scribbling on it, drawing what looked like a simple graph with an X and Y axis. He then explained that the average recruiter there made a minimum of $100,000 their first year, and more than doubled that by years two and three. Stan continued to share that there were colleagues who cleared six and seven-hundred thousand dollars.

These figures were completely foreign to me, and I tried my best to wrap my still-adolescent-like brain around it.

"You're shitting me," I replied without even realizing what I had said. Stan just sat back in his chair ever so slightly and smiled.

Maureen later went so far as to tell me that if I worked hard and found consistent success there, I could possibly retire by the age of forty. All the other recruiters I met with shared the same sentiment. I would be surrounded by like-minded twenty-year-olds, all working hard to make as much money as they could.

Sold. This was my opportunity to make leaps and bounds over what shit money I was making at Boeing before I was laid off. It was a blessing. It was fate. The universe was reaching out to me with unwavering direction. It felt right.

With great luck and a solid reference from my former manager at Boeing, Maureen offered me the job. I accepted with enthusiasm and thanked her for believing in me. In all honesty, I was surprised I got the offer in the first place.

Despite my tardiness to the first interview, Maureen took mercy on me. I would later find out that this was one of Maureen's biggest pet peeves: *don't be late for meetings.* Further, it violated one of my most prized values in life, passed down from my parents: *If you show up early, you're on time, and if you show up on time, you're late. So don't be fucking late* (okay, I added the "fucking").

I would find out in time that after an interview, the entire team would sit around the conference table and debate pros and cons. If there were two or more "no hires" amongst the team, the candidate would be rejected. To say the least, it was an exercise of the utmost scrutiny, many times bordering on ruthless. I recall one occasion where a colleague refused to hire someone because they "reminded him of his ex-wife."

On my first day working at Hall Kinion (HK), I was formally introduced to the team and given my desk and computer, and I attended the morning staff meeting where my education of the staffing world and all its details began.

One of the senior team members, Shelly Holt, took on the role of being my designated mentor during the first three months of training. Did I say training? This was more like bootcamp. She presented me with a highly structured schedule that spelled out exactly what I'd be doing the moment I stepped into the office till I left in the evening, for the next three months.

"We have a proven system here that I need you to commit to," Shelly reinforced. "It's not going to be easy and might possibly push you to the limits. But should you survive the next three months, you'll be set up for lots of success."

For ninety straight days, I would focus on learning "both sides of the desk," as it was presented. One side was sales and account management—the playbook for calling prospective clients (companies that needed tech workers), developing a trusting relationship, and eventually signing them up for our contingent staffing services (contingent just meant that if the client didn't hire a candidate we presented, they weren't obligated to pay us a fee).

The other side was talent acquisition or recruiting—how to call potential candidates for jobs, qualify their experience and expectations, and represent them in the possible job opportunities our clients needed to fill.

For seven hours a day, I would be on the phone, making as many cold calls as possible to prospective companies that might need technology (back then, we referred to it as simply "IT") staffing services. When I wasn't on the phone or in the process of dialing, Shelly would peer around her computer monitor and sternly say, "I don't hear you on the phone," a passive way of telling me to get moving.

I would also spend a week down at the HK headquarters in Cupertino, California, for even more intense training. For eight hours a day, a dozen or so new recruits from different offices across the country sat through presentation after presentation covering cold calling, selling scripts, interviews, dos and don'ts, and company history. We also learned the playbook for HK's sales methodology—a foundation that would help fill my toolbox for the rest of my life.

At the end of the training week, we would be tested to measure exactly how much of the content we had absorbed. It was made very clear before I left for this trip that those coming from Bellevue were top-in-the-class and proved it on the final exam. Talk about pressure. There was no way I was letting down my office.

I took the test and scored top out of the group. It felt good to represent my office, a testament to the quality of training and high bar they had set. I came back and shared the results with Maureen. She said nothing but gave me the look of *you better have.*

The first three months flew by in a heartbeat. I was working my ass off with at least nine to ten hours in the office and another two to three at home. My evening hours were spent researching companies and organizing my call lists for the next day. While at the office, I was dialing the phone, making cold call after cold call, over a hundred times a day on average. With my scripts in front of me, I would call some company that I knew very little about and commence with my spiel.

"Hello, my name is PJ Ohashi from Hall Kinion. Would you please connect me to the IT manager?"

As you can imagine, the responses varied dramatically. Sometimes I'd simply get hung up on. Actually, that happened most of the time. Other times the person who answered would tell me they weren't interested in what I was selling. And on the rare occasion, they would say, "Hold on, let me transfer you."

A voice would answer after holding for a few minutes. "Hello? How can I help you?"

"Hi there, my name is PJ Ohashi, and I'm a technical recruiter with Hall Kinion here in Bellevue. I'm currently working with a candidate who's looking for new opportunities. His skill set includes software development with C++ and Java, as well as some work with database technologies like SQL Server and Oracle. Would someone like this be a valued addition to your team?"

From there, the results were even more mixed.

Here I was cold calling into a hundred or so different companies a day, with little to no research on each one, other than looking at listed phone numbers or the occasional website. I usually wasn't sure if I was calling a three-person mom-and-pop company that sold plumbing equipment, or a larger Fortune 1000 firm selling financial services. We're talking the late nineties, so anything with a dot-com after its name could be the next Microsoft or Google. And given the times, every company had a dot-com.

Again, the responses were all over the board. "Sorry, not interested." Click. Sometimes the person on the other end of the line would get angry and respond with, "Take me off of your list!" Click. Other times it was more cordial. "Well actually, we don't do any software development here, but you might want to call Microsoft down the street, because I hear they're hiring." Click.

And once again, on that rare occasion, I'd hear the words, "Tell me more." This is what they call, in sales terminology, a *buy sign*. Any response or question that furthered engagement with a potential client was always a good thing. It meant press on, but not too hard. It meant something I said sparked some interest and that it would behoove me to qualify the lead further.

From there, my scripts guided me from selling to asking questions. I would dive in with a myriad of questions about the company, the technologies they used, and the capacity of how they used them. "What does your company do?

Where in your organization is your team located? What specific position do you have open, and what are the exact skill sets you're looking for?"

I'd scribble down notes on the yellow legal pad in front of me as fast as I could. Most of the technology-related words might as well have been Greek, as I knew very little of what they were talking about. It was a steep learning curve to understand all things IT. Open-source operating systems, object-oriented programming, Java, TCP/IP, HTML, and the list goes on. But it didn't matter. If I followed the sales process, read my scripts, asked the right questions, and developed rapport with the prospective client, the numbers would lead me to success.

I would learn in time that this sales methodology was applicable to pretty much any industry that sold over the phone or door-to-door. It really didn't matter if you were selling stocks, vacuum cleaners, or magazine subscriptions —the process was the same in spirit. My objective was to get as many prospects or leads as possible into the sales pipeline, and inevitably, a subset of those would continue to the next stage.

Stack the top of the sales funnel with as many contacts as possible through cold-calling, email outreach, or any other creative forms of connecting with people. From there, develop trust and rapport with those contacts via meetings, social interactions, and continued correspondence (nowadays I'm a firm believer that golf is the perfect activity in which to connect). This will lead to qualifying them into different levels of certainty or probability. Is there urgency in their needs? Do they have a budget for hiring? How critical is it that their position get filled?

It was a pure numbers game at the macro level, and our organization was all about the numbers. In fact, they were obsessed with numbers. Stats on every step of the funnel were recorded, monitored, and even posted for all to see. You always knew exactly where you stood relative to your colleagues. It was motivating. No one wanted to be last. Everyone fought for pole position when it came to the numbers. The science of ratios, conversion rates, and sales metrics was the engine that drove us daily. Start with a large very number of leads at the front end, and end with a small number of deals. More calls up front meant more deals closed in the end.

Despite the demanding hours I invested, dialing for dollars so to speak—getting hung up on or berated, gathering information, and following up on leads—sixty days into my employment at HK, I had yet to close a deal. Maureen called me and Shelly into her office.

"Do you enjoy working here?" Maureen asked.

My jaw dropped. For a second, I couldn't speak. An awful and bitter taste of bile began creeping into my mouth. *Is this some sort of trick question? Did I do something that gave her the idea I wasn't happy here?* I gathered my thoughts.

"Yes, very much so," I replied reassuringly.

"Well, in order for you to *continue* working here, we need to see some results soon," was her follow-up.

I tried my best to hold back on responding indignantly with some pithy response like, "What the fuck do you think I'm trying to do?!" Instead, I listened intently, nodding my head in agreement with each observation she shared.

When I walked back to my desk, I was sick to my stomach. *How could this be? I've been busting my ass off, working countless hours, coming in early, staying late, working through lunches, living off Top Ramen, and she has the audacity to question my ability to be successful?! I'm working basically for free, and I'm presented with a veiled threat?!*

I felt anger and disappointment. But most of all, I felt

motivated. The chip on my shoulder reemerged, and it became even bigger. *Fuck her,* I thought. *I'll show her results.*

I dug deep, invested even more energy into my day-to-day work routine, and within a week, closed my first deal. It was a relatively small deal but one that would forever be remembered. I recruited a candidate named Kevin to Iron Mountain, a data records and management company. Two days later, I closed my second deal. Maureen's "pep talk" was apparently exactly what I needed—a little kick in the ass to get me fired up. Maybe my sales would have happened regardless. Maybe not. But I give her credit, despite how her words initially rubbed me the wrong way. She knew it would work all along.

And with every deal closed came a pure adrenaline rush. It was a time for small celebration, to rejoice in the experience and give credit to those involved.

And then, of course, there was the gong. I walked over to the large metal percussion hanging on the wooden stand at the far end of the office, and without warning, I let loose a gentle swing of the rasp—aimed squarely in the middle—and listened with delight as the sound reverberated throughout the office. Cheers and clapping followed.

Closing a deal felt like nothing I'd ever experienced. I'm not sure if it was the endorphins flooding my brain or the adrenaline rush from knowing the follow-up was a fat commission check. The moment I heard a candidate accept a standing offer from a client, I was on top of the world. Happiness. Pride. Elation. Sometimes it came easy. Other times it was fraught with obstacles. But no matter the journey, the result was the same—an unequivocal emotional high.

It's a funny thing, because you can't see a deal. You can't smell, taste, or touch it. It's indifferent to our senses yet affects us with tremendous rapture. I don't care if you're selling stereo equipment, multi-million-dollar software licenses, or pest control services door-to-door—the feeling is the same. A win is a win. A drug of sorts. I was very much like the lab rat who was promptly rewarded with a food pellet after accomplishing a remedial task. I got a taste of success, and I wanted more. A lot more.

As the market became more competitive, it was imperative that I be as creative as possible to differentiate myself from both colleagues I worked with on the daily—and the great many who worked for competitors down the street. So I went to a local Thai restaurant and told the manager I'd like to buy one customer lunch every week. I left a fishbowl on their front counter, so people who came in for lunch or dinner could throw in their cards in hopes of winning a free lunch. My only caveat was that I got to keep all the business cards at the end of the week. This worked well for generating leads.

One evening, I was browsing the technology and computer programming section at Barnes and Noble when I came up with the silly idea of sliding my business cards into specific books. I figured someone who is interested in buying a book on advanced programming languages or network engineering or hardware design could become an ideal candidate looking for a job. I wouldn't say the plan worked well, but I did receive two such calls from candidates who I ended up working with and placing.

The work was a major grind, but I quickly developed two professional characteristics that would help me continue to find success: *perseverance* and *resilience*.

Call after call resulted in small wins as I learned details about a prospective client, such as the name of a decision-maker or budget-holder. And with each small win, I would become hungrier for more. I learned to appreciate them, as I knew they added up to much larger successes. Those successes required relentless effort, a never-say-never attitude, and newly found convictions. I would take the positive energy of the day's wins and apply them to the next day. The flywheel was started.

With my confidence growing, I also learned to grow thicker skin. On the daily, I faced rejection of all types. People hung up on me. People even yelled at me. On one occasion, they even threatened to call the state attorney general for bad business practices, since they had received multiple cold calls from various colleagues at HK. I just happened to be the call that pushed their patience over the edge.

Over time though, rejections were just part of the process, and by focusing on the small (and large) wins, I was able to adopt the mindset of *bigger picture success*.

It was a glorious time, with dot-coms popping up all around the country, all with serious hiring needs based on the short supply of qualified IT workers. Seattle was home to a number of companies like Microsoft and Amazon, all of which eventually gave birth to even more startups (think Expedia.com and the hundreds of "Baby Bill Gateses" that originated from the Redmond-based software giant).

Within six months of starting my role at HK, at the ripe age of twenty-five, I was hitting on all cylinders and closing deals almost weekly. There was never a dull moment, and the money I was earning helped me pay off all my debt and eventually treat myself to a new car. I even started to save some funds, a basic concept that had always been foreign to me.

When I started at HK, I earned $1,200 a month before taxes. To make it more challenging, that $1,200 was "recoverable" by my employer after three months of employment if I didn't sell enough to offset it. Given the duration I was working, my hourly rate equated to well below minimum wage. You see, we were all paid 100 percent on commission, so it was imperative that I close deals, and close them fast. There was no base salary to fall back on. No annual bonus structure to end the fiscal year. We were hunters, and the only food we ate was what we killed for ourselves.

Plus, I dreamt of a lifestyle beyond eating Top Ramen and sleeping in the smallest of rooms in a tiny apartment with two roommates.

Within six months, I was producing hires with my clients, recruiting candidates for my teammates' clients, and earning more in commissions in a month than I had in a year working for Boeing. We all made money off of each other, despite the monumentally competitive and cutthroat environment the leaders created. I even qualified for HK's President's Club, which included an annual award trip down to the Bahamas.

Two Recruits and a New Friend

Which brings us back to Josiah. On a random day in 2000, I made my way down to Nordstrom in downtown Seattle. I was looking for new dress shoes, and Nordies was the place to get them. My go-to style at that time was a chunky, black dress shoe, which I'd wear on the daily. I liked them, because they gave me an extra quarter inch in height.

As I was browsing around, lo and behold, I ran into Josiah Johnson, who was working as a sales associate in the men's shoe department. He immediately recognized me, even though it had been over a year since we last saw each other. Josiah smiled, walked over, and gave me a welcome bro-hug.

A bro-hug is a quick overhand handshake followed immediately by a hug. Some people let go of the hand and then hug. Others keep the hands together, creating a natural pull and transition into the hug. I'd like to think this is a universal standard amongst guys who share some form of brotherhood. It's an important component of social convention, with some inevitable awkwardness as one person reaches out their hand while the other person goes in for the hug. But when done right, each reciprocating party knows exactly how to engage.

Josiah and I did. Or maybe I'm just making this shit up. Regardless, we were glad to see each other. We exchanged pleasantries for a bit, and he asked what I was up to.

I told him about my new gig at the technical staffing company. I shared about the energy of the office, my awesome team, and the income potential. I sensed curiosity in his eyes as I spoke. Josiah was a hard worker and motivated to find a path other than selling shoes for the rest of his life.

"And we're hiring," I said with some enthusiasm. "We're always looking for high-energy professionals who understand sales and have a solid work ethic. The job is hard, and at times very frustrating. But you're rewarded with lots of praise and uncapped commission."

I could tell Josiah's curiosity was growing, so I followed up with, "Hey, if this is something you're interested in learning more about, send me your resume, and I'll get it to my manager and put in the good word."

"Absolutely, and thanks," he replied enthusiastically. "Sounds interesting!"

We chatted for a few more minutes and then parted ways. A couple of days later, I found Josiah's resume in my inbox, and forwarded it to Maureen. I told her about my friendship with Josiah, and she immediately reached out to set up some interviews with him.

Long story short, Josiah navigated the lengthy interview process and was offered a job. He started a couple of weeks later and embraced the long hours, intense cold-calling sessions, and training regimen. Within a couple of months, he was coming into his own there and started closing deal after deal.

A few months later, I received a call from Jesse. He and his girlfriend were interested in moving back up to the Seattle area. Further, he wondered if I knew of any jobs that he might be a fit for.

I thought to myself, *Jesse's a smart guy. He's ambitious, hardworking, and unafraid to take on new challenges. Maybe he'd be a fit on our team?*

I referred him to Maureen, and Jesse found himself in the depths of the interview process with everyone on the team. His efforts paid off, and he was offered the job. Jesse moved back to Seattle and joined our team at HK.

From Jesse's first day, I knew he (and I, for that matter) had made a terrible choice. For starters, Shelly was his mentor as well. Let's just say that her drill-sergeant-like approach and micro-management style wasn't to Jesse's liking. It clashed with his personality, and it only took thirty days for him to hand in his notice. He'd had enough. Beyond that, it was clear that sales didn't suit his strengths and career goals.

Our time working together at HK was memorable for all of us. It set the foundation for our sales and recruiting skill sets that we would use for the rest of our careers. We also developed long-lasting relationships with not only our colleagues, but also a great many technology professionals in the Seattle area (this would prove to be integral when starting a company together eight years later). Most important, though, is we had a lot of fun.

My ride at HK lasted a few years, until a short time after the dot-com crash in 2001. One can argue that the fall was a long time coming, given the craziness of the tech industry and the ridiculous valuations of unprofitable companies. Thinking back at all the hair-brained companies that received copious amounts of venture capital, it's no wonder the shit hit the fan. Inflated valuations. Shitty business models. Irresponsible and frivolous spending. Remember Kozmo.com? Pets.com? TheGlobe.com? I can still recite the short but catchy jingle for Homegrocer.com—♪ "Would you like to have something to eat?" ♪

But to me, the crash felt more like a light switch. I was twenty-six years old, making hundreds of thousands of dollars, and suddenly, the lights went out, the music stopped, and I was left without a chair to be found.

The internet bust of 2001 hit me like a freight train. Total panic before total destruction. This was around the same time the whole Tillie debacle came to fruition, thus adding to the chaos. I was worried about navigating a career path, my prospects as a sales guy in talent acquisition, and the personal turmoil from all the legal troubles involving Lisa's best friend. I searched deep into the network to make more connections.

One day, Josiah reached out to help me find a job. He told me I should connect with John Bergen, a well-connected headhunter with a strong network up and down the West Coast. Josiah knew John from back when they were kids, living just down the street from each other.

I had recently left HK and was looking for some new opportunities. John was the director of recruiting for Devon James and Associates, a company providing talent acquisition services for early-stage companies. Their business model was interesting, as they gave their clients a comprehensive recruiting war-room, consisting of not just talented recruiters, but a full set of best practices and processes.

John and I met on a Saturday morning in 2002 at a downtown Kirkland coffee shop. Triple J's was a busy place, with places to stand or sit and enjoy your morning coffee and pastry. We sat down at a short table.

I immediately liked John. His energy was infectious, and you could tell he enjoyed his job. He shared stories about moving around, up and down the coast, to support different clients. It sounded like a dream job to me—moving from city to city while being involved in several exciting and innovative companies like Cranium—the interactive board game company that was eventually purchased by Hasbro in 2008.

John graciously pointed me to a few of his contacts, but ultimately none of them panned out. The scar tissue was still fresh from the recent market crash, and lots of companies were struggling to stay afloat. Hiring additional staff wasn't in their immediate plans, so hiring me as an internal recruiter was most definitely a fantasy.

We stayed friends though, connecting over email every now and again, keeping tabs on each other's lives.

Roads Leading to Endeavor

Fast forward a couple of years. After Josiah and I had each parted ways with HK, he jumped industries and became a traveling shoe salesman for the swanky upscale brand Gordon Rush. I stayed the course in sales and began work for a technology staffing firm called Comsys. We did our best to stay in touch, but life's distractions made it harder and harder. That was, until I got a phone call from him in early 2003.

Josiah had joined a bunch of former HK alumni and gone to work for a young technical staffing firm called Endeavor Consulting in Seattle. Endeavor was under the umbrella of a private equity company Jesse was involved in at the time. Funny how things come back around full circle.

My once roommate, Jesse, had quit the recruiting industry only to find himself back in it years later as an owner. This was his attempt to get the band back together.

Endeavor offered me a job to help manage their talent acquisition team, and I happily accepted. It felt good working for a smaller company alongside former colleagues and friends. And the market had recovered, so we were actually seeing some success again. We had some rockstars on the team, a couple of whom we'd worked with back in the HK days. There was Ron Combs and Karen Iniguez who worked in recruiting and sales, respectively. (Our paths would cross again with Karen seven years later when we would hire her at Society.)

Around the same time, I was introduced to a mutual friend of Jesse's, Ryan Neal. Ryan was a go-getter type filled with aspirations to conquer the world. He was in law school, and like Jesse, never seemed to ever sit still. We would hang out together at random poker nights or play hoops at the local gym. My first impression of Ryan was good. He had a talent for telling stories, holding the attention of his listeners. He was blunt and straight to the point, a quality I never looked at as a negative. I could always rely on hearing the truth from him whether it was good or bad. Little did I know at the time, but Ryan and Jesse would eventually partner years later, and our connection would come full circle once again.

I ended up working in various roles at Endeavor over the next few years until it became apparent my opinion and perspectives on the direction of the company clashed with the leadership. Josiah had already spun off a business intelligence (BI) consulting company out of Endeavor, so we weren't working together anymore on the daily. And I became disenchanted with some of the leadership that Endeavor brought in.

With one manager I ended up reporting to, the best way to describe our working relationship would be like oil and water. She changed all our processes and challenged me on every point. I'm sure she had some good reasons for the changes, but they felt cumbersome and inefficient. More process. More paperwork. Complicated workflows and the need to get approvals for everything.

You could argue that this was the normal path of a maturing company—a reasonable, if not crucial, move to scale and grow. But I was too stubborn for change and felt stymied, unable to find joy in the day-to-day. It was as if the fun, vibrant culture that once brought everyone together was sucked out of the room, nowhere to be found. I didn't like the direction she and others were taking the company in and decided to do something about it.

I sat in my manager's office while she tried to give me my annual review. She went on about how I wasn't a team player and was struggling in my new role. Her delivery had an awkward silence before she tried her best to say she was disappointed in me. I listened to her evaluation, and she then asked for my thoughts.

"This is complete crap," I said indignantly. "How could you rate me as below average on teamwork when our president presented me with the Team Player Recognition Award just last month?! Further, how can you say that I'm not very adaptable when I've played more roles in this company over the past three years than anyone else?"

I could feel my blood boiling. I continued to give example after example of my performance and contributions to the team and company, but after a few minutes, I stopped ranting and waited for her rebuttal. I'm sure I sounded a bit defensive, even a little confused, but I was seriously pissed.

Deep down, though, I knew I wasn't performing at my

best. My numbers were down overall, and I was finding it difficult to adopt a model I didn't agree with. I knew my attitude was poor. Nonetheless, I tried my best to make a stand.

I could tell she didn't know what to say. She sat there in silence, stunned at my refutation, with her face in her hands. Then she put down her hands, let out a long sigh, and gave a defeated look that said this meeting was over.

I felt empowered. I felt victorious. I'd put her in her place. But those feelings were short-lived, as I quickly realized nothing good could have come out of it.

In the end, I dug my own grave there. I lacked self-awareness. I lacked diplomacy. I lacked political savvy. I was the proverbial bull in a china shop, and even though one could argue I had very valid points on the company's direction, I'd contributed to too much collateral damage along the way. I had outlived my stay at Endeavor.

A few days later, I met with the president, who diplomatically and compassionately showed me to the door. The official news was that I resigned from the company, but most people knew I had poked the bear one too many times and was let go. The chip that remained on my shoulder had gotten the best of me this time. I'd channeled my anger in all the wrong ways. There was no positivity or even productivity. It was a costly learning experience and a stain on my resume.

For closure's sake, I'd like it to be known that Endeavor ended up making a few wrong plays resulting in stagnant revenue, loss of talent, and eventually a fire sale to a competitor. But I'm too mature now to say I told you so. Or am I? My departure would even prompt Jesse to sell his shares of the company, as the writing was on the wall. He would later thank me for giving him some inside stories that allowed him to sell out before the company's revenue plummeted.

After I left, I took a job with an Atlanta-based staffing firm called MDI that wanted to break into the Seattle market. My job was to run the AT&T account in the Northwest, helping to build a strong foothold and then expand from there.

Josiah was off on his own, playing an integral role at ZD1 (Zero Dash One), the BI firm he spun out of Endeavor. They were finding some great success, as this was 2006, and the idea of business intelligence was becoming hugely popular. Spreadsheets, dashboards, and any data visualization was hot at the time (it still very much is, but has evolved with the times), and ZD1 was at the forefront of the movement. I missed working with Josiah but was happy that he found a place where he could thrive.

Jesse and Ryan eventually joined forces and started a small private equity firm together. Their mission was to build a portfolio of small- and medium-sized businesses in which they could operate, establish steady cash flow, and grow the collective value of each entity.

My mid-twenties set the table for a fruitful future—a foundation that I probably didn't appreciate at the time, but years later came to fully understand its value. Learning effective sales methodologies. Fearless cold-calling capabilities, which gave me confidence to handle pretty much any type of rejection and thickened my skin. Knowing how to push and pull the various levers of a sales process and close a deal. The art and science of various sales strategies. A large network of clients, candidates, and colleagues—across a wide spectrum of industry verticals and competencies. The taste of victory and the financial rewards followed. This all only led me to seek out more.

Chapter 4

Stars Aligned

It's June of 2008, and I'm about nine months into my tenure at MDI. "We're going to have to let you go," I hear my boss, David, say on the other end of the line. Within seconds, my mouth and throat dry up, my knees start to give, and a pit in my stomach forms. The conversation continues, words are being said, but they're lost on me. I hear nothing else. I've been fired, I think to myself. Again. What the fuck? I hang up and stare blankly out the window. Holding back the queasy feelings creeping up from my gut, I recall the balance of my savings account. Dwindled down to stems and seeds. How much runway do we have? The mortgage. Food. Bills, credit cards, and car payments. I do the math in my head, which doesn't take long. This is not good. It's happened again, and I'm wondering how this is possible. How do I tell Lisa? I ponder for a minute. We have enough problems, and now this. It's a familiar feeling, one that seems to show its face every so often for me. But it's not a good one. Shame. Failure. Desperation. Yet again, I find myself with my back against the wall.

I'd caught up with Jesse one day in late 2007 over lunch, and he asked me how my job was going. I told him I was enjoying the challenge of building a practice for MDI, but I still didn't love working for the man. I was remote, working with only one other person in a cramped office with no windows, slightly larger than your average broom closet. Jesse could tell I wasn't happy, and he continued to ask me what I was looking for—including how I planned to accomplish it—and I could tell from his tone and line of questioning that this conversation would take a turn.

"Can I say something that might rub you the wrong way?" asked Jesse. He didn't even wait for me to answer his rhetorical question before he shared his thoughts. "You might make a good salary, but the job will never make you wealthy. Making a good income could make you rich, but it won't put you in a position of wealth."

I processed his words as he continued to make his point.

"You might want to rethink your career and how you can accomplish the goals I know you have."

"What do you have in mind?" I asked.

Jesse shared his thoughts on selling his shares of Endeavor years prior, including how it had built the foundation for his future. He and Ryan had recently joined forces and created Pendulum Investments, a small private equity company with a few portfolio companies they operated.

He continued, "I'm not set by any means at this point, but I'm on a track in the right direction. Heather [his wife at the time] and I have a number in mind, and when we reach that number, I'll be able to retire comfortably."

I listened, curious.

"Have you ever thought about starting your own staffing or consulting firm?" Jesse asked. "I've been talking to Ryan about how we built Endeavor, and how the staffing business model works. I'm thinking we could get you and Josiah together, handpick your other players, and with our help on back-office administration, we could kill it."

We parted ways after discussing it for a while longer, and within a couple of months, Josiah, Jesse, and I sat down at Stanford's, a restaurant in North Seattle. The three of us ordered some drinks and appetizers from a highboy table in the bar.

Jesse opened with his thoughts on how we could start another company, what the structure could look like, and why the idea made sense for both Josiah and me. He figured that with my talent acquisition skill set and Josiah's sales background, we would be an unstoppable force in the staffing world. You could hear the excitement in his voice, as he went on and on about not only how cool it would be, but how it could set the stage for a larger financial payout down the road.

Jesse shared some of the inner workings of Endeavor and how he and his partners were compensated. He explained the financials, and how profits and revenue affected overall valuation. It was my first time learning about EBITDA (Earnings Before Interest, Taxes, Depreciation, and Amortization), and its application toward valuing a business with a multiple. I'm sure I'd studied it back in the day at Western, but there was never a need to talk about it until Jesse schooled me that day.

It was a productive conversation, but in the end, Jesse would walk away disappointed, as both Josiah and I concluded the timing just wasn't right.

At the time, Josiah was busy, in the midst of selling Zero Dash One (the BI company he spun out of Endeavor) to a Seattle-based digital marketing firm called Ascentium. There were lots of moving parts, and migrating all ZD1's clients took enormous effort. Plus, Josiah wanted to see how working for Ascentium would play out in his career.

I wasn't preoccupied with any crazy mergers, but I felt committed to MDI and their effort to build a Seattle presence. I'd started to find some success with the AT&T account, helping to build a significant network at the massive wireless company. MDI had taken a gamble on me, so I felt an obligation to see things through and not bail at the first thing that came my way.

Unfortunately, all my effort over the past year with MDI came crashing down five months later. The day started out just like most days. I got up, showered, and dressed. I prepared my morning cup of coffee with my Francis-Francis retro-looking espresso maker. I fed the dogs. I checked my calendar to determine what meetings I had before my commute into the office.

I got the call around 7:30 a.m. the morning of June 23, 2008, which happened to be a Monday. It was my boss, David, and before I even answered my phone, a weird feeling overcame me. We were going to talk a couple hours later—in our standing Monday-morning meeting—to discuss the week's strategy and activities. *So why is he calling me now, at home? This can't be good.*

"Hey David," I answered. "What's going on?"

"I hate to be calling you so early, PJ, but it was important that we connect immediately. There have been some changes to the vendor management relationship over at AT&T, and unfortunately our services contract wasn't renewed."

David continued, "So unfortunately this means that your role supporting the account goes away as well. We're going to have to let you go. I'm sorry to tell you that today will technically be your last day of employment with us. Larry, our human resource manager, will be sending over details outlining your severance package [they gave me two weeks], and he can answer any questions about the separation."

I stood there, stunned, with a whirlwind of emotions racing around in my head. Disappointment. Anger. Hopelessness. *How could they do this to me? I've been busting my ass over the last year, and we were just starting to see some success.* There I was, standing in the middle of our media room on the second floor of my home, looking out at the lush green maple trees in the front yard, trying to get a handle on my frustration. But instead of making the situation worse than it was, I gathered my composure and told David, "Thank you for the opportunity, and best of luck moving forward."

The following week was a very dark period, as I found myself shrouded in a confluence of life's dealings. I'd lost my job. I'd lost a dog to cancer not too long before. My marriage of seven years was showing significant signs of fatigue, despite our best efforts to work out our differences. A constant, gut-wrenching feeling ate at me, as the uncertainty of the future felt bleak and without promise.

I was thirty-three years old, jobless, and completely underwater on my mortgage. I had been the primary breadwinner for my family (wife and dogs), and before long, being on unemployment began doing serious damage to my self-esteem and pride. Beyond that, our savings account was quickly shrinking, as most of it went to pay our mortgage for a house we should never have bought in the first place. We were house-poor, and the looming mortgage crisis was just getting underway.

I liquidated what little money I had in my 401(k) and began tightening up all our expenditures. I'd kept the heat super low in the house, forcing Lisa to throw on an extra sweater. We cancelled all our vacation plans. I cancelled cable TV. We ate Top Ramen. Lots of it. We were scrappy and managed the best we could.

I even sold one of our vehicles for a cheaper version. My beloved Volvo C70, that became a relic of my initial taste of success, had run its course. The whole experience was not only embarrassingly pride swallowing, but a testament to the financial extremes I found myself in throughout my life.

There I sat, in the office of some pompous used car salesman, as he crushed me on the trade-in value of my Volvo, all while boasting the worth of the used, beat-up Jeep I would drive away in. I had no leverage. I was just desperate to be out of the large car payments tied to the C70. I couldn't do anything but accept my fate.

After some healthy self-loathing and general feeling sorry for myself, I began to pivot. I started seeing a therapist to work through some issues with my marriage and overall confidence. I started working out and playing basketball in the evenings. I started reaching out to my network for job opportunities. Self-preservation became my focus.

Survival created fear. Fear begot anger. And anger pushed me to rethink my life. The chip that remained on my shoulder reappeared, giving me inspiration to move forward. I was finally motivated to let go of the self-pity bullshit and get my life moving forward.

Once I started reaching out to various connections in my network, the flywheel began to turn, as dozens of people were calling me about open roles in their respective companies. I set up coffee meetings. I set up happy hours. The calls kept coming. I felt a familiar energy from all the activity, very reminiscent of my cold-calling days at HK nine years prior. I was reliving the numbers game, but this time it applied to my own job search.

By early July, just a couple of weeks after I'd lost my job,

I was close to receiving a few job offers from attractive companies. It felt good to be wanted again, especially given how my previous employer had parted ways. I would have options. Good options.

Even my relationship with Lisa was showing some signs of life. We were more engaged in each other's lives and seemed to find a healthy rhythm in managing our differences. We adopted a puppy. Pepe was a black lab and border collie mix rescued from a shelter north of Seattle. Little did I know, but that dog would be by my side for the next fourteen years of life-changing experiences.

Before the job offers started coming in, Jesse thought it was time we revisit the idea of starting a company. He called me one evening in early July and pitched the idea again. This time, however, he was more assertive with his perspective. Every excuse or reason I came up with was quickly addressed with well thought-out rebuttals. Maybe Jesse was a sales guy after all?

The last thing Jesse brought up was the conversation we'd had nearly eight months prior about building wealth and setting the table for my future. He was well on his way, with Pendulum's growth of diversified investments in manufacturing and fitness clubs. In Jesse-like fashion, he wanted to share the opportunity with those closest to him. And he knew I wouldn't be happy working for the man again. I aspired for much more in life. Not just in material things, but in experiences and relationships. Plus, a significant mortgage and a minuscule nest egg provided plenty of motivation to get my shit together. A well-paying job was never a bad thing, but to someone who thrived on challenges and wanted more out of life, it could lead to stagnation.

That night, I talked to Lisa about the conversation I'd had with Jesse, and the possibility of starting a new company. She was supportive and knew that it meant we'd have to continue to be uber conservative with our expenditures for a while.

The next day, I emailed Josiah and shared my newfound enthusiasm for starting a new company. I had multiple job offers on the table, so I implored urgency for him to meet with us. Jesse, Josiah, Ryan, and I ended up meeting up on the afternoon of July 7, at the Redmond Athletic Club.

As it turned out, Josiah was becoming increasingly disenchanted with life at Ascentium, and now that they had fully integrated ZD1, he felt like it was a good time to entertain new opportunities. It didn't take much to convince him, once the three of us painted a very attractive picture of where we could take this.

"Three years and ten-million dollars in revenue ..." Jesse shared. "And then we sell. We each take our two-and-a-half million dollars and sit on the sidelines for a year till our non-competes are up, and we do it all over again. I've been doing some research, and I'm seeing one-times revenue multiples out in the market for staffing firms." *Multiples* refers loosely to the potential market value of a business, equal to some "multiple" of revenue or EBITDA.

There was little reason to doubt Jesse. His experience starting Endeavor had proved he knew the model and how to execute. Plus, he was well connected to other business leaders in the area.

The plan resonated with Josiah, and he expressed his interest a week or so later. He was bought in, although he would have to give ample notice to Ascentium before starting.

By the middle of July, the four of us agreed that we'd commit to the path of starting a new venture, which we initially referred to as "NewCo." I politely declined four job offers patiently awaiting my acceptance and ordered a new laptop from Dell Computers to signify a fresh start to my career.

The next week, Josiah presented the idea of bringing a fifth partner into the equation—John Bergen. He knew John had an ear to the ground for new opportunities. We listened to Josiah's pitch and felt it didn't hurt to at least meet with him and see how we all gelled. John had reached out to me months earlier about a job there at Jobster, but I politely declined. Given this, I was curious where he was in life.

Over the next couple of weeks, there were several meetings with John, all with different combinations of the four of us. Josiah and John met first, given their personal history as childhood neighbors. Then Jesse and Josiah met with him.

One afternoon in late July, Ryan and I met up with John at a downtown Seattle coffee shop to continue the vetting process. Ryan hadn't met John before, so he was eager to jump into the conversation and get to know him. Ryan shared his vision on what NewCo would look like, as well as the plan to sell when it hit a certain size. After that, we'd do it again and again, over and over.

John was intrigued with the idea but still had some consternation about leaving Jobster and derailing the career he had worked so hard to build. Nevertheless, Ryan and John hit it off wonderfully.

I, on the other hand, wasn't as enthusiastic. Not about the plan, but about including John in the plan. Why did we need a fifth partner? It would mean one more mouth to feed, ultimately diluting our individual ownership by 5 percent. It would also mean one more voice in decision-making, one more opinion, and possibly one more roadblock.

My feelings had nothing specific to do with John or his ability to succeed. In fact, I knew he was a competent recruiting leader with a lot more experience than me or Josiah. It was more about principle for me. I respected John tremendously but wasn't convinced we needed that fifth partner. What void would we be filling? Josiah and I had sales and recruiting covered, while Jesse and Ryan would take care of the finances, legal, and administrative/HR work. How would a fifth partner contribute to our success?

As we continued our conversation, John must have picked up on some of my reluctance. Perhaps my tone wasn't as fervent as it should have been. Maybe I asked too many questions. Maybe it was my body language.

Don't get me wrong, the three of us had a very productive meeting, and for the most part it was filled with agreement. But John is a strong reader of people and knew there was something not copasetic between us. We agreed to take next steps and all meet up again later to discuss finer details and terms of our arrangement.

Little did I know that John shared some of the same feelings as me. He thought, *Why would they bring in a fifth partner when it appears that Josiah and PJ can handle everything sales and recruiting?* But most important, he wondered, *What role would I play, given the personalities?*

John had much more experience leading teams and working in start-ups than Josiah and me. I asked myself, *Where would that put him organizationally? Who would report to who?* Certainly, my ego played a role in this.

I shared my concerns with adding a fifth partner to Josiah, Jesse, and Ryan, but all three were adamant we needed John.

"Bergen brings some solid people leadership and experience navigating start-ups," Ryan asserted. "He also adds recruiting firepower to the mix."

Josiah added onto the debate: "John also has a strong network outside of Seattle, up and down the West coast, which could come in handy as we expand geographically."

"I understand where you guys are coming from," I responded. "Let's move forward."

What Are We Actually Going to Do?

The days and weeks following the decision to move forward were full of excitement and positive energy. But before we got started, we needed to resolve several questions.

We agreed we would start some sort of professional services company with technology and staffing components. After all, it's what we all knew. Then we would evolve with the market demands. Technology flavors would come and go. Some were trendy. Some would stick around for the long haul. Business Intelligence was hot at the time, and Web 2.0 concepts were thriving.

Our underlying service would involve employing our own technical professionals and contracting them out to clients. This was different than the work we'd done at HK back in the day, where our clients employed our recruits. We wanted this different model for a couple of reasons.

First, by contracting our own talent to our clients, this created a residual revenue stream for the duration of the contract. Placing a recruit full-time somewhere meant a large fee, but no ongoing revenue. Our intention was to build a business where we employed lots of techies, thus creating a large base of revenue.

Second, by employing the talent directly, we could establish some sort of eventual brand identity. We also knew we wanted to create a company with a strong cultural connection to the brand. Based on working for several staffing and consulting firms, Josiah and I recognized the frequent disconnect between employers and employees. A staffed contractor might be employed by company XYZ and on a contract with client ABC. Their paychecks are signed by XYZ, their benefits are paid by XYZ, and their W2 is from XYZ—but many times that's where the relationship ends. On the daily, they take direction from client ABC, are integrated into the teams at ABC, and many times are physically located in ABC offices. So, there's an inherent disconnect that is reflected in a lack of belonging and identity. And unless the employer goes out of their way to create a culture of belonging, then it's inevitable the employee could feel more connected to the client's culture. The relationship with the employer becomes transactional. It lacks connection.

This was wrong in my opinion, and a flaw we wanted to solve in the staffing world. How do you build a connection back to the mother ship when your employees are onsite with a client? How do you introduce a unique culture with remote employees? How do you create enough identity with your employees regardless of their day-to-day working environment? How does that identity translate into company loyalty?

These were questions we were eager to answer.

But what about a consulting company? What's the difference between a staffing company and a consulting firm? It's squishy. It's complicated. It's subjective. And depending on who you ask, the differences can be significant or subtle.

Let me attempt to break it down.

The world of consulting contains a wide variety of companies, each representing different service offerings, clientele-base, geographic focus, culture, values, amongst other factors. I like to simplify this world into a spectrum representing the services and relative perception of value.

What are the services offered, and how much money is the buyer willing to pay for those services? On one end of the spectrum, you have your consulting firms like McKinsey, BCG, and Bain. These are global firms with extensive service lines, providing strategy and execution of that strategy. Offerings like change management, corporate restructuring, new product and service analysis, and thought leadership across different domains create a high level of perceived value for the buyer. This is the top of the food chain when it comes to professional services firms, and they're characterized by top-dollar hourly rates, high margins, industry-driving innovation, and prestige. We're talking think-tank level shit. These are the guys transforming industries.

Now to be clear, there are lots of other players in that space, many of which are more boutique in size. Some specialize in very specific technologies or industries, while others only operate and service a few or one geographic market. Regardless of their relative size, big or boutique and everything in between, they all command top dollar.

On the other end of that spectrum are your highly commoditized, low-skilled staffing firms. These companies generally provide labor on an hourly basis to clients looking to temporarily fill roles that are typically blue-collar in nature. These tend to be manual labor focused but not quite at the level of a trade skill or craft. Janitors. Food prep. Agriculture workers. You get the picture.

Companies that provide staffing services for unskilled and low-skilled workers tend to have lower margins, lower overhead, and less prominent market status. It's a volume business where placing a lot of workers equates to a margin large enough to make a net profit. Some of the players include TrueBlue and Express Employment Professionals—each company currently valued in the hundreds of millions of dollars—significant in their own right.

Another difference between most staffing firms and consulting companies is the full-time versus temporary status of employees. Most staffing firms employ their staff, either W2 or 1099 contract, only for the duration of their respective project. Be it three months or three years, when the contract is over, so is the worker's employment.

Consulting companies retain their talent regardless of whether the staffed employee is billable on a project or not. They build in bench time for all their consultants and include it in their overall financial models and pricing. This is generally referred to as *utilization*. Based on projections, or past data, consulting companies target a specific utilization for each of their staff.

When the utilization is above expected thresholds, the margins are gravy. Conversely, when it's below, the margins quickly deteriorate, and the revenue versus cost of an employee can fall into a deficit.

This is a fundamental reason consulting firms charge so much for their services. There is no bench time for those employed by staffing companies, because their utilization is always 100 percent—meaning the employee is either on contract billing or their employment is terminated. This is also why high-volume staffing firms charge less for their services, as the risks are lower. They also lack the ownership of delivering on a project, as staffed contractors are typically individually managed by the client.

Based on this, we knew that we wanted to build a company that possessed the flexibility and agility of a staffing firm, but also had the employee experience indicative of world-class consultancies. Further, given the nature of the market in 2008, we also had to navigate the ambiguity of the imminent collapse of the economy. That idea created a bit of a quandary for us. How do you start a company with minimal investment, at the very beginning of a recession, without overextending or missing opportunities? It was a delicate balance given the market uncertainty, so we decided to start with what we knew, technology staffing, but with a bit more emphasis around employee experience and culture.

You see, the financial model around staffing can be very lucrative, if you manage overhead and focus all efforts on gross margin—the difference between what you bill a client and the salary plus cost of an employee. Further, the model scales nicely, especially when there is scarcity for specific skill sets in the marketplace. Seattle had plenty of need, even though some companies, Microsoft included, were laying people off. Software engineers, data architects, front-end web developers, and data analysts were still in high demand. And sought-after skill sets—including Ruby on Rails, Java, and Hadoop—were hot at the time.

The five of us exchanged emails a dozen times a day as we began sorting out the many remaining business details. Where should we start? We had so much to cover, and the first item on the agenda was the company name.

Naming a company is like deciding on a name for a child or pet. Sometimes it's easy, and other times it's full of strife. There are so many variables to consider in a name. What's the meaning? What are you trying to represent? Is there a reasonable and affordable URL available? Do you want a real word, or something made up (think Salesforce versus Accenture)? Is the name already taken and registered?

For the five of us, the process was difficult. Jesse and Ryan took the first shot at coming up with a list of names based on some simple criteria.

First, the name needed to be memorable—a moniker that anyone would recall regardless of if they used our services. It had to be something very sticky. Second, the name needed to represent a company that was different—something edgy, something that set us apart from the rest. And of course, we had to consider URL availability and cost. We also wanted a name that symbolized some sort of connection or pairing. After all, we were in the business of matching people with business needs.

The initial list was interesting to say the least, with over a dozen possibilities. Names like Cohesion, Evolution Partners, Forté, Fuse, and Tracker made the second cut. We then instituted a democratic process to vote on the most popular choices amongst the five of us. Forté prevailed unanimously.

We now had a name. We were Forté, and excited about moving forward. That lasted less than twenty-four hours, when the very next day, August 5, 2008, Josiah sent an email and basically derailed the entire process. He suggested we scrap Forté and adopt a brand with more personality. I still don't know how or where he came up with his new recommendation, but the world came to a complete stop when I read it. At first, I was taken aback, given we'd all agreed on Forté. This felt like we'd just prolong the process further, resulting in more discussion and loss of time.

Then I read it again.

The Job Mob. It was memorable, edgy, and different. It was completely out there, yet the words symbolized work and a group of connected people. After thinking about it further, I was bought-in completely. This was it: A name that stood out from the rest. A name that embodied connectivity, family, career opportunities, and uniqueness. A name that reflected the five personalities of each founding partner. But the most profound aspect was it represented a company that was playful and didn't take itself too seriously.

And Forté? Really? How could we have considered a name where you need to type a special character on your keyboard every time, otherwise, phonetically it reads "fort." What the fuck were we thinking?

John, Josiah, and I immediately began tapping a few shoulders and asking for feedback to validate the name idea or quickly move on. We all loved it, but would anyone else? From several respected professionals, we heard generally positive responses. Some felt it was a little too casual, but back then, using the word "mob" in a name was trendy and cool. Others felt, correctly so, that branding was critical to exude the edginess.

Jesse wasn't so enamored. He felt it was too casual. Too unprofessional. No one would take us seriously. But we argued that was kind of the point. After lots of debate, the four of us convinced him to take a leap of faith and trust us. We weren't corporate. We were The Mob.

Within the next twenty-four hours, we had consensus on The Job Mob as the name moving forward. On Thursday, August 7, 2008, Ryan filed The Job Mob, LLC, with the state of Washington, and it became official.

Two days after we officially registered our name, Jesse hosted a signing party at his house in North Seattle. The dinner was intended to signify not only the buy-in from the five members, but also from our respective spouses or significant others, from whom we each had received unquestionable support.

The five of us agreed to structure the organization initially as 51 percent owned by Pendulum Investments (Jesse and Ryan), and the rest divided by the three of us, making up the other 49 percent. This was because Jesse and Ryan were putting forth the initial funding of around

$160,000 to get us off the ground. None of us had any significant dollars saved up to invest, so for the time being, it made sense. They were taking a larger risk; they should get the upside.

The plan was to create parity in percentage of ownership (20 percent each) once the original loan was paid back to Jesse and Ryan.

After some more questions and answers, we all enthusiastically signed our names on all five copies of the agreement. It was official. The Job Mob, LLC, was real, and the five of us were united as one entity. There was some hooting and hollering from the other side of the room, as the five significant others cheered excitedly. Then they all joined us to celebrate with lots of hugs and laughter.

A loud pop of the cork from the champagne bottle resulted in more cheers. Heather passed around glasses of Dom Perignon while Jesse handed out commemorative silver money clips that he'd had custom engraved with The Job Mob—a nice, personal touch to kick off our new venture.

The evening went on for a few hours as we continued to celebrate over some good food and tasty adult beverages. The next day, efforts to kick off this company would begin. And so would the stories.

Chapter 5

Starting the Business

It's a Sunday night, and I'm playing pickup hoops at the local Gold's Gym. It's the second game, and an opposing team member checks in the ball at the top of the key. "Ball in," he declares as he tosses the ball to my teammate. Play starts, and I swing around the left side down low, then make my way back to the middle to set a screen for a teammate. Now the guy guarding me rolls off to cover my teammate, which leaves me all alone. I cut toward the basket, hoping to get an easy two points, then hear a faint "pop" and fall straight down to the hardwood floor. Play stops, as everyone looks at me to decipher what just happened. I assume someone stepped on the back of my shoe, causing me to fall forward, but as I look behind me, no one is there. I quickly try to get to my feet with the help of a teammate but find myself back down on the floor. An acute stabbing pain from my right leg hits me hard. My calf muscle is balled up high, and I can't hinge my foot in any direction. Fuck me, I think to myself. This can't be good. I slowly hobble off the court, knowing I've just experienced the mother of all sports injuries.

We had a bit of a rolling start amongst the team members, as Josiah and John were both wrapping up their respective situations with their current employers. As I was unemployed at the time, I jumped in immediately, getting processes in place and beginning the efforts of developing a pipeline of new business opportunities. Josiah put in his two-week notice with Ascentium and was busy handing off accounts and closing out any loose ends with clients. He joined us in the beginning of September.

John, on the other hand, was taking measures to gracefully downsize Jobster, as the start-up was experiencing the effects of the economic slowdown. You see, Jobster developed and sold online tools for recruiting, and as the economy started to show signs of increased unemployment, fewer and fewer employers demanded such tools. As head of people, it was his responsibility to strategize and execute laying off more than a third of its staff. A year prior in 2007, John also had handled a 41 percent reduction in workforce, as the company evolved its business model. He eventually joined the band at the beginning of October 2008.

Despite the downturn of the economy in August 2008, we were able to hit the ground running, signing clients who were still in fact hiring. Even through the worst of what would be referred to as the Great Recession, Seattle remained stable relative to the rest of the country. The housing market cooled but didn't drop out like it did in other markets. And even with some of the tech layoffs affecting thousands in the area, many were quickly rehired with the expansion of anchor companies in the greater Seattle market. Companies like AT&T, T-Mobile, Microsoft, and Amazon.com had trimmed the fat but were still hiring for specific skill sets. Venture money flowed, giving life to a healthy population of start-up companies. The technology sector in the area created a solid foundation of job openings, high salaries, and scarcity of talent. This would prove critical as we commenced our new venture.

I got back into a daily routine comprised of dedicated time slots for specific tasks. I'd really embraced time management while at HK. It's too easy, especially in a start-up environment, to get distracted by shiny objects and tasks. With countless to-dos at hand and only so many hours to execute, everything is top priority. But by blocking out time for each task, I could systematically check things off my to-do list.

The early days were wild and chaotic. Even with Jesse's and Ryan's involvement, it still seemed like we were making shit up on the fly. We didn't have a formal office space, so meetings were held at a coffee shop in Seattle called Louisa's. Since we were all remote, it was imperative we have constant communication—phone calls, conference calls with three or more of us, emails, and text and instant messages—pretty much 24-7.

Most of my early days were spent developing business from either the relationships I'd fostered over the years, or from cold calls into new prospects. Luckily, I held a strong Rolodex of Seattle-area contacts—gleaned from tens of thousands of calls and meetings over my ten years in the business. At thirty-three years old, I was grateful for that heavy lifting I'd done, even though I probably hadn't anticipated how it would eventually pay off.

Within a couple of weeks of calling, we had signed a few clients to run contingent searches and potentially fill some contract roles as well. These searches would produce potential employees of The Job Mob that would then be staffed as contractors to our clients, to work on a myriad of different projects.

From there, I put on my recruiter hat and began hunting. I took great pleasure in the challenge of vetting out and qualifying one's interests, goals, work history, and values. The sales aspect of headhunting is unique, requiring constant communication and continuous supervising, as people can change their minds at the drop of a hat. Sourcing qualified talent was a constant struggle that took up a huge amount of time. Resume boards, professional networks, special interest groups—you name it, they were a possible source for leads. And of course, there were referrals. Lots of referrals.

Word had gotten out that The Job Mob was up and running, and for some reason, we had lots of people reaching out to us with their resumes. Maybe it was the beginning of the downturn of the economy, and people were feeling the effects of the layoffs. Maybe people were just curious what we were all about. We hadn't even established an office, a culture, any level of structure to the organization, or much of what anyone would consider crucial for a company. But we did have our branding.

We had a lot of fun with the branding. Josiah had created The Job Mob moniker and kept a keen eye for what was cool—bringing the most style of us all. Always knowing what was trendy, he applied it to our brand. And once he got the ball rolling, the creative process inevitably sparked for us all.

We started with really funky business cards—oblong shaped, with neon-green coloring and two-tone, lower-case font. The title for each of the five of us was "boss," thus playing off the mob nomenclature. Our simple website showed similar color patterns and messaging that stated the following:

> We started the Job Mob with the primary goal of connecting good people with good opportunities. We're a growing family

searching for like-minded individuals who want to make a name for themselves. So, whether you are actively searching for your next challenge, or simply have an ear to the ground for something cool, please reach out to us in confidence. The Job Mob is here. Consider yourself warned.

We took it even further as we created roles for our first employees. Our consultant employees were called "consigliere," and our first managers "capos." This resonated with everyone, even our clients. Consigliere means advisor, which applied nicely since our employees were providing guidance. All I could think of was the character Silvio Dante in the hit series *The Sopranos*, and how he was Tony's advisor and sounding board. Our first Job Mob T-shirts stole the "Got Milk," slogan and stated "Get Made" across the chest. And with any published content, we made sure to use words like "family," "connected," and "sit down with us," consistent with the mob association.

I must note, our intention was never to be disrespectful to any particular groups, and we tried to be mindful of exactly how far we could push the branding. It was meant to be funny. It was meant to stand out. And it accomplished exactly that.

Applying a Division of Labor

Josiah and I drove most of the sales and business development efforts, while John focused on talent acquisition and human resources. We wanted to ensure that when we finally hired anyone, all components were in place to make the process seamless. This meant our benefits packages, onboarding documentation, payroll, and company equipment forms must all be in order. John even created an employee handbook, complete with company policies, hiring practices, employee code of conduct, and other useful information for any new hires. As things came together, it felt like we were becoming a real company.

Jesse and Ryan would pop in and out on any given day, beyond our standing weekly meetings where we covered the sales and candidate pipeline, established our week's priorities, as well as addressed operational issues. Josiah and Jesse ran with marketing, and with the help of Jesse's neighbor, who just happened to be a graphic designer, organized our website and procured our business cards. We launched the site with very limited content beyond a home page, services page, leadership page, and contact page with instructions on how to apply for jobs. Our close friend and former colleague, Jim Green, helped set up all our technology infrastructure. We also worked with Jim at Endeavor; he led all aspects of IT, so he was very familiar with our needs. He set up a secured network and our email domain, as well as some basic file-sharing servers to electronically store all our documents.

Finding 2815 Eastlake Ave East

By the second week of September, it was painfully obvious that we needed some sort of shared and dedicated space to work effectively. Many times, we'd gather at Louisa's only to find that all the tables were taken. Plus, it wasn't exactly the best setting for discussions over sensitive topics. As much as we were trying our best to keep our costs to a minimum, we collectively decided a formal office was necessary.

Efforts to search for space were driven by Jesse and Ryan, as they had the most experience negotiating lease agreements and terms along with a sound understanding of market rates for commercial space. We looked all over the Puget Sound area but focused mainly on just north of downtown Seattle or South Lake Union. This growing area had major tech and pharmaceutical companies gobbling up every square inch of available space. And this was at least a couple years before shared workspace companies like WeWork started popping up. I don't think we could have afforded them anyway.

Taking a different approach, we looked for second-class commercial property off the beaten path. We weren't looking for a place to show off. We needed a practical space where we could operate with credibility as a legit business with a dedicated, physical address. The five of us also looked at random houses zoned commercial as well as smaller, lesser-quality office space in funky Seattle neighborhoods. We were trying to be as creative as possible given our small budget.

One day, we came across a small, unfinished open space at 2815 Eastlake Ave East, right across the water from Gas Works Park, a nationally registered historic landmark. The single room was rectangular in shape, on the third floor of a shabby office building with an outdated look and feel. It had unfinished concrete floors. A single pillar stood in the middle of the room. Wires hung down from the broken ceiling panels, exposing the rafters above. Any normal person in search of office space would have taken one look and immediately walked the other direction. For us, it was perfect.

The one thing that was absolutely spectacular was the view. The building overlooked the northern part of Lake Union and Gas Works Park. Boats of all sizes cruised by constantly. Amphibious planes took off and landed every hour. Local crew teams practiced in the early mornings.

Every couple of hours each day, you'd see the "Ride the Duck," a fleet of restored U-Boats that offered sightseeing experiences for tourists. With a small balcony off the back, the views from there were the ultimate selling point.

Probably the most important aspect of the space was the price. Our monthly rent was $2,400, a number we felt comfortable with. We didn't require any significant tenant improvements, which made the terms of the lease that much more affordable. There were no individual office buildouts or major tech infrastructure needed. Granted, there was no boardroom or kitchen. There weren't even any cubicles. We had a file cabinet with a laser printer on top, which we bought at Office Depot, along with some basic Wi-Fi routers. Jesse procured a couple of large, four-by-eight-foot whiteboards to hang on the wall as creative workspaces to display ideas, the statuses of sales and recruiting efforts, or messages he wanted to emphatically state for our edification.

One day, Jesse walked in and wrote "Cash Is King" in big, bold letters, making a bit of a commotion as he capped the dry erase pen and slapped it into the tray below. He clearly had something to say and wanted to bring his point home without any misunderstanding. This was his attempt to educate John, Josiah, and me on the concept that we must keep cash flow management in mind as we made day-to-day decisions and considered our business operations.

"A lot of companies go out of business because of cash flow management," Jesse continued. "It's not always about lack of revenue, or even gross margins. Things can be going well from a growth perspective, yet a lack of available cash or access to credit can destroy a company. Make sure you keep this in mind as you consider everyday business expenses."

This simple business concept was stamped into our brains from the very beginning—and we have Jesse to thank. From then on, we did our best to respect the undulating cycle of cash flow and make sound decisions accordingly. Ironically, we didn't realize at the time that we would eventually face this very same problem, even once we were magnitudes larger and more mature as a company.

Given our start-up mentality and minimal funding at our disposal, we did everything to cut corners and save a buck. We needed desks, but office furniture was really expensive. We asked ourselves: *What are our options? Do we lease furniture? Do we make a run down to Ikea and go really cheap?*

John came up with the perfect solution. Given the significant downsizing of staff at Jobster, John worked out a deal with his CEO to buy desks directly from them. I think we got them for pennies on the dollar, and the desks were pieces of art in themselves. Apparently Jobster had the desks specially designed by some famous architect or designer, and man did it show. A combination of wood and wrought iron created each funky and modern-yet-functional desk—seven feet long, with a back shelf at least five feet tall. The primary working surface area was made up of a three-inch thick, solid piece of wood, probably a refinished door of some type. Large pieces of iron served as legs as well as design details for the back shelving. Needless to say, fully constructed, these desks were fucking heavy!

In the middle of September on a Saturday when no one was around, the four of us met up with John at the Jobster offices in downtown Seattle. I walked in, I felt a bit of sadness as the place appeared lifeless. You could tell immediately that this was a business headed for closure.

We brought some tools with us, and carefully dismantled five desks that had been earmarked. We carefully marked all the pieces of wood and wrought iron, as well as the thick steel bolts and nuts that held them together. We used dollies to run the many parts down the service elevator to the parking garage where John had his Ford F-150 parked. After loading everything, we headed to our office and began the long process of hauling the parts back up to our third-floor space—reassembling each one to the best of our ability.

The desks were perfect and provided not only an appropriate amount of workspace for each of us, but a sense of style in an office space that had absolutely no décor. No classy paintings on the wall. No area carpets. Even the off-white paint was nondescript. We positioned each desk on an exterior wall, facing away from each other. John somehow scored the premium spot, facing the only window in the office that had views of the water. I'm not sure how we let that happen. Maybe we drew straws. Maybe we acquiesced, because he was the elder in our group.

Another way we saved money was by parking on the street. We could have splurged for monthly parking passes for the garage downstairs, but that was a luxury we couldn't afford. So we took it upon ourselves to find parking either directly on Eastlake Ave or on some adjacent side street. You wouldn't think it, but parking became a significant topic we had to constantly manage due to the restrictions on Eastlake.

Eastlake Avenue was a major street, relatively speaking, that commuters used to get from north of Lake Union to downtown Seattle. Therefore, any time before 8 a.m., we couldn't park on the west side of the street, as they opened both lanes for commuters. Conversely, we couldn't park on the east side of the street past 5 p.m., as they opened both lanes for commuters heading back north. I remember vividly that tow trucks would line up at 4:45 in the afternoon, just waiting for the bewitching hour of 5 p.m., where they would enthusiastically start picking off unsuspecting individuals and tow their cars away without any warning.

It was a shit show, and inevitably one of us would get towed at least once every couple of months. We'd have to get a taxi or ride from one of the other guys, head down to the impound site a few miles away, and shell out $200 just to get our cars back. The convenience of Uber didn't quite exist yet. This was really nerve-wracking, as we had to constantly think about what time it was, whether we'd parked on Eastlake, and if so, which side. This often resulted in an "oh, shit!"—just before sprinting out of the office, racing across the street, and hoping the tow trucks hadn't gotten to our vehicle yet. Sometimes I got there just in time; the tow truck was loading up some poor victim's car one space ahead of mine. I'd jump in my car, wave to the tow truck driver, and thank my lucky stars; meanwhile he likely thought, *You got away this time, but next time I'll get you.*

After about a month in the office, we realized we needed to make it a little more comfortable and professional. We decided to start with the flooring, as the concrete floors were dingy with various stains in random places. Plus, the acoustics were terrible given the desks were the only materials in the space. Sound would bounce off the walls and reverberate back, disrupting any private conversation, forcing us to talk over one another, exacerbating the situation. Someone came up with the idea of installing hardwoods, thinking they might not only solve the sound problem, but make the office a little more aesthetically pleasing.

To help come up with a cost-effective solution, Jesse and

Ryan used some negotiating power and quid pro quo bartering to procure us some really nice, tongue-and-groove stained-oak floors. I think they traded for some Quantum windows or doors work, leveraging one of their portfolio companies.

One day, twenty or so boxes of dark-stained-oak flooring panels arrived. We let the boxes acclimate to the relative humidity for a week or so in the office before taking on the task of installation. Now I'd done a little carpentry work in my days, represented by a resume that included a couple chicken coops, framing in a wine cellar, and a doghouse. John brought slightly better credentials, and for Josiah, it might as well have been the first time he picked up a hammer.

On a random Saturday, we gathered at the office and knocked out the flooring. John brought a miter saw and set it up on the balcony. Jesse and Ryan helped arrange the panels in an offset manner, while I took measurements for John. We had a pretty sweet system; as each piece was put in place, Josiah used a caulking gun with liquid nails for the adhesive.

We worked all day, late into the evening, toiling over each panel, carefully fitting them into place with painstaking detail. Halfway through the install, Josiah had crazy cramping in his hands, as the caulking gun proved too much to handle. He looked like a ninety-year-old with a bad case of arthritis—hands stricken with carpal tunnel, locked in place from overuse, reminiscent of a dinosaur's claws. He complained the rest of the time, but his efforts were not in vain.

The final product was spectacular as far as we were concerned. Given that none of us had ever installed wood flooring, we admired our craftsmanship as if we had just built a Roman temple. Don't get me wrong; the finished product was not remotely close to the work of a mediocre contractor. There were areas where the floors weren't even, and instead of taking the proper measures to level it out, we just went ahead and installed the panels regardless. So in certain areas, when we walked, the floors would dip ever so slightly beneath our feet. And we didn't install any trim, which gave the area a somewhat unfinished look. But overall, our efforts reflected our scrappy attitudes, knowing we were a startup. We couldn't afford to pay someone, so we had to do the work ourselves. Whether pride in what we accomplished, or disbelief, we got the job done.

As a sidenote, when we moved out of the office a couple of years later, we were tasked by the building management to remove all the hardwoods. What an ordeal that was. Let's just say we applied the liquid nails during the install in the most liberal of ways, so pulling up the panels was excruciatingly difficult. I believe it took more time and effort removing the panels than installing them in the first place.

Work-life at the Eastlake office was full of energy and excitement, as we could collaborate effortlessly in one large room. All we had to do was turn around and ask a question, and sometimes that wasn't even necessary. Even with the newly laid hardwoods, sound would still bounce off the wall in front of each of us and echo back across the room. This was very convenient, until it wasn't. When we needed to have a private conversation, our "conference room" had to consist of the hallway outside or the balcony. Otherwise, we talked over each other in a constant battle. I'm sure we also pissed off the other tenants from our pacing around in the hallways on our phones. Nonetheless, we did what we needed to do, given what we had—a common theme of scrappiness throughout our existence.

In the beginning of October, I suffered a torn Achilles tendon while playing basketball one evening at the local gym. I underwent surgery two days later, resulting in no weight-bearing for the next couple of months. It fucking sucked, as life on crutches was a major inconvenience. Try carrying a cup of coffee while using crutches. To make matters worse, it was my right leg that got injured, so it meant I also couldn't drive. What an inconvenience, not only to the momentum of the business but to my business partners as well. I took a week off to recover from surgery but felt like I needed to get back to work. Cabin fever was setting in, and I had to find a solution.

The only saving grace was a close friend of mine, Jordan Oliver, coincidentally lived just past my house and worked in the same building. For six weeks, he graciously picked me up and drove me home each day—a kind-hearted gesture I will never forget. Luckily, my damaged condition didn't negatively impact our productivity and growth. It only led to yet another temporary nickname from Josiah: "gimpy."

The Photoshoot

One afternoon in November, John, Josiah, and I drove down to Ballard, a waterfront neighborhood in Seattle, in search of some cool backdrops for pictures. We wanted to have individual profiles on the website, but again, in an effort to be edgy, we wanted the pictures to be completely different from what you'd see on your average "meet our leaders" page.

Reflecting back, I seriously ask myself, *What the fuck were we thinking?* What we created was absolute comedy.

We thought it would be cool to find some spots down on the pier where all the fishing boats were moored and take some "spy" shots of us, making it appear we were up to no good. Imagine a hidden FBI agent taking photographs of some shady fellows involved in some sort of nefarious business dealings. There we were, dressed in long black leather jackets and trench coats, trying our best to represent—what we felt was—an overtly macho disposition and a criminal bent. Again, fucking comical. You can't make this shit up.

For some stupid reason, we thought the photos would portray differently than they did. I guess we hoped to be taken seriously, but the sheer buffoonery displayed gave the complete opposite effect. There were pictures of Josiah and John talking in the distance. Pictures of John and me shaking hands—as if we'd just agreed on some shady business transaction. And pictures of me and Josiah standing in front of some random wall with graffiti. We poured every ounce of creativity into creating the appearance of bad dudes up to no good, but our half-ass efforts fell well short of anything impressive.

First of all, there were never more than two of us in a shot—with no fourth person to actually take pictures of all three of us in one shot—and we had no proper photo shoot gear. Great planning, right? Further, none of us had any particular skills with a digital camera. Composition, lighting, and all the other basic elements of photography were lost on us—and it showed in the end product.

And the location ... what were we thinking? What do marinas have to do with criminal behavior? What was up with the graffiti pictures? Was it normal for the mob to conduct their business next to the commercial crab and fishing boats?

Last, I was still on crutches from the Achilles surgery, and my right leg was in a boot. Therefore, taking photos of me became a comical process. First, we'd get into position, and then I'd have to drop the crutches out of sight from the picture, try to maintain a balanced stance with most of my weight on my left foot, then grab my crutches before I fell over. Again, laughable.

We finished our photo shoot, and I took the first crack at editing. I tried to make the pictures appear to be taken from some scope-like lens, giving them a circular appearance with a slightly grainy texture. I was using some basic, off-the-shelf photo editing software—which I had absolutely no experience using. The results reflected this fact.

In the end, we produced three viable headshots for the website. The pictures were low-grade and screamed amateur hour. But the funny thing is, despite this not being our intention, this was exactly what we needed—pictures that were edgy and different, but most importantly displayed the fact that we didn't take ourselves too seriously. The very fact that we looked like a bunch of clowns only added to the cool factor. Mission accomplished, in the most asinine manner.

Building Momentum

By November of 2008, just a few months into the new venture, the energy of The Job Mob was starting to build. We had our office complete with brand new hardwood floors, fancy desks we got on-the-cheap, and large whiteboards on the walls. We even had a little greenery, thanks to my parents who dropped off a potted peace lily as a congratulations-on-the-new-digs gesture. We were proud of the final product, and that translated into positive energy and lots of activity.

John, Josiah, and I were in the office on the daily, with Jesse and Ryan dropping in a few days a week. A Costco order of Keurig coffee pods kept us fully caffeinated, along with the occasional jaunt down to the Hamlin Market across the street for a latte if we felt like splurging. We were busy. Really busy. It was a blitzkrieg effort; all of us were taking any means necessary to get the word out that The Job Mob was here, and we were hungry for growth. The three of us were constantly on the phone, calling up contacts in our respective networks, sharing our company details and asking for business. If we weren't, we were sending out emails or messages through platforms like LinkedIn to make connections.

Within a couple of weeks, we landed our first client, Gist. Gist was a tech startup company that originated out of Vulcan Ventures and their incubator that Paul Allen used to test new technologies. I'm sure that I'm not getting the story completely accurate, but it's my understanding Paul Allen was sitting around with a couple of his leaders, discussing some far-fetched idea of *knowing everything you'd like to know about anything you want*. That conversation evolved into them discussing, "What's important to you?"

People ... relationships with people were what was important. So they asked themselves, *How do we create a technology that can help organize, prioritize, and manage how we connect with those most important to us?* It began with building technology that integrated with applications like Outlook and other data sources, so a user could have all the latest and greatest details of those in their professional networks. It was a very cool idea back then, as the only real option was LinkedIn, which at the time only shared content produced on the platform—versus pulling information from a variety of sources. Their idea was strong enough that Gist spun out of Vulcan into its own entity.

Gist, which was named something completely different prior to spinning off, was the perfect opportunity for us. Josiah had a great relationship with their CEO, T.A. McCann, and that helped set the table for what would become the source of our first revenue dollars. Initially, we conducted some searches for full-time employees for them, along with a contract role for a software engineer.

At first, Josiah drove the relationship with Gist, but gradually, John became more ingrained as he ran point on recruiting efforts. The first role we recruited for was a software engineer with strong opensource and Ruby on Rails coding experience. Josiah knew the right guy and introduced a local candidate, Jacques, to the Gist team. They put him through interviews and gave us the go-ahead to bring him on board—our first taste of success, and it sure was sweet!

The next role Gist needed was a senior engineer with strong experience in C++ and Internet Message Access Protocol (IMAP), and this proved to be very difficult. We searched high and low for weeks and eventually found a candidate named Michael, who lived remotely on the Olympic Peninsula. He had experience working within the Microsoft Outlook technology stack and therefore had IMAP experience. We screened him, shared details of our company and our client, and presented Michael as a candidate for consideration. The interview process was lengthy, as it was difficult to coordinate interview times given the crazy schedules of those at Gist. After multiple calls, face-to-face meetings, and reference checking, T.A. and Steven Newman, Gist's CTO, gave us the thumbs up to hire Michael.

Our second taste of success, and we celebrated over a glass of bourbon at the office that evening. The experience of closing our first deals was magnificent. We were proving to ourselves that despite the market conditions, we could find success. It was the foothold we needed to give us confidence that this new venture was in fact doable.

Our relationship with Gist grew quickly as we became more intertwined with their talent acquisition efforts. They were growing so much and had a very high bar for talent. We eventually worked out a deal where John would be in their office a couple of days a week on retainer. Not only did he help with their recruiting efforts, but he also helped stand up some human resources infrastructure. We billed him out at $13,000 per month—a rate we felt was appropriate, since we'd also make money on the successful placements of candidates. Initially, I loved the fact that John sacrificed himself to be billable. Back then, $13,000 was a lot of money for us. However, over time, we missed his presence in the office on the regular and began evaluating exactly how long this could go on. Luckily, John's engagement with Gist lasted only a few months, resulting in multiple successful placements, both full-time and contract.

Eventually, Gist reached critical mass and hired their own person to run HR, so our working relationship faded in time. We'd be forever grateful for the opportunity to work with them, as the relationships we built would eventually lead us to hiring a senior executive four years later.

As we wrapped up 2008, the five of us were gaining more confidence that this endeavor might actually have some legs, despite the continued decline in the overall economy. Companies were interested in talking to us. Candidates sent us their resumes. The brand seemed to spark some sense of positivity in our community, when everyone was experiencing layoffs, plummeting housing prices, and a global economic meltdown.

Maybe we were so focused on operating the business and evangelizing the brand that we were oblivious to any financial turmoil in the markets. Either way, the market conditions didn't dampen our spirits. I was loving the business we'd created, the clients we engaged with, and the employees we were hiring. At that point, all our employees were billable to clients as contractors, while the owners of our company ran our day-to-day operations. Our culture was beginning to take shape, not necessarily out of intention, but by a natural symbiosis amongst John, Josiah, and me. We were The Job Mob, and whether you liked us or not, we did our best to make our presence felt.

Chapter 6

The Business Evolves

It's around seven in the evening, and it's dark outside, with a February Pacific Northwest chill in the air. I'm in my car, driving away from my house, a couple of suitcases in the trunk, and Pepe is nervously pacing in the backseat. I can see the whites of his eyes contrasting to his black fur. "It's all good, Little Man," I reassuringly say, looking at him through my rearview mirror. He's confused but senses the tone of the moment and eventually curls up into a ball and lies down. Tears fill up my eyes as I second guess what I just did. No, I think to myself. It's the right thing. You need to be strong and hold the course. You just need some space and time to think. I look for a distraction by turning on the radio and hear Kanye West's "Love Lockdown." I listen with incredible detail to each word of the lyrics: "I'm not loving you, way I wanted to. What I had to do, had to run from you ..." The song continues. I'm utterly moved, filled with sadness and sobriety, as I take in every fucking word of the song. I'm fixated on the lines. It's about me. It's about my situation. Kanye knows. He's telling me something. It's fate.

If you're in the business of technology consulting or staffing in the Greater Seattle area, it's likely that you have engaged, are currently engaged, or want to engage with Microsoft. For years, they have leveraged what they call *vendors* and *contingent staff* (temporary workers) to supplement work throughout their giant software company. To many, this presents a potential cash cow, given the stability of Microsoft as a global organization, but also from their quick payment terms. Microsoft has been responsible for the success of many services-based companies over the years.

But engaging in business with Microsoft also comes with several nonnegotiable rules and guidelines. This includes navigating both legal and fiscal requirements, as well as specific engagement criteria like maximum durations and mandatory breaks. Many of these rules are the direct result of a major lawsuit pinned on the Redmond-based software giant for what the Department of Justice described as exploitation of the so-called *permatemps*. This resulted in a $97,000,000 settlement to thousands of workers, along with a slew of new legal requirements instituted by Microsoft to protect them from future co-employment problems.

Despite the evolution of rules for vendor engagement over the years, Microsoft was a key client for us from the get-go. Josiah and I made a ton of calls into the company, letting everyone know that The Job Mob was in business, and we were determined to get on the approved vendor list —no small or easy task, especially as a young company with little track record of success. Call after call, meeting after meeting, we did our best to navigate the complex process that was owned by Microsoft's Procurement Team.

First, we needed an executive sponsor. I recall they had to be at least a director level within the organization and able to justify the addition of a new service provider. Procurement would scrutinize the requests for new vendors and ask why the manager couldn't simply use an existing vendor who provided similar services.

In time, procurement would prove to hold an unreasonable amount of power over us as a service provider, one that would leave a bitter taste. But for now, ignorance was bliss, and all our focus was to find the right person who could provide sponsorship. Lucky for us, we quickly located a few leaders we had good working relationships with.

The second necessity to get on the list was an initial engagement with someone who had a budget to bring us on and open a purchase order. Josiah, Jesse, and I were blanketing the Microsoft landscape with emails and meetings in an effort to land that first deal. Timing was everything, as you never knew when budgets would get approved for any given project.

David Totten was a leader in one of the sales divisions at Microsoft and became a close connection with Josiah. David rattled a few trees in an attempt to get us on the approved vendor list, but unfortunately he didn't have a specific project for us to work on. For some reason, though, it didn't matter. He must have had serious influence given his high-potential status within the large company. His efforts were seriously appreciated, as we eventually reached the correct person within procurement who helped walk David through the process of onboarding The Job Mob as an approved vendor. This process took us over a month to navigate, filling out detailed justification documents, acquiring the necessary insurance and liability coverage, providing tax documentation and extensive company information in an online application, and finally, getting the actual approval from the powers that be.

As we wrapped up 2008, we received our official vendor number from Microsoft, and so began the opportunity to hunt for any business we could find.

The Microsoft master service agreement (MSA) essentially gave us a license to hunt within the giant software company, and we were nothing short of ecstatic to dive in. Since Josiah came from a business intelligence company, he continued tapping the shoulders of every contact he had, especially in groups that leveraged tons of data and marketing technology. Within a short time, he identified our very first client within the MSN business intelligence team, led by a friendly leader named Eleanor. They needed an analyst to help drive reporting and data visualization for some of their internal customers, and we wasted no time getting the right candidate in front of them. David started right away and was our first billable consultant on the ground at Microsoft. He was young, energetic, and eager to learn. He was also a character and fit into our blossoming culture of a dynamic, edgy start-up.

This was a great win for us, as it gave us a nice foothold to leverage. Between our work with Microsoft and Gist, we were able to close out 2008 with total revenue of $139,995, and an overall net loss of over $81,000—results we were quite content with given the state of the economy and the short four months since the company's inception.

A month later in January, we started to experience serious momentum within the Microsoft landscape. Kyle Wagner, a close friend and senior manager within the customer support services (CSS) group, reached out as he was looking to build a team comprised of vendor resources to supplement their full-time staff. We initially brought on Kurt Harris. Then Logan Henry. Then Craig Post. Within a couple of months of landing our MSA, we had a half dozen employees supporting major Microsoft products like

Windows Live, MSN, and Hotmail. Expedia also started to bring us into their database marketing group, giving us a beachhead with our first consultant named Aaron Cozzens. Things were getting busy.

Change Is Expensive, But Worth It

February of 2009 will forever remain an unprecedented time for me and for the business. After many attempts to work out our marital differences on the home front, I decided it was best to take a different direction and separate from Lisa. After eight years of marriage, we had drifted apart. Or at least, I felt we did.

Beyond that, I'd enabled a living situation that couldn't be undone, in my opinion. From my perspective, I had created a future very similar to how my parents dealt with money, and it didn't sit well with me. I resented myself for making this happen, and I resented her more for allowing it.

To make matters worse, she resented me for seeking counsel with a couple of family members during the whole Tillie debacle. All I was looking for was someone to talk to, but she took it as a direct violation of her privacy. This manifested into anger—anger that had been held over my head ever since, nearly seven years later, superseding even what she felt toward Tillie. Between that resentment and the financial dysfunction we shared, I just couldn't continue.

The separation came as a surprise to everyone, as I never aired my personal life to anyone other than Lisa or our counselor. My parents, business partners, and friends were all completely surprised by my move—mostly due to our relentless effort to make it appear like we had a perfect life from the outside. But this charade had become too much work, and I resented my sheer lack of authenticity.

Still, it was a tough decision that I struggled with for months prior. I'd known her since we were teenagers, fell in love with her while we were both attending university, and married her when I was twenty-five years old. She possessed countless talents, was extremely well read, and had a passion to live life on the outer edges of adventure. But despite all the attributes that once made her the woman of my dreams, I concluded I needed change.

Our last meeting with the counselor had sealed the decision for me, an epiphany of sorts that it didn't make sense to try to salvage a relationship when we ultimately wanted different things in life.

"Share with us a time when you were happiest," the counselor requested of Lisa. There was a long, thought-filled pause. I'll never forget her answer.

"I was happiest when I was single, living my life back in New York City."

That was the proverbial straw that broke the camel's back. A mix of sadness and lucidity filled my gut. The prescription was evident. I wasn't going to be the person to stand in the way of anyone's happiness, especially since we had a lifetime ahead of us. We had no children or major assets of any value that could complicate a separation. The choice to move on, create space between us, became soberingly obvious.

"I need some space to think about my future," I concluded later that night as I grabbed some clothes from the closet and stuffed them into a duffle bag. "We are not in a good space right now, and a little time alone is what I need."

The evening of the February 9, after our final session with our counselor, I packed up two suitcases and my dog

Pepe, jumped in my car, and checked into a La Quinta motel. Before I left, I told her not to worry about any of the finances, to live in the house, and we'd reconnect in a month to see how we were both feeling. At the time, it made sense to "take a break," as space and time would help clear our heads and focus on the right path forward.

Little did I know, but that would be the last time I ever saw Lisa in person. A month later, and without warning, she served me with papers in an attempt to take everything in our possession. I was not only blindsided by this move but perplexed that she would go through so much effort just to split up what little we had to our names. I would have been happy to sit down at a Starbucks and hash out the details—since there really wasn't much to divvy up—but her feelings of betrayal and anger led her down an expensive path of retribution.

At the time, she was just getting her floral design business off the ground, and I was working day and night trying to get The Job Mob to a profitable position—which it wasn't even close to yet. Our personal balance sheet was lopsided, with our liabilities completely outweighing our assets. Our house? Underwater. Savings account? Drained to an embarrassingly low balance. I had to borrow money just to hire an attorney to respond to her outrageous suit.

Even worse, the whole legal offensive seemed predicated on her mother's emotional outrage toward me. Her mom had no problem plunking down thousands of dollars to basically fuck with me. "You broke my poor daughter's heart, so I'm going to respond in kind with a nonsensical legal assault; that will teach you a lesson" was the presumed attitude from her. "Hell hath no fury like a woman scorned" is an understatement when you add a disgruntled mother-in-law to the equation. Senseless accusations. Rumors about drug addiction. Pitting relationships of friends and family against me. Ugly. It was a total waste of resources, and all driven by irrational and anger-driven recklessness.

Suddenly, I found myself with my back to the wall, on the defensive, trying to navigate the foreign land of financial restraining orders and legal separation conditions. I was angry. I was confused. But most of what I felt was disappointment. I really respected and cared for her family; they were good, wholehearted people who had been a part of my life for a long time.

But in the end, the separation was my decision, so I was determined to deal with whatever fallout transpired, regardless of any guilt, anger, or frustration. Continue eating Ramen. Sleep on someone's couch. Cherish my true friends who didn't judge. Use work as a positive distraction. Adapt. Hustle. Persevere. Harness the anger that roiled inside of me and the ever-expanding chip on my shoulder as motivation. It was a tough road filled with the collateral damage of family stress, and even worse, lost friendships. Relationships are tough, and no one is specifically to blame for their fate.

Someone once asked me if I knew why divorce is so expensive.

"Why?" I responded.

He then followed up with a pithy, yet weighty, "Because it's worth it."

Years later, I heard someone say it again, and with the unnecessary drama behind me, I couldn't agree more.

Conversely, Ryan and John were doing the exact opposite of me and celebrating their respective nuptials. Both had planned months before on destination weddings that would take them to Thailand and the Bahamas, respectively. Jesse was Ryan's best man and therefore was obligated to make the trip to Southeast Asia as well. That left

Josiah and me to hold down the fort while they were away for the last couple of weeks in February, a time that flew by in the blink of an eye.

The Grind

If you ask Josiah, he will joke, saying that my separation and divorce was the best thing that happened to the business. At the time, I harnessed all my will and focused it completely on the business. We were busy. Really fucking busy. Business opportunities from Gist, Microsoft, and Expedia.com gained us lots of momentum, forcing us to work crazy hours recruiting talent. Josiah and I used every resource we could to locate future Job Mob employees.

Job postings and resume boards, friendly referrals from those in our network, and Boolean search strings on the internet were our hunting grounds for potential candidates. We searched for support engineers for Microsoft, software engineers and user experience experts for Gist, and database marketing analysts for Expedia. In the month of February 2009 alone, we closed a bunch of business, which necessitated the hiring of five more consultant employees.

Clients were committing significant budgets to have our employees work within their businesses on various projects. We would then bill the client based on some hourly or fixed number, pay our employees market wages, and the difference or margin would ultimately be our profit.

I was spending fourteen hours a day in the office, as I'd come in around 8 a.m. and stay until at least 10 p.m. Sometimes I'd be there till well past midnight. I'd eat in the office, with the predominate meal being a Subway sandwich or take-out teriyaki. Pepe would come to work with me every day, offering unconditional love and a listening ear. By the time the other three came back from their respective vacations, Josiah and I had launched the company forward.

Work essentially defined my life. I was alright with it, as it served as a valuable distraction from the turbulent separation I was dealing with in parallel.

I was also living in Jesse's basement, something that I will forever be grateful for, because I couldn't afford my own place. I was giving Lisa over 60 percent of my gross income in what was categorized as "spousal maintenance" —which left very little after taxes and general life expenses.

Even with the closing of new business, the company couldn't afford much for the owners salary-wise. It would be another couple of months before we saw any opportunity to increase that, and even then, it was ever so slight. But every bit helped, as I was clawing my way back to subsistence levels. Talk about motivation.

We continued up a path of steep growth as we rolled through March, ending the first quarter of 2009 by signing new clients and adding more employees. The Job Mob employee roster strengthened by the week, and the overall revenue numbers looked promising. By the end of the month, we had fifteen employees fully billable and over $335,000 in revenue for the first quarter.

The Mob Opens the Books

The pipeline of potential opportunities was healthy, and our graphed-out projections continued to point upward and to the right. We felt it was a great time to hire someone with operational responsibilities, so we posted an open requisition for what we called Captain or Capo. Again, this was our half-assed yet playful attempt to embrace mob-themed lingo.

Creating this role of *engagement manager* was a pivotal move for The Job Mob, as we were starting to become a real company. John, Josiah, and I were in the weeds of the business on a day-to-day basis, and we needed more support in managing relationships with our employee base. Jesse and Ryan were still involved on a part-time basis, but they were also managing a portfolio of other companies. This was our very first operational role we'd fill outside of the founders. Since it would also be the first hire that wasn't directly billable to a client, the thought of this additional cost—complete overhead—was stressful.

But the role was necessary, as we truly believed we wanted to create a great employee experience. Our vision had this person responsible for the care and feeding of all our employees consulting in the field. They would also serve as an escalation point for human resource issues like payroll, health insurance, paid time-off, and other benefits. But most important, the position would help drive a cultural identity to all billable employees working outside our office. This was the impetus for what we would eventually call our *secret sauce* to building a culture to remember. This move would be critical in potentially getting us any prestigious "Best Places to Work" accolades.

In order to check all the requirements, we needed someone with varied experiences and qualifications. We started with those familiar with HR, be it general or specific to benefits. They also needed to understand the dynamics of staffing and talent acquisition—which meant onboarding staff and redeploying them to new projects. And beyond that, this person must have the ability to navigate lots of ambiguity.

I ran point on filling the position, as it originally reported to me, but everyone was involved in the interview and screening process. We posted the role publicly and received many resume submissions. We also reached out to our individual networks for referrals. We ended up with four viable candidates in the pipeline from a variety of sources, mostly friendly recommendations from trusted sources.

One of those referrals came from Ring Nishioka, a friend and former client of Josiah's. Ring ran HR for several start-up companies in the area and employed Lauren Carlton as an HR generalist and recruiter. Lauren had recently left that position and had her ear to the ground for a new role. We exchanged a few emails, as she was evaluating different career options, and eventually Josiah and I met up with her for coffee.

We had a casual yet detailed discussion about the position, our company vision and culture, and our individual backgrounds. Lauren asked very explicit questions, and when she felt she didn't get enough of an answer, she dug deeper. At first, this caught me off guard, as I wasn't expecting that we'd be doing most of the talking. But in the end, she was just what we were looking for—with a tenacious attitude and work ethic, intelligence to think on the fly, and an ability to work independently. We knew this role would evolve over time, and we needed someone who could essentially create and grow the position organically in real-time.

After a bit of discussion amongst the team, it became clear that she was the one. We offered Lauren the position at the end of the month, and she accepted right away.

It didn't take long for Lauren's presence to be felt in our day-to-day productivity. She hit the ground running, taking control of our onboarding process of new employees, as well as some of the general HR functions. We sent out personalized emails to all our employees to introduce her and set up face-to-face meetings over the first couple of weeks.

Lauren's warm personality and energetic attitude were a welcome addition to the team, and we immediately started receiving positive feedback from everyone. She was constantly on the move—bouncing from one client to the next, meeting with employees, answering HR-related questions, delivering coffee and laptops, and ensuring everyone had what they needed to be successful. When she wasn't on the road, she was in the office, grinding away at establishing new processes and best practices for employee experience. I cannot overstate the importance of Lauren's involvement with The Job Mob since these early days.

The end of the second quarter of 2009 came quickly as we continued to ramp up our hiring. With a solid pipeline of projects, we were actively recruiting for several open requirements. At the end of March, we'd employed twelve employees beyond the five founders, but by the time we ended June, we'd doubled headcount to twenty-four. Our revenue also increased substantially over those three months to more than $800,000, a growth rate of over 140 percent.

On July 16, we held our quarterly owners' meeting and strategized how to keep the momentum. We had lots of items to discuss, as we'd started seeing signs of profitability and even a little cashflow.

Jesse drove most of the discussion on year-to-date actuals as they compared to our pro forma. We were now ahead of the models we'd established in both employee headcount and revenue. Given this success, we decided to increase our owner draws as well, a very welcome move given my need to move out of Jesse's basement and into my own place. We also talked about new client acquisition strategies, and decided we needed to add additional revenue firepower to Josiah and me by hiring a director of business development. Despite the fancy title, this was basically a salesperson.

After talking to a few different candidates, we decided to hire a sales professional named Chris. We ran him through several meetings with all the founders, and Chris passed with flying colors. He was very presentable, and when he talked, you listened. He had a charismatic way of engaging with his audience. Josiah had worked with him at a previous employer, and although their tenure together wasn't long, it was enough to have confidence to bring him aboard. Chris started at the end of July. We hoped he could capitalize on our momentum and find new opportunities with local companies.

But for some reason, his trust and credibility never materialized into prospects or opportunities. The five founders did our best to get him on the right track and keep him motivated, but I think he struggled with the whole start-up environment. It might seem like a sexy idea to work for a vibrant, young company like ours—offering a casual and unstructured environment, a scrappy culture and attitude, flexibility of work-life, and the ability to work independently. But what a candidate doesn't see up front can turn that dream into a living nightmare. We didn't have polished marketing materials, like a fancy website or glossy one-pagers to hand out. We had no engineers to support the sales process, as anyone qualified was focused on billable hours and utilization. Ours was an eat-what-you-kill environment, and those who couldn't navigate all the ambiguity and make shit up on the fly would be toast. Also, in a small company with attention to every detail, any weakness immediately stands out. There was no space to hide imperfections or fly under the radar. Everyone saw everything.

This was a costly learning experience for us, as Chris's

employment lasted a mere six months. I think the decision to part ways was a relief for him, as he certainly didn't want to let himself or us down. He just needed an environment that was more mature, with tools to support his success.

Despite seeing little revenue come out of Chris, our third and fourth quarters were stellar. Business development efforts between Josiah and me drove our revenue to new heights. We grew over 12 percent in revenue to finish the third quarter at $917,000 and employed more than thirty billable employees—essentially just one year from our company's inception.

We kept Lauren busy with onboarding new employees, managing some of the tactical HR issues, and connecting with all the existing workers out in the field. Despite all the responsibilities she carried, Lauren still found time to come to the office, adding to the camaraderie.

More Microsoft Love

As we rolled into the fourth quarter, we found and shifted into a new gear, which gave us even greater growth. Our relationships at Microsoft began bearing fruit in the form of friendly referrals to other leaders with projects and more importantly, budget to spend.

We were referred to a senior director named Phil, which opened the door to their customer service and support groups. This led us to onboard a new trusted employee, Dennis Comfort, to help us gain visibility within several new business opportunities and increase our relationships throughout Microsoft. By working closely with Phil and his direct reports, Dennis would provide guidance on various new programs to support Microsoft products like Windows Live, Hotmail, MSN, and other web-based services. He would then bring these project requirements back to me, and we would create delivery proposals to put back in front of Phil or whoever was accountable. This usually resulted in more wins, and therefore the need to hire more talent. Jay, Jian, Devin, Jason, Jeremiah, and Ed were added to our team.

Josiah was also generating new leads throughout the rest of Microsoft and making great headway into various groups, including the Central Marketing Group, Online Services Group, Xbox, The X-Net Team, and MS Advertising. A new manager we got introduced to, Rob Curry, helped us connect with another team needing our services.

This compelled us to hire for a different skill set in the database engineering, data analytics, and software engineering space. Employees like Ketan, Davi, Robbie, and others rounded out a fourth quarter hiring sprint.

Beyond Microsoft, we continued to grow our presence at other companies in the area. Clients like Expedia, Ambassadors International, WidgetBucks, and Gist continued rewarding us with projects ranging from software engineering to project management.

We had a lot to be proud of as we finished our first full calendar year with total revenue surpassing $3.2 million. With strong momentum heading into 2010, we were increasing our level of talent with each hire. We also each found a nice rhythm in our day-to-day roles, which gave us relative accountability and organizational identity.

Beyond all the success, we were really enjoying the ride. John, Josiah, and I got along extremely well, despite our type-A personalities and countless hours together. Whenever we had any disagreement or problem, we handled it with diplomacy and compassion.

Don't get me wrong; there were times of frustration and vehement discussion, bordering on arguing. But we found a way to hash it out quickly, respecting both passion and intensity. When you enter a business partnership with another person, it's very much like a marriage. Trust, communication, respect, and honesty are pillars for success, and they are nonnegotiable. If any are ever compromised, the chances of survival are greatly reduced. We all took abiding by these principles incredibly seriously, and we were rewarded with growth, recognition, and wins.

And with every deal closed came some sort of celebration.

We finished the year with a trip to Maui for some well-deserved rest and relaxation. In this epic vacation, we rented a large house just north of Kaanapali with spectacular views of the ocean. The five founders conducted our annual owners' meeting over cocktails and a delicious meal at The Lahaina Grill. Ryan kept detailed notes on the white butcher paper covering our table, outlining several discussion points including cashflow, our 2010 growth strategy, and leadership.

And as we ended the meeting, Ryan made a couple of notes specific for me—essentially, a list of rules I needed to employ as I began putting myself out there on the dating scene. My divorce was officially finalized after a very difficult and costly process—another reason to celebrate.

After the laughter subsided at my expense, we all signed the large, three-by-three-foot sheet of butcher paper and officially closed out the 2009 Job Mob annual meeting. Even our waiter, a guy named Justin Newman, witnessed and attested by signing the paper as well.

Three years later, I went back to the same restaurant and was serendipitously served by Justin, who remembered all the details of that dinner, down to what wine we ordered. To this day, that paper remains in my possession.

Microsoft: The Good, the Bad, and the Fucked Up

Working with Microsoft up to that point had been both a blessing and a curse. We had plenty to be grateful for given our growing footprint of revenue, new relationships, and talent. We were creating a name for ourselves there, and it appeared the flywheel had started bringing a healthy pipeline of opportunities to our doorstep.

But all that goodness didn't come without a cost.

Microsoft is a huge organization, with lots of moving parts and their share of bureaucracy, making it difficult at times to navigate what would normally be a simple process. We would build a relationship with a stakeholder, gather their business requirements, locate talent for the project, present solutions, and with luck, be rewarded the business. Seems straightforward, right? Not exactly.

Enter the Microsoft Global Procurement Group (GPG). At first, we thought of GPG as just a necessary evil for pushing through our original master services agreement (MSA). But as time went on and our relationship with the giant software company began to grow, it became apparent their influence would play a much more significant role.

GPG consistently postured over us as their smaller vendor, with little regard to the stakeholder clients they were supposed to be serving in the first place. I'd never met more indignant and egocentric professionals. Don't get me wrong; they weren't all bad. It just took a few bad apples to spoil it for everyone else. I worked with some very talented folks there who struck a professional balance between taking care of their internal clients and facilitating their support services—a charter you would think would be not only efficient, but productive. But others seemed to be power-hungry, egotistical assholes with a lost sense of priority. It's as if they couldn't make it in talent acquisition, legal, sales, or HR, so they joined a group where they felt empowered to pump out their chests and beat up on the smallest kid on the playground.

I recall a story shared by a close Microsoft client, explaining his discontent with having to work with GPG. "They came in and basically told me how I needed to run my business," he said. "When I asked them what they actually knew about my business, there was silence. Turned out they didn't have a clue what my organization did, what services we provided, the business impacts we made, or who our customers were. I promptly kicked them out of my office and told them to stop wasting my fucking time."

This was a regular occurrence with many of the Microsoft leaders we worked with. We seemed to run into GPG at every turn of the corner.

The first thing GPG initiated was a $510 per month seat charge for any individual or team member who executed work onsite at any Microsoft building. I completely understand the rationale behind this, as those individuals use valuable resources that could otherwise be used by a Microsoft employee. They sit at their desks. They drink their unlimited free soda. They use their internet bandwidth. But what should be done about work that could only be done on Microsoft campus due to specific technological or data access requirements?

Many of the projects we were involved in couldn't have been done offsite, so we were stuck making the case for exemptions. We had a bunch of them, and GPG made us jump through a series of hoops for each one, when a simple phone call with the stakeholder confirming the details would have been sufficient. It was like pulling teeth to get them to understand each scenario, as we were often handed off to different folks within procurement who only supported a specific task or group. One Microsoft hand wasn't talking to the other, as we flailed our way through each situation. Don't get me wrong; $510 a month isn't a ton of money in the big picture. But it adds up when you have twenty or more consultants onsite.

The second thing GPG tried to do was beat us down on pricing. This was a regular occurrence, questioning our rate cards with all-too-frequent audits and threatening us if we didn't lower our prices, despite increases in the cost-of-living and cost-of-business, and general inflation. With little regard to market rates, they treated all companies the same, regardless of the actual services provided. It was much easier to lump everyone into a bucket versus attempt to understand the difference between a staffing firm and consulting firm.

The projects we engaged in at Microsoft were based off deliverables and a fixed amount, not off an hourly rate—the very definition of true consulting and vendor work by Microsoft itself. Yet GPG was hellbent on treating us like a low-skilled body shop despite the obvious differences.

We fought continuously with them over rates we knew were well within market levels and many times lower than our competitors. Even when we submitted proposals that included rates within our agreed-upon card, sometimes GPG would still jump in and threaten us with sending it out for RFP to other vendors. They rarely took the individual budgets of our stakeholders into consideration, even though the stakeholders were the ones paying for our services.

Our biggest disappointment with Microsoft's GPG happened in their fiscal years of 2011 and 2012. Some whack job within their organization came up with the brilliant idea to tax vendors for increasing their book of business with the company. We essentially started with a baseline for our total book of business and were allowed to grow the next year by only 20 percent. Any revenue above that was taxed and required as payment back to Microsoft. I'm not exactly sure what their motivation was—maybe a last-ditch effort to make procurement look less incompetent by creating a revenue component.

At first, we thought this practice was just a rumor, but then we started hearing about it more and more. One day, Paul, our "category manager" within procurement confirmed the gossip and said it would be going into effect either the second half of fiscal year 2010, or 2011. However, very little guidance was given to us as to how it would be measured, and what the implications would be over compliance. Paul kept his cards close to his chest, sharing little bits of what might happen, but always with an undertone of threat.

We began hitting the network of friends in the business and asked if they had heard of what Microsoft GPG referred to as a "rebate program." It turned out that only a few had heard about it, and that was through the grapevine and not formally through some procurement representative. Even companies we directly competed against weren't aware of any such mandates.

Which brings us back to our relationship with Paul. Was he just fucking with us? Was this his idea, or was he taking direct orders from someone like Tim, the head of GPG at the time? How could a company like Microsoft discriminate against select vendors, and not all of them? We had too many questions and not enough answers.

Paul fit the profile I described earlier with regard to ineptitude and challenge. He was the type of guy who received very little respect from his peers, so he'd probably go home and take it out on his defenseless dog. There was never an easy conversation. Everything had to be an issue of sorts. No matter how direct of a question you posed to him, he'd dish out some bullshit, dance-around-the-answer response that was vague or misdirecting.

After weeks of back-and-forth nonsense, Paul finally provided us with a few very ambiguous details of the program—our baseline and growth limits, along with the fees they would charge us if we found ourselves growing our business even more. What made this worse was that the money we would have to pay back wouldn't go back to our original clients within Microsoft, but into some abyss within GPG. Wasn't this our stakeholder's money? Once we talked to a few clients, they were furious. A few of them escalated it to their leadership, but to little avail.

The first year of this policy was significant, as we wrote Microsoft a check for over $60,000. But year two really brought on consternation, as the information we were receiving about the rebate program was ambiguous at best. Paul continued being cagey about the entire program but would always hint that if we didn't abide by his policies, we could potentially jeopardize our position on the approved vendor list.

Meanwhile, we continued growing our portfolio of business within Microsoft, thinking the rebate program would be cancelled by some rational leader in the ranks, or they would modify it into something more reasonable and collegial. 2011 to 2012 was a massive growth year for us at Microsoft, which based on the thresholds we were given, would precipitate having to write Microsoft a gigantic check back to them. We approached Paul to get guidance on this.

"If we comply with all the requirements of the program and deliver a check to you, will that guarantee us a spot on your approved vendor list?" we inquired. "Further, how will we work with you on determining the exact amount we need to pay?"

These were reasonable questions given the situation. They were asking a lot of us, with little guidance, and we were doing everything we could to stay in their good graces. The answers we received from him were less than reassuring.

"GPG isn't going to calculate what's owed to us. It's up to you to determine the amount through a self-auditing process."

He went on to give vague direction on how the program would be enforced, leaving us with an uneasy feeling that this was some sort of test. Essentially, he made no commitment that Microsoft would police the results, let alone reward anyone for following through.

What a fucking dilemma we faced. Best-case scenario would involve us paying the rebate back to Microsoft, eating the entire amount on the books, and hoping they recognized us as a valued service provider who could remain on the preferred vendor list. The worst case was we would pay the rebate, and they would come up with some far-fetched reason to take us off their approved list. We could also not pay and see what happened. We had no good options in front of us. Paul had us by the balls, and it was apparent he wasn't going to give us any wiggle room.

We decided to take the high road, hand-delivering a check for $180,000 to Paul within the week. Mind you, this was money that we'd legitimately earned by busting our assess and delivering to our clients.

The response we received was less than grateful, as if we had just handed them a paper bag full of dog shit. There wasn't a *thank you for being a great vendor*, or sign that we would continue to be on the preferred Microsoft vendor list. They simply took the money and left us with the familiar, uncomfortable feeling that even though we'd followed through, we weren't guaranteed to be in their good graces tomorrow.

This pissed us off to no end, as we despised the abuse of power they wielded, and how they didn't even try to hide their arrogance. It was extortion in its purest form, and no one gave two shits to monitor it. There we were doing our best to comply with their ridiculous mandates, giving them money that we'd worked hard for, without one bit of appreciation or acknowledgment.

To make matters worse, we talked to a bunch of leaders of other vendor companies, and many of them still hadn't heard of the rebate program, and some who had heard of it decided to not even comply. Yet those same companies never received any sort of reprimand or repercussion. It appeared to be a total scam that left many vendors who did comply bitter and resentful of the whole GPG. In short, it was extortion disguised as a bullshit procurement policy. Those responsible knew they had leverage over vendors and didn't think twice about fleecing them for their own benefit.

And I'm not sure what exactly those benefits were. Did they try to offset some of their costs by creating a revenue stream back into the business? They certainly weren't giving it back to the respective groups throughout the company where the money originated. Maybe they used it to fund some other unsavory projects they had lined up.

Regardless, it took two years before someone with some authority and sense of righteousness must have gotten word of the program, as it quietly ended. Paul told us they were "revamping their rebate program," and that we would "be notified of the details in the future." No surprise, we never heard a word about another rebate program.

Over the years we worked with several contacts in GPG,

and many of them were great. That said, there always seemed to be an underbelly of threat and deceit—a posturing of sorts—forcing us to feel constantly vulnerable. Any day, we could be kicked off the vendor list, despite the top-drawer service we were providing to all our clients.

Working directly with different stakeholders throughout the organization was a blessing, as we developed strong partnerships by understanding their individual businesses, goals, and obstacles. We did our very best to align various solutions to critical problems, and we were rewarded with continued business and lots of internal referrals.

Our Microsoft book of business over the first four years will forever remain near and dear to our hearts. We built it from scratch, growing at a rate of over 1,500 percent, from $9,000 recorded in 2008 to over $14.1 million in 2012. It was all blood, sweat, and tears (maybe more tears than anything), and I couldn't be prouder. We weren't in a position to throw a ton of marketing dollars at them, nor were we an established name with brand recognition. The Job Mob also wasn't included in all the RFPs that GPG sent out for bid for various large projects needing proposals. Instead, every dollar was earned the hard way, by developing relationships with key stakeholders, providing good value with quality delivery, and getting referrals to other groups needing our services. We worked our asses off, and the hustle and scrappiness paid off over time, giving us a strong foundation to build on over the next four years.

Chapter 7

A Time for Change

I step into the entry of the fourth-floor apartment located a block north of Green Lake in Seattle. The empty room smells of fresh paint and is brightly lit up due to its Southern exposure. The kitchen appliances are all shiny and new, hardwood floors unblemished, and I can hear the murmur of traffic in the distance. "I'll take it," I confidently say to the property manager who is standing behind me. "Great, I'll write up the lease and email it over to you," she politely and enthusiastically responds. Standing in front of the living room window, I gaze out at the peekaboo view of Green Lake in the distance. Sunrays reflect off the water, giving the appearance that it's glimmering. Magnificent. I take a deep breath as I think about everything that's brought me here. The legal proceedings and official divorce. Living in Jesse's basement for months. Going into the office with Pepe every day. Eating lots of Top Ramen. Working eighty hours a week for months on end to get the company to a profitable position. I can finally afford to move into this seven-hundred-square-foot apartment. My anger I hold onto has brought me here. This is the first time I've lived by myself, I think fondly. It's a moment full of pride and gratitude. A new beginning.

We rolled into 2010 with a renewed level of energy and plans for growth. This began with the hiring of two new recruiters, Angela and Michelle, along with a new business development director named Brandy. Our hope was that Angela and Michelle could take on a lot of the talent acquisition work from all the business Josiah and I were bringing in, and that in a short time, Brandy could supplement our sales efforts. We were also in heavy discussions with a couple of Microsoft leaders to join us in some capacity to create and lead new business divisions for The Job Mob. It was time to evolve into a more mature company with distinct service offerings, organizational charts, and ultimately, a well-defined go-to-market strategy.

We also started to look at our employees' projects, and some distinct areas of focus became apparent. Most of their work was in the data management space, software engineering and testing, program management, and support and technical marketing services. These primary areas became the blueprint for how we marketed our solutions, as we organically let the market guide us based on our clients' needs. I'm sure some of this work was a direct result of past connections we leveraged when we started The Job Mob, but many were based on new relationships.

As our book of business continued to grow, we identified that some of the folks at Microsoft weren't exactly content with the name of our company. We heard a few random comments about how The Job Mob wasn't professional and didn't represent the sophistication and brand we were trying to portray. Big surprise, the folks within Microsoft's GPG also gave us grief over the moniker. Paul hinted to us that if we kept our name, despite all the success we'd had over there, we would be pulled from the approved list. They just couldn't fathom keeping a company with our name, especially as they were paring down a list of thousands of vendors to just over a hundred. It was a daunting task, but GPG was serious about cleaning out vendors that weren't providing value to Microsoft.

Maybe it was fate. Maybe in the end we should be ironically thanking Paul for being an asshole and forcing our hand to change our name. Whatever the driver, after lots of discussion amongst the owners, we came to agree. The Job Mob had gotten us to our current state. It had been appropriate at the time, given the uncertainty of the economy eighteen months prior when we started. It was different. It was fun. But now we were a real company with real employees, a real culture, and the desire to become more relevant in the consulting world. We needed to start taking ourselves more seriously if we were to grow.

In our rebrand, we followed steps very similar to that of deciding on The Job Mob. Jesse and Ryan came up with a long list of options, and Josiah offered input. After the initial list of acceptable options was established, John and I jumped in with comments. We asked ourselves, *Where do we evolve to from here?* We needed a name that represented quality delivery of project work, a sophisticated culture, brand differentiation, and connection to the five founders. It still had to be fun, while able to stand amongst the other major consulting firms we sometimes found ourselves competing with like Accenture, Slalom, and Revel Consulting.

Our initial list was not very impressive to say the least. In fact, it was downright embarrassing. Names like Resolve, Fuse, Method, and Signal Solutions all screamed desperation and boredom. Even Forté was resurrected for a New York second.

We tried a second pass at brainstorming names, doing slightly better with names like Cohesion (brought back from our original list) and Verity, but those still didn't quite check the necessary boxes.

After days of back-and-forth emails, Jesse finally threw out something that stuck. "What about Pentad? It means five things. Better yet, it can also represent the relationship amongst us as founders." We listened. We liked it. It was original. It represented our story. It had teeth.

But was Pentad enough? We liked the word but weren't convinced it possessed enough grit on its own. Lots of variations came up from there. Pentad Consulting Services. Pentad Strategies. Pentad Systems. And then John suggested Pentad Solutions based on URL availability. It worked. We liked it, and despite our affinity to The Job Mob, it was time to evolve. Pentad became a new entity that would represent a technology consulting firm, while we would keep The Job Mob to cover simple staffing. That said, we now had two companies to run.

In late March, we officially announced the new brand representing not only the five founders and their respective relationships, but also five core areas of discipline that we would concentrate on. The names of these areas were strategically picked as broad, overarching categories that could encompass all our existing projects and talent. This was our attempt to appear to be a sophisticated consulting firm, even though we lacked many of the necessary organizational components. We initially had no delivery oversight, quality control, practice leadership, or specific delivery methodologies. But no one needed to know that at the time.

We quickly launched a new website showcasing our new brand and comprehensive service offerings, with a new leadership page—this time using an actual professional photographer for our headshots. Although we hadn't specifically managed the delivery of many of the past projects we were involved in, they somehow became "case studies" or examples.

The team started putting in the proper pieces to support our new claimed maturity. For starters, we landed 10,000 square feet of office space just down the street from Microsoft's main campus. In fact, we sublet the space directly from Microsoft, as they didn't need it anymore. The place was turnkey with lots of office furniture, a real kitchen, and even a boardroom. We'd have more than enough room to house all our employees and any growth in the short- and mid-term. We even brought in a pool table from Jesse's house to give our employees a little recreation during breaks.

What it lacked was character. We didn't have the funds to invest in lots of bedazzle like kegerators, bean bag chairs, espresso bars, and nap rooms—which would be table stakes for high-tech work environments today. The furniture was basic and boring, and the industrial carpet was worn and tattered in places.

The worst part about it was there was too much room. There we were, roughly fifty employees occupying a ton of relative space, which made it eerily quiet at times. We did our best to position the various delivery teams in areas where they could collaborate and create some level of collective energy. Josiah, John, and I made sure we weren't hidden away in some office, instead situating our desks with the rest of the operations team in a bullpen setting.

In order to walk-the-walk as a self-proclaimed, full-service consulting firm, it was critical that we hire leadership to manage the delivery side of the business. Great thought was put into this process, and we looked at several possible solutions. One idea was to purchase another services firm with the hopes that the company currently employed someone with the proper credentials. We looked at a couple of companies in the area that were slightly smaller than ours, and even threw out a couple of memorandums of understanding (MOUs) initiating a potential acquisition.

Unfortunately, the efforts fell short, as we couldn't find common ground on valuation and terms. That led us to needing to hire someone off the street. We put out some feelers but weren't satisfied with the talent we were seeing. Don't get me wrong; there were plenty of highly qualified professionals, but most lacked the intangibles we were looking for. Namely, we couldn't find someone who exhibited our culture and values.

We quickly realized that the person we needed was already working for us—Dennis Comfort. He was already involved in several projects in support of Phil's group at Microsoft, and he had a successful track record delivering a wide spectrum of projects throughout his career. He understood traditional software development life cycles and possessed an even-keeled demeanor that was genuinely disarming.

John and I sat down with Dennis and walked through the details of the role. We called it a director of professional services, and essentially positioned all our delivery teams and one-off consultants under his direction. Dennis would be responsible for putting in the various systems, quality control, and best practices for all project delivery.

After some light negotiating, he accepted and jumped into the deep end, trying to wrap his hands around all our various engagements. Dennis was a welcome resource, as he gave us strong credibility, leadership for our consultants, and escalation paths for our clients.

Another shift we made organizationally was the

appointment of John as our president, with Josiah and I both reporting directly to him. It was the appropriate move, giving John oversight of everything except finance and legal. Josiah and I were cool with it, as it gave us some structure to operate within. Plus, we didn't have to officially report to one another, which would have been untenable given our respective egos. Jesse played the role of chief operating officer, and Ryan was general counsel.

Working in a start-up environment is one thing, but being an owner is completely different. It's a constant test to function at all levels at any given point each day. You might be in the trenches meeting with clients one hour, negotiating lines of credit terms with a bank the next, and then giving someone their annual review. The need to helicopter up and down depending on the specific business situation was quite taxing but offered unlimited opportunities to learn. Juggling tactics, strategy, and vision were a daily responsibility, and it was expected amongst all of us that we always show up on point. This was one of my biggest challenges during these early days of the company, perhaps for Josiah as well—and John to a lesser degree due to his experience as a leader in many organizations. Jesse and Ryan were used to it, having owned several companies within their portfolio. But for me, it took time to switch gears on the fly. My brain didn't operate at that speed, but over time, I adapted.

You can liken it to a toolbox filled with hammers, screwdrivers, and pliers. In order to be a successful entrepreneur, one must have a wide array of tools at their disposal, knowing exactly which one to use at any given time. The adage, "everything looks like a nail when the only tool you have is a hammer," holds true for solving business problems. I made mistakes, learned from them, and through those experiences equipped myself appropriately. Over time, I added various tools to my repertoire, thus the ability to navigate a wider range of business situations.

Beyond organizing our leadership and securing large office space, we also focused on employee experience as we entered this new phase of the company. For starters, we converted all our employees to full-time, salaried W2 status. This was a tremendous risk, as it meant if a consultant wasn't on project, we'd be eating their costs 100 percent. Overnight, we had to become efficient with the utilization of our consultant base and our pricing methods for varied engagements.

But this was a necessary move to show we weren't just some chop-shop staffing firm that ditched its employees the second they rolled off a project. We also changed our policies around our health benefits and paid 100 percent of employees' premiums, contributing a significant percentage towards any significant others and dependents. Pentad offered three weeks' paid vacation and another week of holidays. Now, some of these items seem like table stakes for most companies, but for us, a self-funded, early-stage professional services firm, it meant we were maturing.

By the time we entered the second quarter of 2010, we began to see another uptick in momentum. The new brand was resonating amongst our client base, and a steady pipeline of new projects was on the horizon. Our support projects at Microsoft kept growing weekly, as did the data analytics work in the XNet group. Pentad was awarded a project supporting the MSN Royalty program, extending our reach within the Microsoft landscape. Brandy was also ramping up her sales pipeline with new companies like Recreational Equipment, Inc. (REI), Clearwire, and a start-up called Twisted Pair. Dennis built out a full team consisting of project managers, software developers, and testers—a group that delivered rapid prototypes to clients when traditional efforts by internal IT resources just weren't enough.

Revenue was steadily growing from month-to-month as new engagements presented themselves. The previous quarter showed total revenue a touch above the $1.5 million mark, which was an all-time best for us. The second quarter was 20 percent higher as we booked well over $1.8 million.

In June of 2010, we made several key hires and investments in hopes of scaling parts of our business. Our goal was to capitalize on some momentum from our new brand launch. For starters, we hired Sarah Bingham as our second engagement manager, as we had simply outgrown any reasonable number of employees for Lauren to manage. Sarah came from a local staffing firm, so she had a strong foundation in staffing, redeployments, and the care and feeding of remote employees. She plugged into our culture and workstyle seamlessly, giving us lots of confidence in ensuring our delivery team members were well taken care of. Like Lauren, Sarah welcomed not only our rapid pace, but also the ambiguity of having to make shit up on the fly.

Other hires included a new business development manager, an office manager, and someone to lead a new subsidiary we called Pentad Analytics. Aaron Fossum came to us from Adobe, where he established himself as a subject matter expert in digital analytics.

The general goal for us back then was to evolve into an umbrella of subsidiary companies that specialized in specific *technology stacks*, or industries tied into a central operations team that provided support like sales, human resources, talent acquisition, finance, and IT. Pentad Analytics was our first of what was supposed to be a multitude of brands under the Pentad Solutions banner. Not only was it the first, but it was also the last, as we eventually decided to pull it back within our parent company a year and a half later.

More Changes

The third quarter of 2010 brought both excitement and new levels of stress, as we now had three separate companies operating simultaneously—The Job Mob, Pentad Solutions, and Pentad Analytics. We had a ton of overlap operationally, allowing us to load balance much of the costs to Pentad Solutions. But it meant three sets of books, three websites, three brands we marketed, and three sets of employees. This, plus the combination of adding new sales team members, creating a whole new analytics-focused business, and changing management structure created many distractions, resulting in our first stagnant quarter growth-wise.

This was demoralizing. We had been doing so well, and to book the same amount of revenue with more costs weighed heavily. We understood it would take time for some investments to bear fruit—a normal expectation, given that people take time to ramp up, infrastructure gets implemented slowly, and new branding takes a while to reach the market. But what we hadn't accounted for was an imbalance of leadership and strategy, and tactics and execution.

Essentially, my lack of experience balancing out individual sales contributions and sales leadership reflected numbers that stood out from the rest. Up to this point, I had been a major contributor to the revenue built off a strong foundation of relationships. Month after month, quarter after quarter, my individual sales revenue rose steadily. After all, I was in the trenches, working nonstop on generating leads, developing trusted relationships, and closing deals.

But I took that for granted and paid little attention to being an actual sales manager. We lost Chris earlier in the year. Our newest sales guy was struggling with our go-to-market and couldn't find much success. And we eventually parted ways with Brandy, as she was dealing with some personal issues that complicated her ability to be successful.

So there I was, essentially zero-for-three when it came to hiring and successfully leading our sales organization. The realization hit me all at once: I was failing for the first time at leadership. It was a time of introspection—and more change.

The next week was lost on me. I was distracted by my guilt and sense of failure. I felt like I'd let the team down, and despite all my success identifying revenue for the company, this responsibility fell on my shoulders. Initially, I asked myself, *Is it the specific people we hired, or truly the lack of sales leadership? Maybe it's the overall structure of our sales organization or lack thereof. Maybe I'm meant to be an individual producer and not a manager. Maybe I just don't have that bone in my body.*

This processing wasn't necessarily a bad thing. Josiah had long before actualized his own professional faculties. He knew he wasn't the best "sales manager," so he just did what he did best: develop trusting relationships, connect others, and serve as culture ambassador. Perhaps it was my time to find a new role within the company that best utilized my skills.

We held the next quarterly owners' meeting around a corner table at a fancy steakhouse in the Snoqualmie Casino. All five of us attended, and the mood was anxious mixed with somber. We all knew our recent performance as a company was less than ideal, and anticipated some of the potentially uncomfortable discussions we needed to have. But the atmosphere wasn't contentious. After all, we were a team, and we always attributed our successes and failures to the team.

John kicked off with an introduction and high-level state of the union, but in typical Bergen-fashion, conveyed his discourse with a positive tone and far too many words. Jesse jumped in and reviewed our income statement, ensuring he noted any specific line items that stood out. A one-off expense for a bunch of computer monitors. An increase in consultant management from adding Sarah to the mix. And so on. He then moved on to owner compensation, quarterly dividends, and our balance sheet.

Then we reviewed our quarterly performance, with John and Jesse facilitating the discussion. The numbers spoke for themselves, but despite our stagnant revenue, we were in fact still turning a profit. That led us to our overall strategic direction including our respective individual roles.

John jumped in and did his best efforts to rip the Band-Aid off with, "Given the latest numbers, I think it would be best if we changed up the roles a bit. PJ, you've shown too much value to our organization with the revenue you bring in, and having you manage a sales team isn't the best use of your time."

We all looked around the table with nods of agreement.

"I propose Jesse oversee our sales efforts for the short term and reevaluate our numbers next quarter," John continued.

There were more nods of approval, and some light comments of encouragement. For a split second, I wondered if I should fight to stay in the sales leadership position. *Everyone has a down quarter once in a while*, I thought. *Perhaps I could approach things differently? Wouldn't my partners want me to put up a fight?*

Then I came to my senses. This was no time to be selfish and let my ego and pride get in the way of making sound business decisions. Plus, John and the others positioned this in the most positive of lights, allowing the focus to be on the upside changes, and not my failures. They knew there wasn't any one of us to blame for the stagnant quarter, despite my feelings of accountability.

My title and role changed to director of recruiting. I would still be responsible for managing some clients, but the bulk of my time would be focused on leading our recruiting team, implementing best practices for talent acquisition, and rolling up my sleeves as a recruiter.

We finished up the meeting with discussions around corporate values, culture, and general company goals. I always loved how so much of our attention was placed on employee experience. What could we do better? What aren't we doing enough of? What are we doing too much of? These questions were always top of mind for us.

After some light, open discussion and a few votes on company investments, we closed out the meeting. As Ryan finished recording the final notes, Jesse casually tossed out the idea of spending some time in the casino. After dinner, we headed straight for the blackjack tables where we spent the rest of the evening.

Even More Changes

I quickly got over the self-pity and embarrassment of the stagnant quarter, as there was just too much to do. Leading the recruiting team came easily, as John had already put in a strong foundation of best practices. Our team was productive and required very little oversight, and I really enjoyed getting back into talent acquisition. There were lots of crossover skills compared to sales in general. Sourcing leads. Cold calling to candidates. Navigating negotiations and closing new hires. These were things I was not only good at, but also relished.

Jesse's efforts to run our sales team didn't come easy. His limited sales management experience was obvious, and his approach was, for the most part, one dimensional. Jesse is a leader, but his understanding of sales methodologies versus business operations was limited at the time. And managing sales effectively requires more than just metrics, ratios, and accountability to hit numbers. It requires a certain level of finesse, motivational support, and guidance on navigating activities that build trusting relationships.

Our new business development hire struggled with exactly the same obstacles Chris had a couple of years prior—the inability to operate effectively in a start-up environment. Having come from a well-established organization with lots of infrastructure, marketing, and technology support, he found himself lost and waiting for direction.

Jesse also took a chance and brought on a new sales guy named Steve. Unfortunately, it didn't take long for us to realize he wasn't the best fit for our environment. Another failed sales professional hire, but this time it was on Jesse's watch, not mine. These examples turned out to be expensive learnings we picked up along the way.

Sales efforts amongst Josiah, Aaron, and myself were also more focused and therefore more effective. We broke into new groups within the Microsoft landscape like the Business Intelligence Customer Intelligence data team, Engineering Excellence, and The Online Services Division. Outside of Microsoft, we began getting more revenue from Expedia and REI.

At this time, some very key employees also joined the Pentad family—Chandra, Michael, Mathew, and Connie to name just a few. We felt not only an uptick in business, but also in the quality of talent joining us daily.

Disaster Strikes

We had many reasons to celebrate on the evening of October 27, 2010. Our revenue had grown on a steep trajectory, the employee talent base had expanded, and we'd added new clients to our already impressive roster. Pentad Solutions was hitting on all cylinders, and it was an occasion to bring the team together for a little happy-hour celebration at Lucky Strike, a fancy bowling alley that doubled as a lounge.

The drinks flowed, employees laughed and engaged with each other, and a few of them went over and bowled a frame or two. As I worked the room, talking to our employees with a drink in my hand (most likely a Manhattan or old fashioned, or some whiskey drink), I received a text message from Jesse telling me to call him. As a partner at Pentad, it was normal for me to receive a few dozen text messages and/or a few phone calls from him daily. I put my phone away, so I could focus my attention on our thirty or so employees who were mingling around, laughing and joking, having fun.

One minute went by, and I received another text, this time from Ryan: "Call me ASAP."

Normally, Jesse and Ryan worked and hung out together a lot given the private equity firm they were partners in. So my guess was they were sitting next to each other saying, "What the fuck, why isn't PJ calling me back?!" And then I got the third text message from Jesse: "Call me back NOW!"

I excused myself from a conversation with Sarah, our engagement manager, and found a semi-quiet area away from the conversations, which were slightly louder than the pop music amplifying from the speakers above. I dialed Jesse's number. In reality, I simply hit Jesse's name in my favorites, and the phone dialed for me.

It rang. Once. He answered. I couldn't even get in a hello, a snarky remark, or question before he jumped in. "Get down to the Redmond Athletic Club ASAP, we have an emergency. Josiah is on his way here, and I'm still trying to track down Bergen." Call ended.

I paused for one minute, racking my brain on what the hell could be so wrong. My mind started to wander. *Did we lose our vendor status at Microsoft? Did someone file a lawsuit against us? Did someone get injured? Was there a problem with our financials, and we somehow found ourselves destitute?* As a business owner, you come to realize that any type of shit can appear out of nowhere, blindsiding you like a quarterback with an ineffective left tackle. I took a couple of deep breaths and gathered my composure, as I didn't want to ring any alarms.

I took Sarah aside to tell her I had to leave for an emergency. She looked puzzled at first (as the festivities had just gotten started) but gave me a reassuring look that said, "Go handle your business. I've got this shit covered." One of the many things I loved about Sarah was she understood circumstances even when she didn't know all the facts. I could always count on her to manage any situation accordingly.

I put my half-consumed beverage down on the bar and walked to my car.

The drive from Lucky Strike to the RAC (short for Redmond Athletic Club) took about twenty minutes, and as

I parked my car, I felt deeply curious yet uneasy, given how little I knew of what I was walking into. Upstairs in their office, both guys were visibly focused on two different things—Jesse at full attention to his laptop, and Ryan shuffling through a bunch of papers on their desk. It was silent, and no one even acknowledged my presence.

After a few awkward minutes, Jesse looked up and asked, "Where the fuck are Josiah and John?"

About ten minutes later, Josiah strolled in, and shortly after came John. I still hadn't heard anything about why we were there. I figured they didn't want to waste time saying things more than once. A distinct discomfort hovered in the room, an uncertain feeling that made John, Josiah, and me a little queasy.

The five of us sat down, and Jesse let out a long sigh. Ryan smiled and let out a short snicker, as if to find humor in the situation and add some levity.

"We've got a very interesting situation on our hands," Jesse continued as he paced back and forth agitatedly. "To cut to the chase, it appears we have a problem with Rob Curry, and our working relationship. I did some research on the two companies that Rob has connected us to for all the reimbursements and purchase orders that he's opened, and I double-checked the addresses for each. After further digging, I discovered that the addresses match Rob's, and the companies are in his name!"

Rob was a trusted client of ours who was instrumental in helping Pentad grow a team within the X-Net group at Microsoft.

"What the fuck?" asked Josiah. "Does this mean what I think it means?"

"I believe so," responded Ryan. "Rob has been using us to funnel money to companies that he owns. I checked the registered agents for Blu Games, and Rob's name is listed. Not sure about Resolution Audio, but I'll check on that in the morning. Without having all the information, I still sense something is fucked up. If Rob is stealing money from Microsoft, we're going to either look like complete idiots or willing accomplices."

As I processed what I'd just heard, I immediately flashed back to Tillie and her embezzlement-scheme-gone-wrong. *What the fuck?* I thought. *Is this really happening again in my life?*

Silence. The five of us just sat there for a minute or two, each processing in our minds what exactly was going on, the implications, how true could this be, and how we hadn't seen it ... a hundred questions and reactions swirling around in our heads. This was obviously a complete and utter shock to hear, given our great working relationship with Rob as a client and the future prospects of engaging in more business with him. For a couple of minutes, all the oxygen was sucked out of the room, as we all stared blankly into space with our own thoughts of despair.

I stood up and began pacing around the office. "So what do we do?" I asked cautiously.

Again, silence.

"We have different options we could take, but each one could lead to the same place," offered Ryan. "We could be silent about this for now and dig deeper into the details to validate whether it's in fact true."

There were nods of agreement.

Ryan continued, "Or, we could escalate immediately to get legal counsel and address this head-on with complete transparency to Microsoft."

More nods of agreement.

I believe the last option Ryan threw out was we could do nothing and continue our business as usual. This was

Microsoft's issue, and therefore we could let them figure it out. We weren't doing anything malicious, so what would be the problem with just acting as if nothing was wrong? Why kick the hornets' nest?

After hours of discussion that night, we all agreed that the best course of action was to do a combination of options one and two. We would dig deeper into the details, while escalating the issue to our attorneys to address this situation directly. It was the right thing to do, despite the myriad of potential devastating effects it could have on our business.

We were already busting our assess to stay in the good graces of Microsoft's procurement group, appeasing their every command. Something like this could derail all our efforts, with the possibility of one person in authority crushing our working relationship and therefore seriously jeopardizing our survival.

Would they think we were somehow an accomplice? Or would they think we were so hungry for business that we simply overlooked morality? Questions would certainly be raised. This was all that someone in procurement would need to justify an act of retribution or authority. We could be made an example of for all vendors.

This situation had revealed itself after working with Rob Curry for over a year, since August 2009. He was a director at Microsoft who we were introduced to by several trusted contacts, all of them telling us that Rob was a high-potential leader with growing responsibilities and lots of work he needed help with. An Air Force Academy graduate and Yale MBA, Rob seemed to have the world at his fingertips. He was climbing the ranks at Microsoft, and he quickly made a name for himself as a go-getter with connections all the way up to Bill Gates.

Rob's primary role at Microsoft was in the X-Net

Strategy team, where he led analytics and measurement to drive adoption (downloads and installs) of the Bing search toolbar. Downloads and usage of the toolbar meant significant advertising dollars for Microsoft, so Rob was a key player in the blossoming search space that Microsoft was trying to move into (Google was the primary player in that space). He had shared with us his plans to build out a sophisticated data infrastructure and analytics layer on top, and said that Pentad would be a key partner in accomplishing his goals. Big plans meant big budgets, and we were a hungry company looking for large contracts and opportunity to shine. Why wouldn't we want to partner with someone like that?!

Josiah was the primary person who corresponded with Rob on the daily. Within two months of introduction, Josiah had built enough confidence with Rob to award us some business building out a SQL data warehouse for his team, as well as connecting various disparate data sources.

Two months later, we doubled the business by adding some business intelligence/analytics services. By March of 2010, we doubled our revenue within his team once again. At the end of 2010, Pentad was providing nearly one-and-a-half million dollars' worth of data consulting services to Rob's team.

In April 2010, Rob reached out to Josiah and asked for our help with a vendor payment for an Xbox event the month prior. Some audio equipment was supposedly purchased for the event, and Rob asked us to use a purchase order that he'd opened to pay the third party directly. The amount was $49,800, and Pentad wouldn't be making any money off the transaction; this was simply a pass-through to help Rob. He requested we cut a check to Resolution Audio, a third-party vendor he used for the

Xbox event, and invoice Microsoft via an open purchase order that Rob oversaw for the same amount. We were led to believe it would have been a hassle for him to set the audio equipment company up as a new vendor in their system—something we knew could be true, given Microsoft's long processes with procurement.

We paid the vendor and thought nothing of it. It was business as usual with Rob, and all the data work we were engaged with continued as planned.

Two months later, in June, Rob presented a second request for a third-party vendor payment—this time at $26,400. Again, we executed on the request, paid the vendor, and didn't give it a second thought.

Over the following three months, our consulting services with Rob steadily grew, and our working relationship became stronger yet.

Do you ever reflect and think back about a very bad situation you found yourself in, and realize exactly where things started to go from good to bad? The beginning of October 2010 was that moment for us.

Rob gave Josiah a call and shared an idea around "adding another component to our partnership." He continued to describe an arrangement wherein Pentad would help account-manage several distribution partners of Microsoft. We would then receive compensation for the distribution of Microsoft search results via several ways—Chrome browsers, browser address bars, company sites, or other properties. Essentially, for any advertising revenue generated through Microsoft's search results as a direct result of Pentad's involvement, we would receive some sort of revenue share. Further, Pentad would be given additional compensation for every Microsoft Search toolbar installed based on our influence.

Now I bet you're wondering what this has to do with data and technical consulting services? Not a fucking thing.

Josiah brought the idea back to the partners, and we discussed it ad nauseam. Sure, it wasn't in our wheelhouse, but the revenue opportunity could be huge. Really huge. Based on the way Rob explained it, we were talking potentially millions-of-dollars huge. Rob wanted to move quickly, as he already had "budget approval on a million-dollar purchase order." All we'd need to do is invest in this business as a parallel service, offering it along with our consulting. Maybe hire a couple sales engineers to focus on this new vertical.

Picture this: We have a client who's asking us to partner on some new business opportunities, and what exactly is the hesitation? I guess we all had the thought, to a certain degree, that some things were too good to be true.

The group came to an agreement that we'd investigate further, but not let this new shiny object of an opportunity lead us astray from our core competency—professional services in data and technology.

On October 7, 2010, Rob Curry sent over the draft contract for us to review. Ryan ran point and worked with Josiah and John on the finer details of the document. But around the same time, Rob had issued an approval for payments to the tune of $459,000—again, money to be paid to Blu Games and Resolution Audio.

Little did we know that by the end of October, we'd all be having a very different conversation.

Which brings us back full circle to Lucky Strike, happy hour, celebration, and the discovery of an elaborate embezzlement scheme and unsuspecting accomplice: us.

Jesse and Ryan led conversations with our outside counsel, and with their assistance, we took the first move in reaching out to Microsoft's legal team. It was our intention to be 100 percent transparent and basically tell them that we discovered something concerning about one of their leaders, and it would behoove them to take a deeper look. And we felt that since we hadn't reached the point of signing the partnership agreement with Microsoft, we hadn't received any money from the payouts to the two third-party vendors, and all our consulting business with Rob's team was totally legit—that all these things didn't point to any nefarious activities on our part.

We retained outside counsel who reached directly out to Microsoft's legal team and shared the suspicious behavior we'd uncovered. Ryan also got involved and was the unlucky participant in multiple follow-up meetings as the investigation began to uncover all the details. Even Brad Smith, Microsoft's executive vice president and general counsel, got involved.

It would take quite a bit to unnerve Ryan, but those meetings did the job. The level of questioning and scrutiny was granular. In the end, we had nothing to hide, so ultimately, we felt good about taking the appropriate action.

Nevertheless, the fuse was lit and the ambiguity of whether this would result in a catastrophic explosion, or a slap on the wrist, was killing us. We thought about the worst-case scenario. We thought about every other scenario. None of them look good for us. We could very well be fucked.

On January 13, 2011, Rob Curry was officially fired from Microsoft, and news of the offense hit every technology publication, blog, and local newspaper.

In order to head this off at the pass, we sent out an all-employee email explaining how we were involved, how Pentad never benefited from Rob's actions, and how to navigate any conversations that arose. We detailed our legitimate data work with Rob's team and all the praise we'd received. We further explained that we were responsible for uncovering the unlawful behavior and escalated it to Microsoft's proper authorities. We were the heroes. We were the ideal partner. The shining example of what Microsoft would expect out of a vendor. Our integrity stood tall, and each and every employee should be proud. It was crisis management at its finest.

Unfortunately, the media didn't exactly share this sentiment. I believe the word "unwitting" was used in a few articles describing our involvement. Another said we were "duped." Regardless of how you described our involvement, these reports didn't represent the facts, and this made us both a victim and informant.

A few employees asked further questions, but after hearing us out, didn't give it a second thought. A couple of clients also asked about the incident, and again, once they heard our side of the story, it was business as usual.

Even Microsoft came around with a little "atta-boy" for Pentad. The legal team at Microsoft wrote an internal memo to all our individual stakeholders there, praising us for how we'd handled the situation and going so far as to tell them they should be engaged in more business with us. This felt good. We were a small fish swimming amongst hundreds of much larger fish in the Microsoft Ocean. They could have easily eaten us for lunch. But they took the high road, giving credit where credit was due.

Rob was eventually convicted on multiple felony counts and sentenced to a couple of years upstate. He paid back the money he stole and showed much remorse for his acts of malice.

Apparently, he had been disgruntled over a beef with one of his supervisors, which led him down a path of retribution. I imagine there was a component of greed in there as well. What started out as a snowflake quickly snowballed out of control. Rob said in the proceedings, in front of the judge, that he knew he would get caught.

A Strong and Heartfelt Close

Our 2010 finished on a high note with record revenue, getting us all back on track to our annual projections. We ended with more than $2.2 million for the fourth quarter and seventy-five employees—a 22 percent jump over the third quarter. Overall, we closed out our second full year of business with over $7.5 million in revenue, over 134 percent growth since the previous year.

Even more important, November closed out with a celebration outside of the office, as John had experienced fatherhood for the first time.

We also ended the year with the introduction of charitable giving during the holiday season. The team chose the Wounded Warrior Project, an organization with a charter focused on providing comprehensive support for veterans who were wounded in service. In this instance, we chose to sponsor five different families based out of Fort Lewis.

On two separate occasions, a group of us drove an hour south and met with each family individually. A Starbucks parking lot became the agreed upon meeting place. I didn't know what to expect, but I'd never been so moved in my entire life. Our team was greeted by some of the most gracious human beings I'd ever met. There were lots of hugs and tears as we bonded with the wounded veterans and their families. We listened to their stories. We heard about some of their many struggles, both physical and mental. We thanked them profusely for their sacrifices to uphold the very freedoms we took for granted daily. They all responded with humility, despite what it may have cost them personally.

The children lit up with excitement as we carried boxes of wrapped presents to their vehicles. Their parents broke down crying with gratitude. One family in particular had experienced such hardship, we had to wire them money ahead of time to cover their fuel to get to us.

From then on, charitable giving became a major tenet in our company culture. Over time, all our employees would participate by donating their time, money, and energy for such worthy causes as Treehouse for kids, The Obliteride bike ride for cancer, Northwest Harvest, and the YWCA.

Revenue growth for the first half of 2011 continued to be strong, as our investments in our infrastructure, sales team, and talent acquisition began bearing fruit. Karen successfully took on some of my accounts and uncovered new projects for us. Josiah continued to bring in opportunity after opportunity. Aaron was kicking ass getting our analytics practice off the ground. And I managed to allocate some of my calories to our sales efforts. All in all, by the end of June, Pentad Solutions recorded over 50 percent growth and over $5.1 million in revenue.

Most of our net profit immediately went back out into various investments for the firm. This business philosophy was vital to continuing a steep growth trajectory. We weren't interested in pulling more cash out to fill our pockets. We wanted to scale, sacrificing short- and mid-term profit for long-term gains. We intentionally put every dollar of profit back into the company. I hired two new recruiters for our team—Jana Salamanca and Patti Phipps. Again, both were known and highly valued professionals we had worked with from Endeavor. We knew they would slide into our scrappy and dynamic culture with little effort.

Everything seemed to be headed down the right path for Pentad, as many of our investments were starting to pay off. Revenue, profitability, culture, delivery, and strategy all appeared to be gelling nicely.

Little did I know, an opportunity would soon present itself that would completely alter our future in the most unexpected of ways.

Chapter 8

From Five to Three to Four

It's March 1, and Mary Ellen and I are celebrating her eighty-eighth birthday. We're sitting in a booth across from each other at Hector's, her favorite restaurant in downtown Kirkland. She's enjoying the panko-breaded fish and chips along with a side of the orange vinaigrette, her preferred dipping sauce for French fries. We talk about our history of being neighbors, how she'd sold me her house once it became too much work to maintain, and stories of her childhood. Mary Ellen is my adopted grandmother, a woman with no children, no living relatives, and only a handful of friends. I say adopted, as we're not related in any way other than we once lived next to each other. I look out for her, as there isn't anyone else in her life she can depend on. She's lived a long and hard life full of mischievous adventures and traumatic misfortune. She appears content though, happy with the simple pleasures of a casual meal and some lighthearted conversation. There's a sparkle in her eye, reinforced by her curmudgeon-like attitude mixed with a playful demeanor. I tell her about the business and some of the success we're finding. She tries her best to understand every detail, but I know all she cares about is my happiness. I listen intently to the stories she shares of her past. The multiple husbands. Growing up in a foster family. The various jobs she's held. Mary Ellen is a woman who has faced all that life can throw at her from abusive relationships, financial turmoil, and life-threatening health scares, yet she perseveres forward without the slightest hint of regret. She's delighted when the waitress surprises her with a slice of apple pie with a candle in it, a great way to cap off a memorable occasion.

It was a Friday in early June 2011 when I jumped on a call with Jesse to chat about plans for the weekend. It must have been around 5 p.m., as all but a few of our employees had already left for the day. I had a habit of pacing around while on the phone, probably attributed to my early days at HK when I was told that standing while talking would project more confidence. Or perhaps it was just my nervous habit.

As I walked around the large oval conference table, doing slow laps in the very back room where there was more privacy, Jesse and I chatted about the usual stuff. How did our sales projections look given the week's productivity? Any employee issues. Deals pending. Deals closed. Hoops on Sunday evening. Maybe a casino run to play a little craps and blackjack. And probably dinner one of the nights.

Once I caught him up on all the business updates and we solidified our plans to hang out, Jesse steered the conversation in a direction I wasn't anticipating.

"I'd like to share some thoughts on Pentad and Pendulum's involvement," Jesse said. "When the five of us got together, our plan was to work our asses off and build a ten-million-dollar company within three years, and then sell it. We've come a long way and are now approaching the three-year anniversary as well as our target valuation. I've been talking to Ryan about this, and we're considering selling our shares back to you guys, assuming we could work out some sort of agreement. Pentad is at a good spot right now for you, Josiah, and John to continue operating moving forward."

Jesse continued, "Plus, our other companies under Pendulum are now requiring more attention, and severing ties with Pentad would give us the necessary time and resources. What do you think?"

I continued to pace around the table but couldn't say anything. A rush of different emotions flooded my brain. What I'm sure was a few seconds felt like an hour. I struggled to answer. My throat dried up. There might have even been a slight prepubescent crack as I opened my mouth.

"Uh, I guess," I responded awkwardly. As soon as those words left my mouth, I reversed gears. "Wait, why would you want to do that when we're doing so well?" I asked insistently. "I get our original plan was to sell, but this thing could get much bigger. Plus, you and Ryan play integral parts in the company. How would we replace you? We started this together and feel we should end it together."

My immediate response was to talk Jesse out of it, convincing him it was a bad idea. I tried to tug at his heartstrings. Maybe he would reconsider and just forget he ever brought up the idea in the first place. We were a team, right? A band-of-brothers who had experienced the trials of combat together. Metaphorically speaking, we'd shared foxholes, stormed beachheads, spilled blood, and seen our share of death. And we'd also tasted victory together, taking out the enemy and conquering new frontiers. We were connected by a bond few would understand. Something sacred. Something spiritual. Something that would keep us united for eternity. A covenant that couldn't be broken. We shared similar chips on our shoulders. And the war wasn't over, as far as I was concerned. Far from over.

My effort failed miserably.

"PJ, this is just business, and Ryan and I must look out for what's best for Pendulum. We've got three other businesses on our plate to operate, and Pentad is getting too big for us to manage. It makes sense. You guys will be just fine moving forward, and you'll have complete control of the business."

We chatted about it for a few more minutes and decided it was best to continue the conversation later. I put my phone down on the table, gazing at the pattern on the dingy, reddish industrial carpet. Pepe had followed me into the conference room and was balled up under the table. He raised his head and watched with curiosity as I followed the linear patterns in an obsessive-compulsive manner and continued my pacing.

My heart sank. I felt like one of my best friends was giving up on me. Giving up on the team. How could he even think a buyout was a good idea? I understood his point about the need to move on, but where would that leave the rest of us? It represented a change I wasn't prepared to process. I was at a loss for words. But most of all, I felt very, very scared.

When it came to our personal friendships, everyone was on an equal playing field. Our personalities all jived for the most part. We were all equally competitive in business and in sports. We all played poker regularly and hung out in the same circles. We had fair play with snarky remarks or juvenile pranks on each other. We were five guys who not only worked together but hung out constantly.

The most significant factor was that our skill sets complemented each other. John brought operational leadership. Josiah was the white elephant hunter in the group.

Ryan's legal prowess helped us manage many issues internally. Jesse brought finance and organizational leadership. And then there was me. I was a bit of a utility player for the team. If you needed me to sell, I would sell. If you needed me to recruit, I recruited. A jack-of-all-trades. We all operated in our own individual swim lanes for the business, which resulted in a combined product larger than the sum of its parts. We were a team built off of equitable proportions.

But when it came to our professional relationships, I had always put Jesse and Ryan on a pedestal. They operated on a different level than the rest of us. Their business conversations. Their strategic thinking. The responsibilities they took on. The transactions they closed. The two of them just had more experience, which made me recognize a huge chasm of knowledge separating us. I thought we would be lost without them, and this dependency made me even more uncomfortable.

That's why I was scared. My own insecurities, combined with the realization that my experience was limited to executing and not leading, conjured up fear and ambiguity. Sure, I managed a small team, and I tried to be a leader. But all my efforts fell short of my self-imposed target.

This was my professional wake-up call. I needed to get my shit together. I decided, *Turn this fear into anger. Create bad thoughts about what if. And use those bad thoughts as motivation.* This would prove to be a pivotal moment not only for the company, but for me (and my business partners) to elevate our game to the next level.

Later that evening, I called John to update him. "Jesse and Ryan are thinking of selling their shares in Pentad and moving on," I revealed. "I think it's a bad idea, and I'm a little frustrated they would drop it on us now when we're doing so well. What do you think?"

I anticipated a similar response from John—something like, yeah, that doesn't make any sense. Or what are those guys thinking? But after a few seconds of pause, John came back with, "Hmmmm, that's interesting. I figured they would bring this up eventually. And it makes sense, given we're now three years into this venture and hitting numbers we had ultimately planned for."

"You think it's a good idea?" I asked with surprise. "The two of them play significant roles on the daily. How would we fill the gaps? Who would handle all the finance and accounting? What about legal?"

I could tell John's brain was cranking away at the significance of the moment. He was methodical on how he processed situations, never one to overreact or jump to conclusions. I always respected this about John—not just as a trusted business partner, but as a friend. I could rely on his grounded nature, his pragmatic approach, and his even-keeled way of thinking. He was a rock, and I was the turbulent and uncertain waters.

John and I discussed for a while, and he continued to make very valid points for why buying them out was a good thing. "When you think about it, we could replace their respective roles, given they're more operational. We can hire someone to run finance, and we could leverage our outside counsel for any legal matters. That pretty much covers the bulk of what Ryan and Jesse do."

I started to rethink my initial response as John continued.

"But for this to happen, we would seriously need to step up our game. Jesse has been a good sales leader, so you or Josiah will need to fill that void. We've got strong momentum, and we need to keep it going while figuring out how to effectively transition them out. And we need reasonable terms for the buyout, so we're still able to grow the business. You know Jesse and Ryan are going to make a case for top dollar."

Then John threw out one of his famous John-isms: "But let's not rathole on the details tonight; let's discuss with Josiah tomorrow." We called them John-isms, because he would inject metaphors into the conversation, and as odd as they were, we always knew what he meant. "Rathole" meant over-focus. Sometimes he'd throw out "chewing on glass," which meant the process would be painful.

The next day was business as usual, although I couldn't stop thinking about the seed Jesse had planted the night before. My feelings of betrayal, frustration, and hurt turned into nervousness and loss of direction.

Later that day, Josiah, John, and I sat down in the Pentad conference room to discuss. I shared the details of my conversation with Jesse, with Josiah bringing him up to speed. I continued with my concerns, although I was tempered in my position this time, and less agitated. Still, deep down I didn't like the uncertainty of where this could go, and my own insecurities were evident to both.

John jumped in and began sharing his perspective. Overnight, his pragmatic position of *this might not be a bad thing* had turned into a *this is an opportunity we need to take advantage of.*

"I've been thinking about this all night, and assuming we could work out a reasonable deal with Ryan and Jesse, I don't see why the three of us can't blow this thing up. The three of us are the face of the company, to clients and employees, so separating from Pendulum shouldn't create any negative impact to culture and productivity."

Josiah sat back in his black, faux leather high-back chair and listened intently. I thought his initial reaction would be similar to mine. Frustrated. Even a bit annoyed.

But he came through in typical Josiah fashion and displayed nothing but excitement.

"Let's do this," Josiah said abruptly, slapping the table with the palm of his hand. "And I have an idea of someone who could join the three of us as leaders of the company. I've been talking to Chad Richeson over at Microsoft, and he's thinking of moving on to something new."

Josiah's idea was intriguing, despite the fact that John and I had little interaction with Chad. We knew he was a senior director at Microsoft and was responsible for a considerable-sized book of business in the online space there. His legacy up to that point at Microsoft was taking their proprietary big data technology called Cosmos out of the labs and applying it to all the processing for their online data analytics and business intelligence.

But beyond that, we knew very little. Josiah was the key point person managing their relationship and had spent quite a bit of time with Chad, learning his business over the years, and helping us navigate the Rob Curry situation that had almost collapsed our company earlier in the year. We trusted Josiah's opinion and made plans to see how this could play out.

We closed out the first half of 2011 with another 17 percent spike in revenue over the previous quarter, and respectable growth to more than ninety employees. But as we pushed into the third quarter, we began to experience a staffing phenomenon between onboarding new talent and losing people due to churn. This resulted in stagnant growth, because we were backfilling roles and contracts at an equal rate to their falling off. As soon as a new consulting gig was filled, an old contract ended.

This vicious cycle was common in the industry. Different variables can contribute. Short-term engagements can often lead to quick talent turnover, hiring talent that isn't committed to staying, clients stealing talent (try-before-you-buy objectives), and insufficient sales pipelines relative to revenue goals. For us, it was a combination of all the above, plus the fact that new employees focused on sales and recruiting weren't fully up to speed.

Retention of employees was a constant struggle for us for many reasons. Some left due to their performance, while others hunted for greener pastures, often in the form of larger compensation. Occasionally, our clients would poach them by offering something we couldn't. Although this bothered me at first, I took it as a sign that we not only hired a great employee to begin with, but now had a loyal advocate inside our client's organization. People's lives change over time, and therefore their respective needs change. A new baby might require a move to a larger company with extended paid parental leave. Or a geographic move may be necessary. We did our best in retaining employees, but sometimes it was simply out of our hands.

In addition to our struggle to replenish ending contracts, we as owners were now distracted with a potential buyout of 40 percent of Pendulum's ownership stake in Pentad Solutions.

John, Josiah, and I met often to discuss our thresholds and level of comfort with various financial, time, and legal terms and conditions. How much cash did we have access to? What terms would we be willing to accept, and which ones were nonnegotiable? What valuation would we give the company and why? How would we finance the remaining balance after depleting most of our cash? This was our first foray with a business transaction where the three of us needed to be in complete lockstep. Division of labor. Setting priorities. Communication lines. Decision-making. All were mission critical. It was also time for fiscal-year contract renewals with all of Microsoft—a significant and mission-critical effort endured by the entire sales team.

The third quarter of 2011 flew by in a flash as we juggled a shit ton of priorities, each seemingly more important than the next. We continued hiring operational staff, including a recruiting coordinator to help execute marketing efforts like branding and social, and a new director of finance. Onboarding and ramping them all up took significant time and resources, but it quickly took a lot of operational responsibilities off our plates. We also hired some very key consultants—all of whom brought valuable data and analytical prowess.

The five owners were ready to begin discussions to hone-in on agreeable terms of the buyout. From the get-go of the negotiation, the two parties had obvious tension and frustration.

Email after email, meeting after meeting, the various terms were individually but painstakingly checked off and agreed upon. The only thing left was the overall value of the company. With each meeting came heated discussions. Jesse and Ryan used their experience and models to determine what they believed to be a reasonable valuation. Their number was a shade under $10 million. We used our own methods and third-party resources to calculate our own numbers.

Based on each party's estimates, we were more than $1 million off.

Jesse and Ryan had applied a simple multiple of EBITDA to the valuation, essentially dumbing it down to simple math. Our calculations had utilized a similar approach but accounted for much more risk and general ambiguity, coming in initially at $8.5 million. We felt that part of our success could be attributed to Jesse and Ryan's involvement, and that by losing them, our overall productivity could be negatively impacted in the short-term, as we would need to replace them with either full-time employees or outsourced services. After all, Jesse managed our sales efforts on a day-to-day basis. In addition, all these distractions were already sending our sales numbers down as we forecasted into the third quarter. This only added to our stance that the value was somewhat lower.

John drove most of the communication to Jesse and Ryan, ensuring he had Josiah's and my buy-in on any detail discussed. Our plan was to take an eventual agreed-upon value, apply Pendulum's 40 percent stake, and break it into two tranches—the first being 70 percent cash up front based on a Small Business Association (SBA) loan for Pentad, and the second consisting of a personal note we would carry for the remaining 30 percent. Interest over the next four years at a reasonable 6 percent would give us plenty of runway to eventually refinance all the outstanding debt and sever any contractual obligations to Pendulum.

Jesse and Ryan countered with a higher valuation, somewhere in the $9.5 million range, and slightly different terms to get them more money up front—a reasonable move to reduce some risk on their side. After some more back-and-forth, we all settled on an overall valuation somewhere just over $9.1 million, giving the two Pendulum partners a combined sum of $3.66 million for their 40 percent stake. John and Ryan worked out the finer details of the purchase and sales agreement with the help of our respective outside legal counsel, and by the end of October, we closed the deal.

Pentad Buys Octane

In parallel to the Pendulum buyout shenanigans, John, Josiah, and I were busy vetting out Chad Richeson and his fit for joining our Pentad team. The move necessitated zero doubt from any of us. With Jesse and Ryan out of the picture, we shared dreams of grandeur—exponential growth, a dynamic and sophisticated culture, and the market presence of a world-class consulting firm.

We met with Chad individually and as a group, ensuring that both dynamics could be measured all around. It was very clear from the get-go: Chad brought a resume of experiences that significantly complemented ours. We were owner-operators who could tactically execute day-to-day operations with precision, build an intimate culture, and lead by example the various business functions.

Chad brought strategic thinking. A vision. An MBA from Tulane. Meaningful finance knowledge. Wisdom developed over years working in global, mission-critical environments like Microsoft and FedEx. Further, he brought maturity to our leadership team—a welcome addition, given our intention to take the company to a new level.

After several meetings, including some moderate negotiations, we decided that hiring Chad would be the first critical step in elevating Pentad. His conditions were reasonable. A CEO title. Ten percent ownership. Compensation equivalent to ours. Done deal. In order to navigate the tricky tax implications of bringing on a new partner to an established company with real value, we formulated a plan for Chad to start a company, and we would then subsequently buy it. Octane Data, LLC, was born and, in a very short time, acquired by Pentad Solutions.

The company was entering a new phase in its lifecycle,

and despite all our distractions, excitement was brewing. The chip on my shoulder returned, as I was determined to find success without Jesse and Ryan's participation. I felt some sadness that the original five wouldn't be continuing together. But that sadness quickly turned into spite. And the spite transformed into motivation. I felt personally challenged to prove to myself—and to them, for that matter—that we were capable of continued growth without them.

Chad brought new energy to our business like a stiff wind to a sail. It was palpable; you could hear, see, and feel the buzz amongst the employees. Our infrastructure was primed to help us scale. The sales pipeline was strong. Our talent acquisition team was ramped up. Our engagement management team was solid. And Dennis and Aaron were each building incredible delivery teams.

But there was one thing that didn't fit—one small but significant detail that stood in the way of our progress: our name. With four owners now in the mix, the Pentad Solutions moniker no longer made sense. This time we wouldn't change it out of reluctance or provocation, but inevitability and necessity.

Chapter 9

#WeAreTeamSociety

It's December 11, 2012, and twenty-five Society employees pile onto a school bus destined for the local Target store roughly twenty minutes away. Excitement and joy fill the air as champagne bottles pop open and glasses are passed to everyone. We raise our glasses in the air, clinking them in celebration. We've waited a year for this occasion: the annual Society shopping spree to support the Treehouse for kids foundation. We arrive, and everyone grabs shopping carts—lists in hand and Santa Claus hats on—and disperses to different sections in the store. Customers look on with curiosity at the disruption we've caused, not knowing exactly what to make of it. I find myself in the toy section grabbing board games, Lego sets, and a couple of bicycles. I see Josiah over in the electronics area buying up pretty much the entire inventory of iPod Nanos. After just thirty minutes, I find myself with a full shopping cart, along with a dozen of our employees, standing in a dedicated line just for us. A Target manager approaches me, thanking me for not only the business but for the cause we're supporting. He hands me a bunch of coupons for our purchases, thus increasing our purchasing power. I look down at the receipts and add them up *in my head the best I can. $15,000 give or take, I think. Pretty cool. We eventually head back to the bus, hauling bags of clothes, toys, lunch boxes, school supplies, and electronics. Tomorrow, all the purchases will be delivered to Treehouse's storefront in Seattle, where thousands of young people in foster care can acquire many of life's necessities for free.*

With Chad officially on board as CEO and the Pendulum partners slowly pulling back from the business till the end of 2011, Pentad's motivation for growth was unprecedented. We now had a multi-million-dollar bank loan that made up most of the buyout price. With this came strict bank covenants that needed to be reviewed and satisfied quarterly. Additionally, Jesse and Ryan carried a personal note for over a million dollars, with monthly payments plus interest. Further, we had invested in our sales, talent acquisition, engagement management, and finance teams, thus significantly increasing our overhead.

But first things first. We needed a new name. Uh, third time's a charm, right? *Here we go again.* Like Jay-Z said, "On to the next one."

This time around, the process was much more streamlined and professional. There were no random names pulled out of our asses. No, this time we were serious about establishing a brand that could outlive all of us. A name that was not only memorable, but stood for something.

Chad spearheaded the rebranding efforts and hired a local design firm, Turnstyle Studios, to help us navigate the process. Once again, we started with a long list of names ranging from Silverbow, Amper, Clutch, and Society. We batted around each option amongst the ownership group as well as with Tanna in marketing, measuring each one against a variety of qualifiers. URL options. Pronunciation and spelling. Word association. Global meaning. Uniqueness and memorability. Chad was hooked on Silverbow, as he felt there could be very interesting branding opportunities tied into it. The rest of us were lukewarm at best. Amper had some potential.

Then there was Society. Just say it. *Society.* Think about it. Marinate on the idea. The more we said "society" out loud, the more it resonated from within.

"When you really think about it, society describes who we are as an organization," John explained. "By definition, we're a diverse group of people who came together for a common goal. Sure, it doesn't necessarily spell out technology or data analytics services, but who cares?"

"I love it," I casually responded, doing my best to hide my true enthusiasm. "Everyone else?" I looked around the boardroom table at Josiah, Sarah, and Tanna.

"Let's do it," exclaimed Josiah. Sarah and Tanna gave their respective approvals. Chad, seeing everyone else's enthusiasm, quickly jumped on the bandwagon in an effort for solidarity. We were now Society.

Towards the end of October, John, Josiah, Chad, and I hosted our very first company-wide state of the union. Its purpose was to share the many changes and significant updates with our entire employee base. John drove most of the content, focusing on all things positive. Our revenue growth. Profitability. The promotion of Sarah to director of operations just weeks prior. The addition of Chad as our new leader.

John then announced that starting January 1, 2012, we were rebranding to Society Consulting. Cheers of approval and clapping filled the room.

John's final announcement was that we were officially closing our Redmond office and moving everyone to a new headquarters in downtown Bellevue. More cheers erupted, as the location presented lots of nearby restaurants and urban living, plenty of parking, and lots of retail shopping.

We closed out the remainder of the year with around ninety-five employees and a dash over $3.1 million for the quarter. Our 2011 total revenue came in at a respectable $12.4 million, a 65 percent jump from the previous year, just three years since our inception.

We had much to look forward to as we approached the new year. A new CEO to lead us forward. A new brand that represented our core identity comprised of people. A new vision upleveling our go-to-market strategy. And finally, a new headquarters in a prime location.

Enter: Sherry

In addition to all the excitement around the company's evolution, my personal life would forever change, as I met my future wife and partner in life, Sherry, just as 2011 closed. The backstory is amusing. Sherry moved right next door to me into a high-rise apartment building in downtown Bellevue, just months after I moved in. She had relocated from Toronto as she transitioned roles within Microsoft.

One random day in December of 2011, we were leaving at the same time, so I introduced myself and did my best to engage her with typical questions. How are you liking living here? What do you do for a living? I noticed her Microsoft badge hanging from her belt. For a split second, I thought, *She might be interested in Society's services. Maybe she leads some business unit that requires a lot of analytics consulting services. Maybe she's got budget to spend.* I know it's a bit smarmy, but hey, I'm a sales guy at heart and therefore always thinking about leads.

Sherry explained that she was an executive coach who

ran leadership development for Microsoft's global sales and marketing. All I heard was *coach*.

Ironically, I was looking for a new coach. I had been working with one for the past year, but she had moved away to the islands, making it inconvenient to meet face-to-face.

I pressed on and asked Sherry if she happened to know any coaches I should talk to. Perhaps someone she could refer me to. I knew this wasn't a question she could easily answer. I might as well have asked her what car she thought I should buy. Lots of specifics would need to be flushed out in order to effectively qualify which coach was right for me.

Sherry said she'd think about it and get back to me with some thoughts. I figured that would be the last time I would hear from her, so I took it upon myself to push the interest. I was, after all, a professional headhunter, whose primary job was to find and connect with people.

At the time, I had access to Microsoft's internal global address list (the GAL) due to my credentials as a vendor. I used it daily to access clients' calendars, which made scheduling meetings easier. So I found Sherry's contact information in the system and sent her an email to her Microsoft alias. I can imagine how surprised, and possibly a bit uneasy, she felt seeing my email come out of nowhere: *How the fuck did this weirdo get my email?*

With luck, her reaction didn't come in the form of a restraining order, but a page full of qualifying questions to determine exactly what type of coach I needed. I tried my best to answer as many as I could but found myself stuck, unable to articulate, given what little experience I had working with a coach.

We eventually made plans to grab a cocktail and talk about my answers to her laundry list of questions. It was the evening of December eighth, after Society's annual charity shopping spree for Treehouse. We'd had such a good turnout of employees that we finished earlier than planned.

I texted Sherry, "Hey, I finished early with our event, so I'm wondering if you're open to dinner instead of just a drink? There's a great Italian restaurant off Main Street."

She replied with, "That sounds great."

I picked her up in front of the building and drove to Cantinetta, just a couple of miles down the street. We ordered some wine and talked about everything. Work. Backgrounds. Family. Everything. Everything except coaching.

We would later joke about that evening with playful accusations that the coaching request was all a ruse, and that my true intention was to get her out on a date. I really was looking for a coach at the time; that's the truth. But I can't help but think perhaps my motives to identify a coach and have dinner with a beautiful blonde weren't necessarily mutually exclusive. In a short time, I would discover that this magnificent woman was also extremely intelligent, possessed the kindest of souls, and had a hunger for living to the fullest.

From that very first dinner, our commitment evolved at a rapid pace. Within a month, we went on a whirlwind trip to Las Vegas, and within six months, we purchased a condo together and moved in.

But the one thing we were not in any hurry to do was get married. We had talked about it almost from the very onset of our relationship, but both of us were firm believers that twice for her and once for me was more than enough. It's not that we had anything against being committed to each other. Marriage just seemed like an unnecessary ritual neither of us found convincing.

That lasted about two years, as various friends were celebrating their own nuptials, compelling us to rethink the idea altogether.

In 2014, Sherry and I eloped on a secluded beach in Washington with the presence of only an officiant, a photographer, two dear friends from British Columbia, and of course, Pepe. The ceremony was only five minutes long, as we stood on the beach amongst the driftwood and seashells, and officially consummated our nuptials. One week later, we celebrated with a large group consisting of family and friends, many of whom were Society employees.

Growing Up

Chad joining our team as CEO brought an immediate impact to all aspects of our business. We rolled out a new organizational structure, formalized our go-to-market strategy, and established our 2012 goals and overall vision. It was very clear that Chad not only thought about leading the company in a much more sophisticated manner, but he possessed an astonishing ability to organize and articulate his vision. Years working within large corporate environments provided him with these tools. He could provide complex ideas in digestible ways—be it through a PowerPoint, spreadsheet, or even email—elevating our existence. We liked to call it "marketecture," the art and science of presenting ideas in aesthetically pleasing ways.

Beyond Chad's management skills as an executive, he brought serious credentials and vision as a data practitioner. Just like Gretzky, Chad knew exactly where the puck was going to be. He knew of interesting events in the market—like the confluence of mobile devices, social media, cloud computing, big data, and customer relationship management—and how we should make the most of those opportunities.

After all, Chad had been responsible for taking Microsoft's internal big data solution and applying it to online customer advertising, Bing search, and other properties. We're talking petabyte levels of processing at a time when only the big dogs like Microsoft, Amazon, Google, and large research institutions were involved. This type of experience was critical in setting the stage for more investment in data analytics and business intelligence offerings. He gave us serious street cred, but even more so he gave us a vision.

We started 2012 with a restructuring of the go-to-market practices by having Chad oversee all our consulting practices. This allowed proper oversight of delivery while John, Josiah, and I concentrated our efforts on operational duties including sales, talent acquisition, and human resources.

Next, we focused on establishing an annual goal along with strategies and plans to support it. We broke our plan into three areas: grow revenue and profit, drive operational excellence, and invest in future capabilities. Each section had its own set of key performance indicators (KPIs), all driven by even more specific tactics: build strong, connected consulting practices across strategic verticals and geographies; differentiate our brand around business acumen and agility; and develop key partnerships with software vendors. Breaking it down like this helped us divide all the various initiatives amongst ourselves, measure progress on each, balance them based on our individual workload, and most importantly, hold each other accountable.

The new Society headquarters at 901 104th Avenue Northeast brought a breath of fresh air. The downtown location gave us an urban feel, yet the small, unique, two-story building removed any impression of a stale, corporate environment. Small workstations and lots of natural light comprised the upstairs. Previously an architecture and design firm, lots of cool office furniture, storage units, and space to grow became ours. The downstairs was vacant, once occupied by a boutique women's clothing shop. All the walls, dressing rooms, and large mirrors remained.

A buzz rang through the new office. Plenty of people coming and going. The sound of keyboard strokes and mouse clicks. The smell of a freshly brewed cup of coffee from the Keurig machine in the breakroom. A refrigerator full of soda. Dogs wandering around saying hello to neighboring employees. Phone conversations. Conference rooms filled with employees discussing complex, technical scenarios written on a whiteboard. A mix of dance, hip-hop, and pop music playing in the background from someone's computer in the recruiting bullpen. The energy was infectious: the feel of a start-up with lots of momentum.

If you asked John what he is proudest of with regards to the company's history, it won't be the early days of laying our own hardwood floors. It's not the acquisition. It's 2012.

In retrospect, so many things happened in 2012, many of which were unforeseen or out of our control. Legal and tax disputes, poor hiring decisions, and continuous churn overwhelmed our already over-filled plates. Yet, despite all the obstacles we faced that year, we grew our overall employee base, upleveled the talent with key hires, invested in a variety of strategic company initiatives, began an expansion project for the lower section of our building, increased our top-line revenue, and if that wasn't enough, successfully migrated to a new bank and refinanced all our debts to Pendulum. John wasn't wrong.

Lawyer Up

In Spring of 2012, Jesse and Ryan brought to our attention the obligation for Society to write them a $90,000 check in support for 2011 taxes, given the buyout. Their argument was that the company historically set aside funds to pay for our individual member taxes, and therefore should be on the hook to contribute to theirs.

We disagreed. The buyout had triggered income taxes for them, versus the capital gains tax they assumed they would be paying as a result of the acquisition—a significant amount of dollars and oversight on their part. We stood our ground and retained the services of a tax attorney to help us navigate the details. We also leveraged the good folks at Cairncross, our outside general counsel. They reaffirmed our position as not being liable.

In meeting after meeting in our conference room, we'd essentially come to the same point of disagreement. We were at a stalemate, each party with their own justification and heels dug in deep, with little hope of compromise.

One day, Josiah, John, and I were in our conference room with Ryan and Jesse, discussing the details. Up to this point, even though the discussions hadn't necessarily advanced, we'd kept an element of professionalism and mutual respect. We were all friends after all, and the buyout was, for the most part, accretive to all parties. Ryan and Jesse were happy to focus on their own portfolio of companies, and we were happy taking the company in our own direction.

But that came to a quick stop when, out of sheer frustration during a spirited discussion, Jesse stood up from his chair, grabbed his backpack, and declared, "Alright then, get ready to lawyer up." Silence. He and Ryan walked out of the office without saying another word. John, Josiah, and I just sat there dumbfounded, looking at each other in disappointment, anger, and confusion. *What the fuck just happened?*

Eventually, this issue became a major distraction, so we put Chad as point person for all communication and negotiations. A week later, Jesse and Ryan came back to the Society offices to try to put this dispute to bed through some equitable resolution. The two were calm and collected and approached the conversation in a tone that was more *let's all rise above all the bullshit and come to some reasonable compromise.*

Then Ryan recapped exactly where we all stood, the hard lines that had been drawn, and the financial chasm in between. He brought up the idea that we should all look at the differences not in the spirit of the law, but in the spirit of friendship. He hoped this would lead us down a softer path, a gentler approach to finding an acceptable middle ground. Ryan was diplomatic, and as a seasoned attorney and born negotiator, displayed a sincere and commendable effort to move forward.

He was quickly interrupted.

"Are you kidding me?!" exclaimed Josiah. He was furious. "How the fuck can you sit there and reasonably say anything about the *spirit of friendship*, when not a week ago you told us to lawyer up! That's complete bullshit. No friend tells another friend to lawyer up."

At first, I was completely caught off guard by Josiah's reaction. In fact, I'd never seen Josiah as pissed off as at that very moment. It was like watching Dr. Banner suddenly transform into his alter ego, the Hulk. Tension and annoyance grew with each word spewing from his mouth. His reaction also caught Ryan and Jesse off-kilter, as they weren't expecting it either. Then it all caught up to me: he was right for calling them out.

Silence. Jesse and Ryan picked up their belongings and walked out the door. I ran out and met them in the parking lot where Ryan was still waiting. Jesse had driven off.

"Well, that was a bit intense," I joked in hopes of finding a brief moment of levity.

"There's nothing I can say to that," Ryan replied while gazing blankly. "Josiah's reaction was justified, and I'm stuck here in the middle having to manage both sides. *Lawyer up*," Ryan murmured to himself. "Those are two words I need Jesse to get out of his vocabulary."

Ryan and I discussed the details a little further, talked about playing hoops the coming weekend, and parted ways. I wanted to play a role in the diplomacy given my friendships with both Jesse and Ryan, but also in our fiscal connection due to the buyout.

Deep down, I knew Jesse wasn't serious about suing us. His "lawyer up" comment was simply a reaction to his frustration, as the negotiating hadn't made much progress. But I know it pissed off Josiah and John, leaving me in a precarious position to mitigate as much risk as possible.

It was a delicate situation for us, one that required careful weighing of options. On one hand, we were convinced that Pendulum wasn't owed a dime, and that the surprise tax bill was a direct result of their own misunderstanding of how the IRS would categorize the buyout. They messed up, so why should we be responsible for cleaning up their oversight? Our attorneys gave us even more confidence that this was the case.

However, Jesse and Ryan carried the note for the buyout —millions of dollars that we still owed them. It wouldn't exactly be in our best interest to piss them off over a relatively minor dispute, only to have them hold our feet to the flames when it came to the note. What if we ran into some bad luck and had a down quarter? What if we were late on a payment or missed one all together? All good questions with potentially dire consequences, should Pendulum decide to play hardball. An angel was sitting on our other shoulder, whispering reason and rational advice in our ears.

A couple of weeks later, we came to a reasonable compromise where all parties involved were happy. We added $75,000 to the principal balance owed to Pendulum to represent the tax credit. Pendulum, in turn, reamortized the note and extended the terms to forty-two months, giving us more wiggle room for cash reserves.

The result reminded me of my first marriage and the divorce proceedings that led to binding arbitration. The arbitrator said something to me as he wrapped up his judgement. "You know how I know I've done a good job?" he asked. "When both parties walk away disappointed with the results. This means it was probably a fair outcome for both." It would be easy to think that in this case. Ryan and Jesse didn't get as much as they originally wanted. We ended up paying for something we weren't responsible for. But in the end, I looked at it as a win-win; the most significant part was salvaging our friendship.

Burning the Candle at Both Ends

The hiring of new talent continued at a rapid pace, as the Bellevue office provided ample space for new bodies. It seemed my calendar was filled with various stages of interviews throughout any given week. The recruiting team was slammed, as our practice leaders kept opening new headcount. Within a couple of months, we began to test Sarah and her operations team's ability to be creative in finding space for new hires. Something needed to be done.

After everyone left for the day on a random Monday in

spring of 2012, Josiah, John, and I changed from our work attire (which was very casual) into workout attire and proceeded downstairs to do some light demolition. Recall the vacant downstairs portion of the building that was formerly a boutique women's clothing store, with most of its infrastructure remaining? Our plan was to eventually expand into two floors, but a little manual labor was required prior. And who better to do it, saving a little money while getting some well-needed stress release? The same scrappy guys who installed hardwood floors in our first office not three years prior.

This time, armed with sledgehammers and crowbars, we smashed down wall after wall, tearing through sheetrock and metal studs. Dressing rooms demolished. Old track lighting destroyed. We had the most fun demolishing the gigantic eight-foot-tall mirrors that were essentially glued to the walls from floor to ceiling. If breaking a mirror brings seven years of bad luck, the three of us have a few lifetimes' worth of shitty fortune coming our way. To be honest, it was really fucking fun. We'd toss the sledgehammer as hard as we could in axe-like throwing fashion, smashing glass from across the room. Shards from the mirror flew everywhere like shrapnel from a grenade.

By the end of the night, the place looked like a bomb had gone off. Dust from the gypsum covered absolutely everything, including us. Stacks of broken-down walls and strips of metal from the studs piled high on one side. Large industrial plastic garbage bags filled with glass stacked next to them. We spent the final hour sweeping up the remains and hauling everything out to the dumpster. Mission accomplished. Hard work, but it's what you do in a startup.

With the downstairs wide open, we began discussions to connect the two floors and build out the lower level. Josiah was close friends with a couple of fellas who owned

Build, a local design and architecture firm that specialized in simplicity and function. Andrew and Kevin jumped in and brought a clean yet artsy vision for the space, and a way to connect the two levels with a functional staircase and sitting area. Over the next year, we would work with intermittent levels of construction noise, sometimes causing significant distractions to our employees. Hammering. Sawing. Drilling. A bit of an inconvenience. Some worked from home. Others set up a workstation at their client's office. Most just dealt with it. Some brought in their noise-cancelling headphones and didn't give it another thought.

But the finished product was an absolute masterpiece in my mind and therefore worth every distraction. Bright walls, accented by our Society colors of gray and two tones of yellow, connected both the upstairs and downstairs. An L-shaped staircase led down to a set of built-in bleachers with lots of comfortable seating for breaks or a change of venue. At the base of the interstitial staircase was a large stage-like platform we would later use for all-company meetings. Four long worktables provided dozens of workstations. Three small rooms tucked around the corner offered up privacy for individual conference calls. And a large conference room, lined with multiple windows looking back into the office, emphasized the clean presentation and minimalistic feel of the space. All in all, the office represented exactly what we desired: a fun, casual yet functional space offering a variety of work options, places to collaborate, and spots to relax.

The rest of 2012 flew by at light speed as the four owners dialed in our operating rigor in hopes of capitalizing on a bunch of new investments. Josiah continued to crush our business development efforts by landing us new logos including Cisco Systems, T-Mobile, and Zulily. We grew our sales teams, added talent to lead our data engineering practice, and increased headcount in our finance department.

But all this momentum wasn't immune to some hiring mistakes. A new leader of talent acquisition lasted only six months before we parted ways. I replaced my role overseeing sales with a business development executive who didn't last much longer. Luckily, the hiring errors didn't compromise our continued growth trajectory.

Dennis and I continued growing the product development division by adding a large team of support engineers after winning an RFP as Microsoft outsourced their GetHelp organization. We also were rewarded with work from Microsoft's digital crimes unit on a product very few people knew about—including us.

We closed out 2012 on a high note, achieving record revenue of more than $16 million, with well over 130 employees. The company awarded its top performers with an all-expense paid trip to Maui the following spring. We were also recognized with our first "Best Places to Work" accolade presented by *Seattle Business Magazine*, and a spot on the "Fastest Growing Companies" by the *Puget Sound Business Journal*—honors we received again over the following few years.

Team Society's momentum into 2013 felt unrelenting based on all the pieces being put into place. Refinanced debt, a healthy balance sheet, top-notch talent, and a strong sales pipeline gave us encouragement that we were making the right moves.

Chapter 10

Growth and Growing Pains

It's the closing hours of Society Days, and the whole company is gathered downstairs, taking in the stories and teachings of Chase Jarvis, this year's keynote speaker. He paces back and forth on stage with a casual yet passionate presentation. Everyone's attention is locked in as he shares his perspective on creativity and art, capturing unique moments that nobody else can artificially recreate. To further his point, Chase unexpectedly reaches to a can of sparkling water sitting atop a small table on stage and intentionally tips it off onto the floor. Thud. I cringe as I watch the bubbly water pour out onto the area carpet and onto the hardwoods. What the fuck? I think to myself. What nerve. Go get a towel and clean that shit up. Sarah, our operations director, looks over at me with satisfaction, as she can tell I'm uncomfortable and a bit perturbed. She flashes me a smile indicating she's laughing inside. Chase then explains the value of living in the moment and collecting moments of creativity—the spilled can of water, despite my indignant feelings, is art.

The year 2013 started out with a renewed energy and sense of mission. Besides our remodel, within less than a year from the buyout of Pendulum, we had completely refinanced our debt, allowing us to place bigger bets back into the company.

The ownership team adopted and rigorously applied a practical approach to investment dollars. Our philosophy was based on a set of criteria that gave us common priorities. The top of the list was *revenue*. Was the investment going to directly impact potential revenue streams? Next was *operational efficiency and cost management*. Then *employee experience*. This framework allowed us to measure the progress or impact that any dollar spent was having on the company. From here, we would gauge whether to continue a path or cut bait. The fail-fast mentality was an important aspect to saving money in the long run, while quickly applying the resources to other areas of need.

Along with numerous investments in our talent base, we also invested in developing our very own intellectual property. This was part of Chad's master plan not only to fine-tune our services, but to inject our own proprietary technology to the mix. We weren't sure if this would entail any licensing, or if we would simply use our technology to increase efficiency while executing client projects. Best case scenario, we could do both.

Our first investment was a mobile application for internal employee use called Society Engage.

Dennis ran point on the project and worked with a few people on his team to execute. The app was a portal for our employees "to all things Society." Given the remote nature of consulting, the application empowered our employee base with access to the latest company information and events, a complete directory of employee profiles including a skills inventory, and easy-to-navigate peer-to-peer interaction. The service became a valuable tool, as anyone could locate anyone in our organization through meta search capabilities.

Another major investment for Society was the development of Amper, a piece of software to help democratize data analytics. Initially called Nexus, this became a significant investment with multiple engineers working on it. The idea was driven by Chad, and the overall concept was nothing short of genius. Amper's primary function was to provide analysts with a nonprogrammatic user interface so they could access disparate data sets, build and schedule data pipelines, cleanse data, and turn around insights with less time. Through a drag and drop interface, an analyst could build complex data pipelines from various sources, execute the pipeline, and point it to any business intelligence or analytics tool of their choice.

In addition, Amper's backend was built to leverage Hadoop, a big data technology used to handle massive data sets, thus increasing the bandwidth for most analysts. It essentially empowered the front-line analyst with capabilities normally provided by corporate IT.

You see, it could take days, weeks, or depending on IT resources, months for a typical analyst to access data, apply it to some sort of analytical tool, report on it, and then gather insights. Requirements gathering, countless meetings, permissions, and often politics were all part of the typical corporate process. One's reliance on IT department resources was a major obstacle, preventing frontline analysts and data scientists from quickly iterating off their data sets. Once they eventually got their data, often it was already stale, or the business requirements or use case had changed.

All-in, the ownership team invested roughly $1.5 million over a couple of years of development; however, the ultimate returns on the product were minimal at best. It was a great conversation starter, and clients were most definitely interested. We pitched it to a variety of clients like Microsoft, Expedia, T-Mobile, and others. But Amper never reached commercial-grade levels, and therefore no major company was willing to take the leap to use it, despite its very cool functionality. We were services people, not product people, so Amper suffered from our own shortcomings. The market was ripe for a product like Amper; we just weren't able to capitalize. In retrospect, we should have spun it out into a whole new venture with its own leadership, engineering, sales, and marketing teams.

Despite the disappointment in Amper's lackluster success, the rest of Society continued to grow at an aggressive pace. We matured as an organization, especially during 2013 and 2014—through our new processes and best practices, caliber of talent we hired, quality of delivery to clients and new methodologies, and most of all, vast number of investments in employee experience.

Doubling Down on Team-Building

John, Josiah, and I made it clear from the get-go that culture was king; we wanted this to differentiate us from our competitors. And with our newfound company identity, aspirations for growth, and investment mindset, the time had come to double down on our people.

We scheduled regular, free catered lunches for all our employees. We hosted special breakfasts where the executive team served up freshly made pancakes and waffles. There were wine tastings, company picnics, ad hoc team lunches, and surprise happy hours. We attended Seattle sporting events and hosted annual holiday parties. Josiah added to his many "fun" titles with a designation of CCO—

Chief Culture Officer—and began a tradition of booze-cart Fridays.

As our employees finished up their Friday work, Josiah would load up a booze cart and wheel it around the office, making specialty cocktails for everyone. He took great care in offering a wide variety of spirits, wines, and non-alcoholic options—something every employee looked forward to toward the end of the week. Everything was celebrated. A birthday. An engagement. An employee having a baby. A promotion of a team member. We took every opportunity to bring the team together as a family.

Culture, however, wasn't just about booze carts and wine tastings—although they certainly didn't hurt the cause. Culture, for us, was the most important aspect of our leadership, even beyond strategy. We wanted to create a purpose for all our employees, something they could tangibly grasp and hold onto. Coming to work was supposed to be productive, but also fun. We wanted our employees to look forward to coming into the office.

Our executive team embraced and propagated that culture seamlessly into the rest of the company. At our peak, Sarah's engagement management team consisted of six employees fully dedicated to employee experience and culture. In time, I even witnessed some of our competitors emulating our model, which felt good.

Further, John spearheaded the establishment of our company values, distilling them down to four distinct yet representative words that embodied our ethos. People, Growth, Excellence, and Fun became our bedrock of values that every employee would embrace moving forward.

In an effort to drive sales activity, operational excellence, and quality delivery, I worked with Josiah, Chad, and John on our recognition program, the President's Club. This entailed incentives to all employees who wished to adopt new skills related to lead generation, above-and-beyond delivery to clients, and leadership. Annually, the owners hosted an all-expense paid trip to Hawaii for those who were nominated or qualified through preestablished performance criteria.

The executive team also hosted monthly new-hire lunches for new employees joining the Society family. Each casual luncheon offered high-level company information, a little history, and an overview of our values. We continued our quarterly all-hands meetings called the state of the union, where we would share the latest in our company financials, investments, and programs and initiatives, while taking time to recognize and reward employee achievements and promotions.

One of those events annually became a part of what we called Society Days. Our employee base had grown not only in size and talent over the past couple of years, but also geographically, with at least 20 percent based out of other cities around the country. So in this event, we flew everyone in to corporate for a few days of team-building, brown bags and tech talks, and cross-functional training.

Often, this was the first time many of our employees put a face with a name. We closed the event by hosting our state of the union. We would share comprehensive details pertaining to company direction and annual sales contest announcements, closing with a keynote speaker. Local industry icons like Chase Jarvis and Richard Tait shared inspirational thoughts on creativity, overcoming life obstacles, and success.

Eventually, we also integrated what we called the SVA, which stood for Society Value Awards. Employees nominated and voted on their colleagues who most exemplified any of the four stated values: People, Growth, Excellence, and Fun. Not only did the award-winners get recognition and a nice commemorative piece of crystal, but they also immediately qualified for the following year's President's Club trip.

Our overall revenue also continued to grow significantly. Quarter after quarter, we signed new clients, upleveled our projects, and grew our presence with existing clients—steadily increasing our top-line revenue from $16 million in 2012, to $21 million in 2013, to $28 million in 2014. Company headcount also grew proportionately, ending 2014 with close to 200 employees.

One of our most significant organizational changes was the creation of individual practices led by managing directors. These leaders owned specific service offerings as well as designated geographic regions. Many of Society's investments were in the big data and digital analytics services realm, leading us to hire as soon as we found the appropriate talent.

In 2013, we were able to hire Steve Newman, former client and once chief technology officer of Gist. He decided to move on from BlackBerry and found a perfect home with Society. I can't begin to tell you how lucky we were to have Steve, as he not only was a well-respected technology leader in the area, but a wonderful human being who brought compassion, respect, and integrity. Steve drove most of the efforts around our individual practice development and eventually hired Frank Huynh, Charlie Shoemaker, and eventually, Felix Chen. Each of them owned individual P&Ls and were given reasonable autonomy to hire, invest, and manage all aspects of their business. The model worked, as revenue continued to soar.

Searching for an Identity

It's safe to say that even though the company was doing well, my own professional trajectory could only be described as stagnant. I was a bit lost. My role had evolved into a multifaceted position involving varied responsibilities, but it lacked a specific charter.

You could argue that this is life in a startup, and after five years of grinding away, growing the company at a rapid pace, selling, hiring, firing, and just straight hustling, I would have been used to it by now. Everyone had to wear a variety of hats throughout our evolution—a critical component for our business success. John played a billable role in the beginning. Josiah put on his recruiting hat every so often. Jesse tried to manage the sales team. We displayed countless examples of do-whatever-it-takes maneuvering.

But over time, the individual roles of Chad, John, and Josiah seemed to fall into a specific function with their own respective identities. Chad was the visionary CEO, and although he also oversaw our financial well-being, his primary responsibilities around strategy were well-known. John led all things people and operations. Human resources, talent acquisition, engagement management, and general facilities all fell within his oversight.

And then there was Josiah. Although he also wore a significant number of hats over the years, he eventually fell into a clearly-defined cadence of responsibilities. In fact, he ring-fenced his own set of responsibilities himself, knowing his own strengths. He was a pure business development savant, a white elephant hunter, who recognized very early on that his talents didn't lie in people or process management. Instead, he focused 100 percent of his efforts on driving new clients, and therefore revenue, while being an ambassador for company culture.

I, on the other hand, continued to struggle with my own role within the organization. I crossed swim lanes often, assisting anyone and everyone when the opportunity arose. Sometimes I was asked to do it, and other times it happened organically. But with each move, questions would manifest in the back of my mind: *What role do I play in the overall success of this company? What do I need to do to gain an identity and ensure I'm positively contributing?*

Sure, I had a "vice president" title, but what the fuck did that mean? I wasn't a VP of anything specific. If anything, I was the VP of nothing. An empty title. A token title with no specific people management or delivery responsibilities—despite the enormous pressure I felt day-to-day. And this gave me angst regardless of my other official title: cofounder.

Scott's tenure as our recruiting director ended up short-lived, so I eventually took over that team's leadership. The talent acquisition team worked well together, so they took very little of my time. Our new executive led our sales team, so I played more of a conduit between his day-to-day management of the team and coordination of larger sales initiatives like responding to large proposals, coordinating cross-team delivery components, and establishing formal partnerships. I also kept my own book of business, which involved lots of business development, account management, and general administrative bullshit. So an average day still consisted of varied tasks with little focus on any one major area.

Towards the end of 2014, my role would change once again, as Chris, the VP of sales we hired not a year prior, would prove ineffective and therefore move on. I became the new SVP of revenue, not to be confused with Josiah's title, SVP of business development. Within a short time, we fell into a healthy rhythm of responsibilities. Josiah focused solely on landing that next client, while I focused on our sales team leadership, sales excellence, workflows and reporting, and some marketing. The divide and conquer strategy for sales worked wonderfully, as it not only created a very clear delineation of responsibilities, but it also let the two of us focus on our strengths. John also played a key role in managing me over that timeframe, giving me guidance on where to focus as well as navigating the minefield of my blind spots.

A Victim of Our Own Success

The first half of 2015 almost brought the entire company to its knees, as we struggled to keep pace with our own success. Geographic expansion to Austin, Chicago, San Francisco, and New York stressed our financials as investments took time to produce returns. Additionally, our consultant base also grew, thus creating the need to invest in even more operational staff.

Sarah added more engagement managers to her team, along with a manager to lead the talent acquisition team. Steve Newman also added to the madness as he created a new delivery excellence group, focused on quality control of all project deliverables, standardizing delivery methodologies, and creating a playbook for all future engagements.

Dennis at this point was leading our largest book of business and provided us with capital to reinvest in other areas throughout the organization. He grew the business organically, not specifically due to targeted investments, but through word-of-mouth referrals and the help of my sales efforts.

In spring of 2015, Dennis and I were contacted by a couple of Microsoft leaders who owned support for many of their enterprise services like SQL Server, SC Operations

Manager (SCOM), Azure, Office365, and many others. They were looking for a new vendor who could help them with a new model to support their customers across different Microsoft products and services. A week later, we set up a meeting at our Society corporate office and hosted three Microsoft leaders.

At this point, we weren't sure what to expect, but once the meeting kicked off, things couldn't have gone better. We began with a deep-dive investigation into their business, including their challenges and potential solutions. The three Microsoft managers were surprisingly transparent, sharing intimate details about their daily pains. We shared the Society story, focusing on our capabilities, past successes, aspirations, and a healthy dose of company culture.

The managers, seemingly satisfied with our dog-and-pony show, changed gears and unleashed a blitzkrieg of questions, ranging from employee retention rates and benefits offerings, to support methodologies and office space. They wanted to know about our engagement management model, and the intricacies of how we cared for our employees. They even went so far as to comment on the vibe of our office, as Pepe was silently curled up in a ball underneath the conference table.

Dennis and I fell into a routine like Lennon and McCartney. We bounced back and forth, complementing each response with supporting commentary like facts and data, fielding all the questions as if we had rehearsed them all prior. You could tell they were impressed and interested, but just how much, we didn't know.

That was, until one of them said, "Okay, we've heard enough. How long would it take for you to create a statement of work, get all the infrastructure in place, hire the talent, and have everything ready to go?"

Holy shit. Dennis and I looked at each other. "When would you like us to be ready?" we asked.

"Is one month realistic?" they responded.

"Most definitely," I concluded, despite knowing exactly how enormous this request was.

We finished the meeting with a short tour of the rest of the office and a couple of introductions to key employees. I immediately walked down the hall to Chad's office to find him sitting at his desk.

"Dude," I said giddy with excitement. "Dennis and I just closed a substantial support engagement with Microsoft's Enterprise group."

"That's great," Chad responded. "What's the size and timing?"

"Uh, we're still figuring out the specifics, but my guess is around thirty people and three or four million dollars."

Chad's mouth dropped and eyes grew as he processed what I had just said. I could tell he was equally giddy with excitement but also terrified of the immediate implications. He knew the long-term revenue benefits would help our crusade in investing in other areas of the business, namely analytics, big data, and customer experience. But the more business we generated that involved support services, the more it diluted our direction toward being a pure play data-services company. A true quandary of sorts.

Plus, this deal was much larger than the typical engagements we won over the years. A large deal might be around a million dollars and only a handful of people. But thirty people and over four million dollars associated with one project was monumental to say the least.

Once we dialed in all the details of the new engagement, the whole team jumped into support. Sarah's recruiting team began sourcing and interviewing candidates. I focused on creating all the statements of work encompassing all the deliverables and financials. Dennis drove most of the qualifying and onboarding of new employees along with organizational structure. John helped locate additional office space for us to use, as we were already bursting at the seams. And then there was Chad, who was busy negotiating with the banks for our credit lines, cashflow, and covenants.

Remember Jesse's proclamation that "cash is king?" Here we were, a thirty-million-dollar company with strong cashflow and an equally strong balance sheet. We were much larger than we had been. More mature. Nothing like the fledgling startup in a cramped office off Eastlake years prior. But when you add over thirty new employees in a given month, plus all the infrastructure, office space, desks, laptop computers, technical support, beverages and snacks, the amount of cashflow expended is tremendous. This puts a significant stress on a business, as any revenue to offset the expenditures is at least thirty to sixty days out. Imagine having to navigate all the expenses plus three payroll cycles before receiving a dime from the client. It was painful, and we as owners would have to forego a few months of pay till our cash cycle caught up with everything—a small but necessary sacrifice.

We had daily calls with the banks who were uneasy with our balances. The entire team was taxed, as we were all working night and day to coordinate all the hiring, office space, computers, and general necessities. That's what we faced, and if it weren't for our scrappiness as an organization and willingness to find a new gear of productivity and creativity, we could have easily imploded from our own successes.

A New Mission

By the middle of 2015, Chad led the company through yet another stage of maturity. He shifted to a more refined go-to-market strategy that best reflected his vision.

Chad, along with the other founders, created a new mission statement, one that would resonate with our employees, clients, and partners: *Society's mission is to help our clients compete on customer experience.* This new statement gave all of us a North Star from which to navigate. Chad broke it down even further by reorganizing our practices into three distinct but highly complementary divisions —what we called A-B-C, which stood for Analytics, Big Data, and Customer Experience. Stitched together, the new practices resonated with how our clients consumed our services.

Chad's forethought was brilliant to say the least, and the story helped take the company to even higher levels. With Steve Newman's oversight, the individual practices, along with our geographic expansion, were ready to scale. We didn't have anyone focused on customer experience, so Chad drove most of those conversations, given his experience activating data for various customer touchpoints.

And then there was Dennis. He had essentially been with us from near the beginning, helping to grow his product development division to record levels. With the latest win at Microsoft adding over thirty new employees to his already substantial roster, Dennis's overall book of business stood above everyone else's.

But where did it fit in the company's new mission around customer experience? There was A, B, and C, but where did that leave Dennis and his team? Sure, the margins were larger in our booming analytics and big data practices, and the growth rates were certainly higher. But none of the investment would have occurred without the successes of Dennis and the legacy business he managed. This is where things started to turn ugly.

The ownership team did its best to figure out how Dennis's group played into the overall strategy and mission statement. The support engineers were certainly customer-facing, and we could justify it somehow as part of the customer experience practice. But it was a stretch. A square peg in a round hole. An outlier to the direction of the company, despite its importance to the top and bottom line. Then there was the rest of his team—again, a mixed bag of one-off software engineers, project managers, and testers. Some were involved in actual deliverables, but most were staffed on individual, random consulting gigs. Where would they fit in to the Society equation?

We ended up creating what we called the enterprise support operations (ESO) team as a separate practice. But it didn't resolve the larger problem. A sentiment grew that no one cared about the successes, history, or overall impact Dennis and his team had on the current state of the company. Nor did it seem like they belonged in the future state. Unfortunately, Dennis didn't help the situation.

In defense of the owners, Dennis was tasked with figuring out the strategic direction of his practice. Meaning he was given plenty of opportunity to collaborate with the other managing directors, brainstorm on future-state synergies and go-to-market tactics, and bring some high-level plan back to the owners. It wasn't an easy task by any means, but it was a task only he could have accomplished given his knowledge of his entire organization. But in the end, Dennis failed to produce a viable proposal, so Chad made the decision to simply move on with a plan he felt was best for the company.

As owners, we found ourselves in a serious dilemma of

sorts. We now had a stake in the ground: A vision and strategy to take the company into the future. A plan to capitalize on the latest trends in the marketplace. An opportunity to be the next major player in big data and analytics. But on the flip side, a significant piece of our business was vital in its revenue and profitability but didn't align to the new direction.

Further, Chad had published what we called the Society Black Book—a long-range plan that encompassed mission, vision, strategy, values, culture, and investments; a roadmap of who we were and who we were going to become. He sent it to all employees, ensuring both transparency from the ownership team as well as a rallying call for solidarity. For the portion of the company that was involved in A, B, or C, it was well received. But for some who were part of Dennis's team, it presented a question we could never fully answer: what did it mean for them?

As you can imagine, this ignited a spark of dissention amongst Dennis and the rest of his more vocal and loyal employees. It was innocuous at first, but as whispers around the water cooler and general red-headed stepchild sentiment spread, the cancer grew. My guess is it all began as simple criticisms amongst each other—small complaints about how the leadership team didn't care about them; or how we only focused on the shiny objects, paying little regard to Dennis and his team. This, of course, wasn't the case, as every employee residing in his organization was treated with equal value, respect, and inclusiveness. But the discord continued and eventually led to the recruitment of other dissatisfied employees in other divisions.

The leader of our big data practice fell prey to the whispers and rumors and joined them in their jaunts to a local bar, where they would swap perspectives and lament on how poorly the owners were leading. Things seemed to get worse when one of Sarah's engagement managers even joined the fray.

When asked directly if there was a problem, each one kept quiet and denied having any sort of beef. But we all knew the truth. You could see it in their eyes. In their level of energy and enthusiasm. In the tone of their voice. In the random yet frequent rolling of their eyes in response to something company-oriented.

It was obvious to the owners that something needed to happen. But what?

Chapter 11

Divestiture

It's absolutely dumping rain, but our spirit and effort are undeterred from finding matsutake, a mushroom that only propagates in old growth forest. We're in the Cascade Mountains, six miles down a gravel forest service road in the middle of nowhere, a location we know as one of our secret family hunting grounds. My sister, two brothers, father, and I meander through the forest, poking our walking sticks at the base of rotten tree trunks and mounds of pine needles in hopes of discovering the hidden fungi. This year, the conditions aren't ideal, and only a couple of mushrooms are found. Unfortunately, mother nature has brought the rain a little too late in the season. But the hunt is only part of the experience. Afterward, the five of us find shelter by huddling together under the raised tailgate of our SUV and feast on several picnic items. There are onigiri, or balls of rice filled with pickled plum, hot green tea, and cold fried chicken. We never deviate from the menu. This is a family tradition, passed on from previous generations.

During our January 2016 quarterly board meeting, Chad, John, Josiah, and I discussed the idea that it might make sense to divest the entire product development practice. We could potentially sell it on the open market and pass all the contracts, and therefore employees, over to the buyer. I guessed that several competitors in the space would love adding tens of millions of dollars to their top line, along with a pool of exceptional talent. It could be a winning situation for all.

On paper, everything seemed to add up. Dennis and his team would get to work for someone else. Society would remove an entire group that didn't exactly fit in our new go-to-market. The buyer would get revenue as well as talent. And we would create some liquidity that we could use to expand our other practices even more. We decided to investigate further.

Our first step in investigating our options for divesting the practice from the company led us to finding a broker who could counsel us throughout the process. We made a bunch of calls, set up meetings, and listened to their respective pitches. We settled on Cascadia Capital, a well-established, full-service investment institution with a strong mergers and acquisitions division. Three of their employees worked closely with us—a managing director named John, and two middle management analysts who did most of the heavy lifting.

We all knew there were challenges associated with selling just one piece of the business. And at our very first meeting, John and his team emphatically reinforced those risks. First, finding a buyer who would be willing to navigate such a complicated transaction would be extremely difficult. Peeling specific contracts from the company, providing assurance that employees would transition, and placing a dollar figure on it all was damn-near impossible.

Other potential risks included the impact on company morale and Microsoft's reaction to the sale. And even if we were able to get a potential buyer, we would be taking pennies on the dollar for the true value of the practice. Which convincingly led us down a different path: sell the entire company.

At first, the idea of selling the company was unappealing to all of us. 2015 was on track for record levels of revenue. We were just starting to see some of the fruits of our labor. Plus, we still weren't sure how the geographic investments were going to play out. But the more Cascadia touted the market conditions and potential multiples they were seeing for services companies, the more interesting things got.

Promises of top-market valuations were presented. Assurances of a top-tier buyer list and network in our space further intrigued us. Connections galore. This would be a slam dunk. Dollar signs began swirling around in our heads. We were enamored to say the least and bought in to all the hype they were dishing out.

Confidentially, we agreed to sell the entire thing.

We should have known from the very get-go that something wasn't quite right. The companies they were bringing to the table didn't seem all that interested. Many of them were equally uninteresting to us. The valuations weren't what they should have been. The suitors lacked natural fits for our services and organizational structure. They didn't like our client concentration. The Cascadia folks kept backpedaling, making excuses for this or that. It was a frustrating experience, as one potential buyer after another fizzled early on in the process.

Finally, they brought a London-based technology consulting firm to the table called Ebiquity. After several calls with their leadership team, an initial meeting between

Chad and some executives, and lots of discussion amongst the owners, we received a letter of intent outlining the high-level aspects of the purchase.

The opportunity was dubbed "Project Swan." The four owners secretly coordinated a whirlwind trip to London to meet with the various leaders for two all-day deep-dive sessions covering every aspect of the business. The meetings, for the most part, were promising, as we would quickly recognize the quality of leadership in Michael, their CEO of the Americas. He even went so far as to commit to us a couple more years of leadership before he retired, if the deal went through.

The deal looked promising, but after some back and forth negotiations, it became clear that Ebiquity, Society, and Cascadia were not on the same page. We learned of some backdoor conversations we didn't know about—discussions that would complicate expectations and handcuff our ability to have an open dialogue. Although the initial cash payout of their offer was attractive, the planned earnout over three different tranches appeared unattainable, opening us to too much risk. They pressed us on EBITDA minimums that would have a serious impact on our ability to reinvest in growth, and in the end, it proved to be a showstopper.

After lots of internal discussions, Chad reached out to Michael and shared the news that we wouldn't be moving forward. Although disappointed, Michael understood and extended his appreciation for the opportunity.

Over the following month, Cascadia brought fewer and fewer opportunities to the table. All the promises of grandeur were eroded by what we felt was their inability to position us in the right light. We took for granted the idea that they actually knew how to sell us to potential suitors.

This proved to be incorrect, given the low valuations and general lack of enthusiasm.

Eventually, this led us to decide that it was best to put the sale on hold and refocus our efforts on growth; hence we broke off our relationship with Cascadia. This was a significant relief, as the extra meetings, correspondence, and sneaking around were a major distraction to our normal day-to-day operations.

But we walked away with profound insights related to how a company might value us. We were unique in our story and would require a unique buyer where all the stars aligned. The conditions needed to be perfect, very similar to those required for the elusive mushroom my family foraged for all my life.

A Tough Decision

Even though we weren't actively working with a broker, our reputation as a growing analytics firm had spread throughout the market. Companies that heard through the grapevine or happened to be on the hunt for a company like ours continued to tap us on the shoulder to see what we were all about. Most didn't lead anywhere and were quickly dismissed by Chad, who fielded our inquiries.

As we closed out 2015, Josiah, John, and I refocused on managing the dynamics of our employee-base and remote offices across the country and ramping up our sales team to capitalize on our latest go-to-market strategy. Several moving pieces required delicate management, proper communication, and strong leadership coordination.

Unfortunately, our big data practice director decided to leave to pursue his own aspirations of building a product company. He left on good terms with the ownership team, giving us plenty of notice while ensuring none of his projects were negatively affected. Ilya's departure was a hit to our big data practice, as his leadership and knowledge in the discipline would be difficult to replace. But knowing his heart wasn't in the game, as he continued to harbor ill feelings towards the rest of the leadership, made it the right move for the company in the long run.

Shortly after he left, the ownership team began dealing with some of the other company dissidents. We parted ways with one of Sarah's engagement managers who was not only radioactive to the company culture, but somehow managed to stir up drama via multiple interoffice flings. Her tenure with the company was so short, it isn't even listed on her LinkedIn profile.

Then there was Dennis. His situation posed a complicated predicament that required deft handling with kid gloves. Dennis had been with us for so long and was especially effective in propelling us forward with our projects at Microsoft. We all adored his personality—almost father-like, with a casual and calming demeanor. Further, his practice entailed a significant portion of revenue that we were dependent on for investments made in other parts of the company. But the practice he led had become a catch-all for one-off consultants and the enterprise support operations (ESO) work we did for Microsoft, requiring lots of resources to manage, unnecessary overhead, and a distraction to our company direction.

Our philosophy as owners was to always have an open-door policy. Every employee was empowered to escalate concerns, share ideas, and provide feedback. As employee headcount grew along with some geographic expansion, this philosophy became more difficult to sustain.

So, despite all his effort and successes, Dennis was partially responsible for the undercurrent of dissent. This became cancerous and something we needed to contain.

Company culture, employee sentiment and retention, and our industry reputation were all on the line.

Within a short time, we decided it was best to part ways with Dennis. This was bittersweet, as I'd worked with him more than any other owner. He and I had closed millions of dollars' worth of consulting services over the years. We leaned on each other in handling employee and client issues. We shared many late-night working sessions, pumping out proposals and negotiating deals. Usually, we'd close out our efforts with a glass of bourbon and sharing of personal stories. I considered us friends.

We sat down one afternoon and presented an appropriate separation package reflecting Dennis's significant contribution to the company over the years. Although disappointed, he understood and respected our decision. I can imagine that, in a way, he felt some relief given his frustration with us. It's never easy parting ways with employees, especially those you considered family.

A Suitor Emerges

Chad kept busy, as he fielded one inquiry after another from unsolicited potential buyers of Society. As we wrapped up the final quarter of 2015, a constant stream of suitors lined up to meet with us. Again, most were short conversations with one or both parties realizing a difference in strategic alignment, general risks, valuation, or culture.

But one particular outreach on LinkedIn sparked Chad's interest. Jay Leveton, an executive at a Washington, DC, based company called Stagwell, reached out directly to Chad in hopes of starting a dialogue. Jay said his inquiry was a recommendation of Mark Penn, the CEO of their firm and former chief strategy officer for Microsoft. Mark was a serious player, having led various major initiatives—first under Microsoft CEO Steve Ballmer, and then Satya Nadella when he took over that role in 2014. Prior, Mark held various leadership positions supporting both Bill and Hillary Clinton through their respective senate and presidential campaigns.

"Mark Penn knows us," Chad proudly remarked as he forwarded the email to the rest of us. He was smitten at the idea that someone of his caliber and status within the industry knew of some small data consulting firm called Society. Apparently, our branding and business reputation preceded us enough to prompt his interest.

We would soon discover that Stagwell was well positioned, with a healthy war chest of funding from various investors, including Steve Ballmer, who had the utmost confidence in Mark's abilities. Mark's mission was to build a powerhouse digital agency through the acquisition of specialized capabilities, allowing Stagwell to offer and compete with global marketing, advertising, and research firms. Society was identified as a viable target for their digital analytics vertical.

As the year ended, Stagwell pushed forward with Chad to discuss our strategy, professional service offerings, and general financials. Things looked promising, as Stagwell was on a complete terror, buying up advertising and marketing companies nationwide. We eventually set up some meetings after the new year with hopes this opportunity would bear fruit.

Despite the growing internal opposition of a few employees, significant hiring sprees to support geographic expansion, and secret discussions with multiple companies about selling, the company had grown to new heights in 2015, increasing revenue to a record $36 million and employing close to 250 people. We ended the year with trending revenue that would easily take us well over $45 million for 2016.

I added firepower to the sales team to support the various geographies in New York, Southern California, and Texas. New clients joined the Society roster, giving us even more credibility as an industry leader. We also added another managing director who would lead our big data service offerings, and we promoted Tanja to managing director, Frank to vice president, and our controller Kristin to director of finance.

Despite the wooing of Stagwell, our trajectory continued up and to the right, giving us lots of confidence that 2016 would be an interesting year.

Chapter 12

Project Seahawk

It's March fourth, and sixteen Society employees along with their significant others fill a long table right in front of the stage. There's Polynesian drumming in the background as we watch the ceremonial entrance of the roasted pig carried by four substantially large men in traditional Hawaiian dress. Everyone at the table cheers with encouragement as the luau gets underway. Thoughts of work are absent despite the fact that we sit amongst colleagues. Today, we celebrate Society's annual President's Club trip attendees and pay tribute to their professional achievements and hard work. A buzz fills the air as tropical drinks made from pineapple juice and rum flow liberally around the table. Hula dancers glide between tables and ask for volunteers to come on stage. Without hesitation, Josiah stands up and is all in. He tries to goad me and John on stage, but we convince him that won't be happening. We all cheer in support as he does his very best to emulate the flowing and rhythmic movements of the hula dancers. The evening festivities continue throughout the night with plenty of laughter, revelry, and camaraderie.

We had steadily worked our way down the path of a deal with Stagwell when one day Chad got the call from Gary Angel. Gary was a veteran in the analytics space and had started Semphonic, a digital measurement and web analytics firm back in the late nineties, which was subsequently acquired by Ernst & Young (EY) in 2013. Their paths crossed occasionally, and there was mutual industry respect, which is why Gary had referred the corporate development team at EY to look at Society. He also knew that EY was on the hunt to acquire smaller, specialized consulting firms to beef up their service offerings and talent in the digital space. Chad and Gary reconnected first over email, and then over a call, where Gary shared his experience being acquired by EY as well as perspective on being a partner with the firm.

On February 8, 2016, Chad sent an email to the founders with a summary of all the activity with the various suiters. He included a list of each company, the latest status of discussions, and general thoughts and comments for us to process. HCL, one of the companies pursuing us, had launched a new business unit called Beyond Digital a year earlier, and as much as we liked what they had to say about their ambitions, we were at a standstill just signing their NDA, as it left us a little too exposed for our liking. They had expressed interest in taking next steps, but we were slightly reluctant given how hard it seemed to be to work with them. POSSIBLE, a creative agency that eventually got acquired by the powerhouse Wunderman Thompson, was also interested in furthering discussions. Chad included EY but offered up little hope, as we knew little about the organization and guessed they wouldn't be interested in our financial models and client concentration.

That was the general sentiment we had heard from other companies we talked to over the past year and a half.

They loved the space we were in and were attracted to our go-to-market strategy, culture, and talent base. But some didn't like the fact that nearly 60 percent of our revenue was based off one client: Microsoft.

Most would argue that this poses higher risk—having most of your eggs in one basket, so to speak. And that made sense, given any changes to our working relationship with Microsoft could potentially be significant if not fatal to the business. It's not a business model we targeted; it just worked out that way given our services, the way Microsoft leveraged vendor companies like us, and our geographic proximity to their backyard in Seattle.

But our perspective was slightly different. We felt that our Microsoft business was solid and well diversified within the giant software company. Around that time, we were providing $23 million of services to them, and it's not like they could just simply cut it off. And this was spread out amongst more than fifty separate engagements. We were relevant enough for them to be somewhat dependent on us for various business functions, and simply cutting off our services would seriously impact many of their business units. Plus, we had official status on their pared-down, approved vendor list—meaning we had proven our value as their vendor.

Nevertheless, we received this consistent feedback time and time again. You see, valuing a company, as complex as it can be, comes down to a simple formula where its perceived value is equal to future cash flow minus risk, sometimes described as discounted cash flow. And that risk of client concentration was affecting the valuation that these companies were applying to us.

We were a consulting firm, so future cash flow could only be projected with certainty for the duration of our client contracts. In our case, that was usually a year.

Without knowing much about how EY valued companies, we simply assumed they would feel the same way, and this assumption was reflected in the tone of Chad's email to the founders.

But by the following week, Chad would be advocating a new tone. As point person for all merger and acquisition discussions, he scheduled conversations with both the EY corporate development team (their internal group that focuses on acquisitions), as well as one of their digital leaders, Woody Driggs, a veteran partner with the firm.

Chad first set up a call with Derek Gustafson, a leader in the mergers and acquisitions group at EY. Talking to Derek gave Chad a good sense of how EY typically structured their deals, as well as an education of their acquisition track record in the digital space—I believe close to thirty companies globally over the past five years. Very impressive. Derek also walked Chad through a high-level overview of how they would proceed. The overall process wasn't all that different between EY and other firms we talked to, but there certainly were unique components.

A Little Taste of an Acquisition

Once a company is identified and contacted, typical acquisitions start with some get-to-know-you meetings to feel out owners' motivations, service offerings, finances, and other company facts and figures. They may go so far as to understand a company's culture, but usually the "touchy-feely" stuff is overshadowed by the hard numbers as the process gains momentum. At this stage, it's usually some sort of dog-and-pony show where both the acquirer and acquiree put on their best faces, showcasing everything wonderful they can offer. The message is pretty much the same: this is why you should consider selling to us, and this is why you should consider buying us!

Assuming there is mutual interest from both parties in continuing discussions, the conversation begins to get more granular, and usually the parties sign some sort of mutual non-disclosure agreement (NDA). Confidentiality is paramount. That said, with an NDA in place, there is trust and comfort in providing the potential purchaser with significant and confidential company information like a financial pro forma, employee skills breakdown, and listings of all clients. I like to think of this as the courtship period of the relationship. The two parties continue to woo each other, putting everything in the best light, and trying hard not to show too many warts.

After that point, there usually is some form of letter of intent (LOI) or memorandum of understanding (MOU) to purchase, with general numbers and high-level terms. Is it a cash deal? Is it in stock? Or both? What are the payouts? Is there an earnout tied to performance over time? Are there any bonuses associated with the selling owners? What are the buyer's plans for the employees? Are there any purchase price adjustment terms? Is this a stock purchase or an asset purchase for the acquiring entity? An LOI might even spell out the due diligence and transaction timing.

Note that an LOI and MOU are not usually binding contracts. They offer a high-level overview, in good faith, outlining the major components of an offer should things move forward. But they don't represent the beginning of negotiations, which can take countless hours of back-and-forth clarifying of questions, calls with respective attorneys, and continuous communication.

We streamlined this entire process with a divide-and-conquer strategy. It worked well, as Chad ran point on any formal communication, while John, Josiah, and I focused on day-to-day running of the business. Chad would summarize any significant discussions he had in either an email or bring it up as a talking point in one of our founder check-ins that happened pretty much every other day. Then each of us would share our respective feedback or opinions—and from there, Chad would respond to the suitor. He also worked directly with our outside counsel team over at Cairncross & Hempelmann as legal matters became more complicated.

Once two parties mutually agree on all the high-level terms of a transaction, then the really complicated negotiations commence. This involves hashing out the nitty-gritty, granular details that outline the conditions of the purchase, which typically are many, and dialing in the legal language that satisfies both parties.

From here, due diligence begins. John described this as "fully opening up the kimono." The acquirer usually sends over a long list of items to prepare and deliver back. This can include but is not limited to audited financial statements over the past three to five years as well as lease agreements; all employee records and files outlining all details like salaries, titles, certifications, and education; organizational charts; detailed copies of active and executed contracts and master service agreements with all clients; any intellectual property; and any other information that impacts company infrastructure integration.

I liken this process to the saying, "no stone goes unturned," but I replace the word "stone" with "grain of sand." Specifically with EY being an audit firm, this couldn't have been truer.

In parallel to due diligence is usually some integration strategy. This entails a comprehensive plan to bring all significant aspects of the business into the fold. How are the employees integrated into a structure that is different than their current? Titles? Salaries? Where will they physically work from? What specific IT requirements are needed to keep servicing the existing or future projects? What are the go-to-market capabilities, and how do they align with those of the purchasing company? The factors to consider are dauntingly complex and significant in number.

Once all the details of a deal are negotiated and agreed upon, a formal purchase and sales or definitive agreement is drawn up. Both parties review with their respective internal and outside legal counsel, and the contract is executed with signatures. Major milestone achieved. You're now committed to sell. Now the real fun begins.

With EY and many other companies that provide services including financial audit and assurance work, there's an additional layer of regulation that must be navigated with extreme care. Ever since the financial calamity in 2001 caused by the fraudulent practices of companies like Enron and WorldCom, hefty regulation and compliance laws have been in place—like the Sarbanes-Oxley Act. Beyond setting a new stage for responsible accounting practices, internal controls, and IT systems for all companies at a global level, a new level of scrutiny was placed on consulting firms in the assurance space. This helped to ensure a clear delineation between services provided: those related to providing *advisory* services to a client, and those specific to *auditing*.

For sake of simplifying the nomenclature, I use the words *advisory* to describe traditional consulting services, and *assurance/auditing* to describe something different.

In our world, this translated to the simple fact that if EY had an audit client, they could not provide any advisory services to that client. And the same was true for the reverse. If EY had a client they provided advisory services for, they could not be their official auditor. Although there's some gray area in the definition, the rules ensure the elimination of conflict of interest brought on by conflicted services provided. Essentially, the government realized there's something wrong with a company like EY advising its client to take certain actions, while at the same time, auditing their books for compliance. This makes sense, as lack of regulation mixed with greed had resulted in catastrophic economic fallout including the eventual demise of many companies, including Arthur Andersen.

We'll cover specifically how this affected us later in this chapter. For reference's sake, EY used the terms *channel one* for audit clients, and *channel two* for advisory clients—a very important distinction. But for now, let's get back to our courtship with EY, and how an unlikely and unexpected suitor became a lead contender.

Codename Seahawk

The conversation between Chad and Woody was eye-opening. Woody shared the EY vision (coincidentally called Vision 2020 at that time) and their digital strategy, and how they differentiated themselves from other competitors. He also offered some feedback on why the firm was interested in Society. They loved our West Coast presence. They also liked that we had a large footprint with Microsoft (I would come to learn that EY was not only a top customer of Microsoft's, but also a top service provider and official partner). Woody was determined to push EY to adopt a modern culture that embraced digital thinking, and Society's influence could help that cause.

Chad followed up again with the three of us, sharing summaries of each conversation as well as some enthusiasm to continue talks with EY. My initial response was shortsighted to say the least.

Why would we sell our company to an accounting firm? I thought. It was an important question fueled by my ignorant ideas of what EY was all about. I immediately thought of accounting, tax, and audit. I thought of your grandfather's accounting firm. I also thought of stodgy, boring CPAs and bean counters wearing cheap suits and pocket protectors. Somewhere along the way I'd picked up preconceived notions, and they couldn't have been further from the truth. Perhaps it's because I really didn't know any EY employees, or maybe it was the thought of a former in-law who was an accountant, who I held little regard for as a human being. But I digress.

Sure, accounting, tax, and audit were a part of EY, but everything else I thought about them wasn't accurate. In fact, my ignorance couldn't have been further from the truth. EY had a significant consulting practice that provided advisory services to clients globally—ahead-of-the-curve services that helped shape the landscape for modern-day business operations.

Who knew that EY was building some of the first commercially viable blockchains for the global shipping industry, or that they invested hundreds of millions of dollars acquiring digital technology service companies around the world? We didn't, but we would learn in a short time that they were a major player, boasting close to ten-billion dollars in advisory/consulting services—separate from their assurance business, which was well over double that figure. Yes, these guys were serious players.

Chad explained how EY was positioned as a formidable company in the digital space, as well as the numerous acquisitions they had made in the past few years—companies very similar or complementary to Society in nature.

"We're not so far down the path with Stagwell and others that we couldn't entertain other options," stated Chad. "It makes sense to see what EY could offer, and it never hurts to have options on the table. If they can't move fast enough or give us a reasonable valuation, we always have Stagwell to fall back on."

We eventually all agreed to take the next steps with EY, which meant all four of us engaging with the various organizations within the giant company.

The following weeks flew by in record time. Weeks turned into hours, and days into seconds. It was all a blur, as meeting after meeting was scheduled between representatives of EY and Society. We were quite surprised at the efficiency and speed of the massive company. They knew we were expecting an LOI from another company and didn't let their size and bureaucracy get in the way of the process. We figured when they said they would move fast, it was all relative. *Fast* for a global company with more than 220,000 employees means something completely different than *fast* for a 250-person firm. But they did as they said, and their efforts were appreciated.

But the process of considering EY required a lot of sneaking around and some smoke and mirrors to ensure confidentiality amongst the owners of the rest of the company. Meetings were held "off-site," at either the EY office in Seattle, some third-party location, or after hours at Society's second office down the street. The founders had to be creative with perceived obligations, schedules, and communication.

I hated lying, so it was important to come up with relatively reasonable excuses for missing meetings, or just being unavailable in general. In retrospect, I'm truly amazed at how we were able to navigate the numerous calls, meetings, and dialogue given that we were all burning the candle at both ends.

For starters, in late March of 2016, Society participated in Adobe Summit, a conference we typically attended annually as a formal partner. However, this year we were a sponsor, so the number of moving pieces seemed exponential. Nonetheless, this was a big deal for us not only as an official partner with Adobe, but from a public relations standpoint as well. Josiah and I helped quarterback Society's representation, swag, client meetings, accommodations, entertainment, and booth in their vendor convention hall. Luckily, various team members assisted in coordinating communication, setting up and managing meetings, streamlining decision-making, and marketing/design initiatives.

This was a major investment of funds (six figures) and took an enormous amount of time—organizing the fifteen or so attendees, and various activities. Happy hours. Breakfast meetings. Lunch meetings. Dinner meetings. Entertaining clients at a nightclub. Dozens of moving parts to coordinate.

On the final day of the conference in Vegas, John, Josiah, Chad, and I snuck away for a breakfast meeting at Jardin in the Encore Hotel with Bob Patton, who at the time was EY's Americas vice chair of advisory services. This was huge for us, as Bob represented the highest-ranking partner we would meet prior to the acquisition.

The meeting went well despite the previous night's festivities. I'd spent the evening hosting clients at a late-night dinner, with plenty of Wagyu steaks and silky California cabernets, at Delmonico Steakhouse. I believe Josiah didn't actually sleep, as he was entertaining clients with a VIP experience at a club all night. Nevertheless, Bob appreciated our efforts to show up the best we could, and we had a productive conversation that led to his stamp of approval to move the process forward.

We kicked off February by launching Key Employee Equity (KEE), an important and time-consuming effort aimed at extending shares of ownership to team members. This rollout of a non-qualifying equity program was created for a select group of five executives, and with the hope to add others as the program and company evolved. With the help of a close friend and advisor, Pierre Gallant, we created a program that incentivized each leader with an equity vesting model based on growth of profit and revenue for each year moving forward. This allowed participants to obtain future shares in the company without any significant and immediate tax implications, since their basis was zero. And because it was nonqualifying, it meant we could set the guidelines around vesting schedules, valuation, and performance requirements.

Between February and April of 2016, I was traveling quite a bit. Business trips took me to New York City to meet with clients and employees. I also went with my partners for a quick thirty-six-hour sprint to meet with the Stagwell team in their offices just down the street from the White House in Washington, DC. Columbus, Ohio, was a quick twenty-four-hour stop to meet with an executive coach I'd hired to help me with sales excellence. And on the personal side, I made trips to Reno, Nevada, for a family celebration as well as a whirlwind getaway to Sydney, Australia, with Sherry.

The other three founders had also become heavy road warriors. Chad had moved his family to Southern California and was commuting back and forth consistently. John had trips to Mexico, as well as other destinations around the country. And then there was Josiah. He was constantly on the move to wherever he was needed—which pretty much meant everywhere. San Francisco, New York, Chicago, Austin, and Los Angeles were all on his docket. But somehow, we were all able to align our schedules in complete confidence to the needs of the process.

At the beginning of March, Society also held its annual President's Club Award trip, this time in Maui. Roughly twenty employees and their significant others attended. Celebratory activities ranged from a luau, whale watching, lots of extravagant dinners, and some well-deserved rest and relaxation. I got in a round of golf as well as some snorkeling at Black Rock Beach, which is known for its sea turtles.

The lease for our corporate headquarters was up in a year, so the time came to investigate possible new office space options. John spearheaded the search and worked with commercial brokers he knew. We must have toured at least a dozen buildings, considering both Seattle downtown proper, as well as the Eastside where we currently were in Bellevue. Again, we considered tons of variables, most importantly what our employee base would be happiest with.

In the Greater Seattle area, probably like most metropolitan areas, there's a distinct Eastside versus Westside preference. Seattle is separated from the Eastside by a lake, with only two bridges that connect the two. This poses absolute opinions based on where an individual lives, but also the relative distance of their commute.

John was extremely sensitive to the preferences of the employee base and took great care and consideration when making decisions. As president, all things human resources, facilities, and operations were in his direct responsibility. And he took that shit seriously. So John created a heat map consisting of every employee's home address and relative commute to locations on either the

Eastside or downtown Seattle. This laborious task proved useful, as it displayed the level of consideration we had for our employees. Plus, we were an analytics company, and we loved sexy data visualization.

Nonetheless, taking time each week to view the newest office buildings in Bellevue or recently renovated vintage space toward Pioneer Square took copious time. Sitting through everyone's spiel, we'd hear how green the building was, how it rated on the walk scale, or what type of coffee shop would be in the lobby.

In March, we also launched a much more modern website to showcase our A-B-C (Analytics, Big Data, Customer Experience) service offerings. It showed a much more mature and sophisticated presence as a consulting firm and displayed our employees' pride in our story.

And finally, as if we didn't have enough spinning plates, we were also in deep acquisition discussions with a local design and creative agency, with the goal of adding immediate firepower to our customer experience offerings. The fit would have been extremely complementary to our services, and we would have moved forward with the acquisition, but progress became stagnant the further along we found ourselves with EY and Stagwell.

As we were finishing the first quarter of 2016, we looked at our overall performance, and the numbers were less than stellar. We'd ended the previous quarter with record revenue and gross margins, despite Ilya and Dennis leaving. But a weak sales pipeline and a few year-end projects put a strain on both revenue outlook and gross profit for the quarter.

This was disconcerting, given our conversations with multiple suitors; could we course-correct in time, or would a downward trend affect their respective valuations or general interest? Tension was high, and we pressed all our team members to increase productivity. Everyone was operating on all cylinders.

March 2016 was busy, as we met with many of the partners and principals at EY. For a while, it was downright confusing. EY was highly matrixed, and unless someone came from one of the Big Four, it could take some time to fully understand its intricacies. I liken it to a scenario where you first meet your significant other's entire extended family. We're talking aunts, uncles, second cousins, grandparents. Names, faces, relationships—drinking out of the proverbial firehose—you try your best to keep it straight. Who's related to who? Who's so-and-so's mother?

I was dizzy just thinking about it. You almost needed a Venn diagram to understand the complexities of such an organization. There were leaders of services. There were leaders of sectors. There were leaders of markets. Then there were also leaders represented from a central and shared business group. And all of them seem to have their own agenda and charter.

Saj Usman, a senior partner with EY, came into the picture early in the process. He would eventually become our overall endorsement for acquisition, as well as our direct leader within their analytics competency. Saj was articulate, and the five of us hit it off immediately. He shared his vision for the organization and did his best to address our questions.

As both parties became more interested in each other, Derek crafted a code name for all of us to reference the acquisition: *Project Seahawk*. The four founders loved it, given our fandom for the Seattle NFL team. All our meetings were titled "Seahawk Discussion."

By late March, we had great momentum with both EY and Stagwell, as both companies expressed that formal offers would be forthcoming. Things were getting very real, and our day-to-day lives were about to get even crazier.

Offers

On March 28, we received LOIs from EY and Stagwell, outlining their respective details of the transaction. Up to this point, EY didn't specifically know about Stagwell, and vice versa, but they both knew they weren't our only option on the table. We were diligent enough to keep it that way to incent each company to bring us their very best offers.

The next day, we set up calls with both EY and Stagwell (separately of course) to walk through each proposal, so we could completely understand the components.

The first call was with Derek from EY and the four Society founders. Derek walked through the agreement, explaining each section in great detail. Overall, the offer was to purchase Society Consulting's assets, and not make a stock purchase of the company itself. This meant EY was offering to purchase the contracts, employees, and any intellectual property, not specifically the shares that made up the legal entity of Society Consulting. The founders would retain the company, but effectively it would be worth nothing, given post-acquisition it wouldn't have any employees or assets. The rest of the EY offer didn't disappoint in the least.

The first notable item was that this offer was an all-cash deal, nearly all of which was paid out up front. This was huge for us, as many companies attempt to offer up some sort of earnout, where they stagger payments in tranches over time. That's also a way to keep individuals motivated to perform and continue growing the business. There's usually an upside with an earnout, but for us, getting paid up front without any strings attached was very attractive.

Second, EY offered retention bonuses for the four founders, as well as for our key employees and leaders. For the founders, these were significant, seven-figure bonuses paid out for the first three years. To make it sweeter, they set aside over $2 million to be spread out to our executive team and select employees over the next couple of years. This was an extremely important piece of the offer, as we knew the Key Employee Equity Program, which we'd launched a month earlier, would come to a standstill if the acquisition went through. We wanted to make sure our people were taken care of, and this would provide them with real dollars at the close of the transaction and moving forward.

The third piece outlined the compensation for the four founders as well as acknowledged our future principal status within the firm. We were blown away, as EY offered seven-figure annual distributions for each of us, essentially our salaries, a move that tipped the scale in their direction. We would learn in time that principal and partner were essentially the same within the firm—the only difference being that partners had CPAs. Being a principal also meant we had voting rights in the firm—a privilege, should the firm ever reach that magnitude and decision.

We asked many questions. For example, we wanted to better understand how debt would impact purchase price. We also hoped to increase the retention bonuses for more of our key employees. Derek gave us very specific answers to each question, and we closed out the conversation with a "we'll get back to you soon, thanks, goodbye."

Later that day, we connected with Mark, Jay, and Jason of the Stagwell executive team to review their LOI and address a list of questions we'd sent over ahead of time. It was a productive conversation, driven largely by Mark. He was clearly excited about the prospective acquisition, as he jumped into every question with enthusiasm. The Stagwell offer wasn't as compelling as EY's with regard to amount of cash up front, but it included a long-term play that, if we performed and the numbers worked out, could be much more lucrative financially.

Unlike the EY offer, Stagwell presented the desire for a stock purchase. In this case, they offered up an eight-figure number for 65 percent of the company, leaving the remaining 35 percent to the founders. Two years later, a second tranche of an even greater amount would be paid to the founders—contingent on company performance, more specifically EBITDA targets.

The real meat of the offer was the potential longer-term (five-year) plan to take Stagwell public, and the payouts were projected to be almost a hundred million dollars. Essentially, the plan for Stagwell was to build a comprehensive portfolio of digital marketing, technology, and creative services, and Society would plug in as their data and analytics service line. We would operate independently with our own brand, but under the umbrella of the Stagwell parent company. This had some appeal, as it would allow us to retain much of what we'd built in our culture and brand.

Other components of their offer were standard and didn't present any major concerns or selling points.

That evening at 5 p.m., John, Josiah, Chad, and I sat in our shared office to discuss the day's meetings and our thoughts on the offers. I was running on fumes, trying my best to keep the details of the two offers straight. Shit was getting real. With two solid offers on the table, it was a win-win, regardless of which direction we went—which was a relief. Either would dramatically change our lives financially, while offering tons of opportunity for our employees.

But this was not going to be an easy decision, so I also

felt an overwhelming pressure. Having the others there helped, as we broke down the offers with a simple pros and cons list.

Chad kicked off the discussion with, "The guaranteed cash up front is a major selling point for EY. It's almost double that of Stagwell. A million dollars a year in distributions on top of that is quite appealing."

We all nodded in agreement.

"And the three years of retention bonuses really sweetens the deal," I added confidently. "How does everyone feel about our potential to use EY as a springboard for our services?"

"The opportunities are massive," John replied. "EY has offices and clients all around the world. There's no doubt we could grow our business and become the tip of the spear for their analytics services."

Additional nodding in agreement continued. Then Josiah spoke up.

"I'm also interested in how Society could influence EY and help them adopt a more modern and digital culture. They made it clear they wanted us to rock the boat."

We discussed growth opportunities for our employees, increases in their compensation and benefits, and potentially global career moves to different countries.

We then moved on to the cons.

"I'm sure we'll lose the Society brand in short time," claimed Chad. "We've worked so hard on building it, I would be lying if I said I wouldn't be sad about it going away."

"There's also the ambiguity of how our employees would react to the news we're being acquired by EY," John added. "Many of them love the small, tight-knit family we've created, so there's no telling if there will be a negative reaction to becoming part of a massive global company."

Probably the largest con that we discussed was the impact to our client-base due to EY's internal controls on audit-versus-advisory clientele. Recall the aforementioned legalities that dictated the type of services that could be provided to a specific client? Any client EY was providing audit services for would be ineligible for EY's advisory services, and vice versa, in order to avoid conflict of interest and satisfy regulatory mandates. That meant if we moved forward with the EY transaction, we would be forced to let go of clients we serviced that were existing EY audit companies. And at this point, we didn't have visibility to the entire list of companies that would be impacted. We knew it didn't include Microsoft, as Deloitte was their auditor, but what about the rest of our clients? More to come on this later.

The Stagwell offer had its own list of pros and cons. The discussion continued with everyone jumping in to share their thoughts. Chad continued.

"Although the guaranteed cash up-front is less than half of EY's, the long-term potential of going public would result in a much larger windfall of cash for all of us. Mark's a smart guy, and his reputation could positively impact our street cred. He has a deep Rolodex and is politically connected."

"His Microsoft ties could help us build stronger relationships with executives," I added. "Could we keep the Key Employee Equity Program for our executives?"

Chad jumped in with, "The deal structure would be a significant motivator for the participants, as the upside is much greater. Beyond that, we could keep the Society brand and culture, as well as move forward with buying the creative agency."

"There's something appealing about taking some chips off the table for the time being, yet still having the opportunity to swing for the fences down the road," John acknowledged. "The idea of two bites at the apple is attractive."

The cons of going with Stagwell were substantial and took up most of the conversation. Most importantly, there was a lot of risk given the ambiguity of the longer-term vision. Would there be an actual IPO? And with such focus on EBITDA, we might struggle to keep reinvesting dollars into growth. We would be looking at a five-year time frame from the date of acquisition for any significant payout, assuming all went well, versus three years with EY.

Also, Stagwell was just starting to build its portfolio of services, so there wasn't a proven track record that the model would even work. Lastly, we knew Mark was well connected and could potentially impact our growth, but it was unclear how the rest of Stagwell's reach would influence business development opportunities.

Then Chad threw out a curveball, one that I certainly wasn't considering.

"We have a third option that we should discuss. We decline both offers and stay the course."

We processed what he just said in silence for a moment.

"It's not an unreasonable path given our momentum, but it's also a way to preserve all the goodness we've built. It could be our opportunity to be the next Merkle or Sapient [companies that were magnitudes larger in size]," Chad continued.

"I like the idea of calling our own shots, investing how we'd like, and retaining the brand and culture. That's not an insignificant outcome," John added.

Chad elaborated, "And with continued growth, there could be an opportunity to sell for a larger amount down the road. Maybe we go big and search for outside funding, and even an IPO?"

I sat there, starry-eyed, pondering the many details of

each option. And despite all the goodness of each opportunity, I began to feel panicked and overwhelmed. Regret and guilt churned in my gut. But the potential dollar signs dancing on the horizon brought hope and promise. I scanned the room, gauging everyone's expressions. Everyone appeared to be in deep thought but had slight smiles reflecting the positivity of the moment. *Am I the only one feeling this?* I wondered. *Get with the program, and see the goodness in all of this.* I snapped my attention back as Chad jumped into the cons of staying the course.

"Keeping Society as is would mean a delay in any liquidity event for us as well as the KEE participants. We'd also be taking on some general risk due to market conditions we aren't able to anticipate."

We all sat back and pondered. What if there was another crash like in 2001 and 2008? What would happen if Microsoft terminated our contracts for any reason? What if a new virus resulted in a global pandemic and shut down our economy? A myriad of situations could negatively impact the health of our company, which created an uneasy feeling for all of us.

After a couple of hours of discussion, we decided to head home and take the night to ponder the various implications, outstanding questions, pros, cons, and feelings in general. Chad provided general feedback to both Stagwell and EY, giving them the opportunity to fine-tune their respective offers.

While walking back to my condo roughly three blocks from the office, I took an out-of-the-way route to allow myself time to process. Then I began circling the walking path in a nearby park. The early spring, evening air was cold and crisp, and the maple trees were just starting to show buds. It was getting dark, but the path was illuminated by overhead lights. With my hands in my pockets, I continued to walk and deliberate.

The decision felt very emotional, regardless of the hard numbers in front of me. I had put all I had into building the company, and when I thought back to the countless wins, losses, and drama, it felt bittersweet. The Job Mob. Pentad Solutions. Pentad Analytics. Society Consulting. The evolution of each brand meant so much to me that I also felt a bit of betrayal.

Am I being selfish? Was this all for nothing? Was I the picture definition of a sellout? In reality, doesn't everyone sell out at some point in their lives? And who should care if I do? No one else is going to look out for me, so I should take whatever I can get, right? I had received exactly what I had wanted and planned for, but I was having second thoughts—doubts like, *Maybe we really should entertain option three and not sell.*

Chapter 13

Calm Before the Storm

I need to get some fresh air, I think to myself. So I walk out onto the upper patio just outside the shared founders' office. I'm alone and take a seat at the picnic table overlooking the parking lot. There's lots of talking and commotion inside, but out here it's peaceful. I can hear myself think. The warm July sun shines down on me as I pull out my phone and log into the Fidelity application to verify the funds successfully transferred. Fuck me. Beads of sweat form on my forehead. For a split second, the old adage, "Be careful what you ask for, because you might just get it," hits me hard. I can't hold back. What am I supposed to do now? I never thought I'd be rich. I mean, I dreamt about it and scratched and clawed my way toward the goal but never put much thought into what it would mean should I achieve it. Feelings of momentary inadequacy and guilt fill my heart as I fight back tears, hoping no one comes out to see my like this. Luckily for me, everyone is distracted with the massive changes: today we're Society, but tomorrow we're not. I take a few deep breaths, gather my composure, and head back inside to join the madness.

The next day was full of the typical day-to-day business distractions. This was good, as it helped take some focus off the looming decisions we had to make. I had a one-on-one with Francisco, a recent sales hire out of New York. I also had a sync with Elizabeth Brothers, one of our rockstar consultants, to discuss her current engagement at Microsoft, and how to navigate a particular situation. In the afternoon, Society held its monthly happy hour at Tavern Hall, a local sports bar and grill down the street—a nice break from all the acquisition madness dominating our brainpower. A couple of drinks and some tasty bar food was the perfect escape for an hour, before the four of us reconvened around 6 p.m.

But throughout the day, there had been constant back-and-forth amongst the four founders, emails and calls hashing out our individual sentiment—new intel that one of us would present or a perspective that hadn't been brought up. With the guidance of our outside counsel, it became clearer which levers we could push and pull to get to an offer we felt good with. Chad circled back with Derek in the morning and gave him some feedback on the retention pool and how we would like to see it increased. He also tried to negotiate the time and amount of the indemnification window to reduce our exposure.

EY came back with new terms that addressed both of our requests. The retention bonus pool for our key employees was increased significantly, totaling three-and-a-half million dollars, and they reduced the indemnification period to eighteen months, versus twenty-four—which meant we would be paid out on the remaining balance at that time. It was obvious that the EY team was listening to every detail and making efforts to address all our concerns.

Chad also went back to the Stagwell team with some feedback. He shared we had a significant alternative offer on the table, and something must be done with regards to the cash up front for them to compete. The result was less than compelling, as they came back with an offer to increase the cash at closing by 30 percent, but they reduced the two-year payout by the same amount. Sure, it was nice that the guaranteed payment went up, but our incentive for the second tranche was lowered dramatically. It felt like a rob-Peter-to-pay-Paul scenario—but we appreciated the efforts to be creative and construct a satisfactory offer.

For the next hour, we shared our final thoughts on each offer. Chad had communicated that we would have an answer for both EY and Stagwell the next day, so it was imperative the four of us come to some conclusive agreement.

"So, let's hear everyone's latest thoughts on both options," Chad requested. "Both companies generously improved their offers based on our feedback, but now's the time for us to make a collective decision."

"I'll go first," Josiah enthusiastically stated. "Both offers are compelling, but I think one stands out above the other based on a balance between compensation and overall opportunity. I think we could kick ass at Stagwell if the stars aligned perfectly, but EY seems more like a sure thing—for us, for our employees, and for the growth of the business."

We all looked at each other in agreement, thoughtfully nodding our heads. John leaned back in his chair, and with a handful of Red Vine licorice, continued the conversation.

"I agree. What really compels me is the fact that EY stepped up when asked to increase the retention bonus pool. They delivered, allowing us to take care of our people. They knew this was an important piece of the deal."

"I guess we've got our answer," I said assuredly. "Let's put this to a vote."

Chad proclaimed the voice vote, "All those in favor?"

"Aye," was said in unison by John, Chad, and me as we all raised our hands enthusiastically.

We all looked at Josiah, who was sitting across from us at his desk leaning back in his chair looking as stoic as he could. For a New York second, I felt he was going to derail the conversation and point us in a different direction.

"I abstain," he joked with as straight a face as he could muster. We all couldn't help but erupt in laughter.

"Holly fucking shit, guys. We did it," I uttered in disbelief. "Congratulations and thank you for everything."

In the end, the offer from EY was just too compelling to pass up. It wasn't an easy decision by any stretch of the imagination, and after lots of deliberation, we were all in agreement. The combination of cash up front, no earnout, significant retention bonuses for our employees, and joining forces with a global powerhouse consulting firm overshadowed the potential grand-slam offer from Stagwell.

At 7:06 p.m., Chad sent Derek the LOI with all four of our signatures. Within minutes, we received confirmation of receipt from Derek, congratulating us and sharing their excitement on next steps. And to top it all off, validating our decision, Chad received a text message from Bob Patton expressing his congratulations and enthusiasm. We all had that warm and fuzzy feeling, but we knew the hard work was just beginning.

The next day, we followed up with CEO Mark Penn and the Stagwell team to tell them the unfortunate news that we would not be moving forward with their offer and had formally accepted another. Mark took it better than we anticipated and wished us the very best. He also concluded that should things not work out for any reason, we should reconnect and continue acquisition discussions—a gesture that left a sense of positivity and professionalism.

Josiah also jumped on a call with his contact at the creative agency we were looking to purchase and shared the unfortunate update that we wouldn't be proceeding. The owner was bummed but completely supportive. It was too bad, as I really think they would have been an incredible asset under the Society brand.

The Calm

Due diligence started immediately, with Derek sending over a series of meeting requests with the four of us, as well as an employee data spreadsheet template to capture detailed information about every one of our staff. The level of detail we needed to provide for each employee—every aspect of information imaginable—was excruciating yet necessary, and as head of all things human resources, John ran point. This would create the basis for how we mapped all of the Society employees to respective levels in the EY ecosystem.

Although we'd brought Kristin McNeely, our director of finance, into the dome of secrecy a bit ago to help with gathering some financial data EY requested prior to the LOI, it became apparent that we needed to carefully bring in others. This was a precarious proposition, given if word of the pending acquisition spread into the employee ecosystem, the ramifications could be catastrophic. Employees might consider leaving, nervous clients might start looking into other service providers, and strategic partners might start questioning our focus.

After thoughtful discussion, we decided to share the news with both Steve Newman and Sarah Bingham, our respective VP of delivery and VP of operations. We knew both of them would treat the information with kid gloves, and we felt that getting their unique perspectives would be beneficial to how we managed the process. Plus, we needed all the resources to help us with due diligence. It would have been nearly impossible to accomplish all the requests without them, plus we knew they were so in-tune with the business that they would have suspected something in little time.

John and Chad met with Steve and Sarah and shared a comprehensive list of talking points to give them a full understanding of the moment. As expected, they were both excited to see where this path would take all of us. Their ability to handle the delicate, confidential details was absolute, which reinforced our decision to bring them into the fold.

By early to mid-April, we were in full sprint mode, which meant an additional ten to twenty hours for due diligence on top of our normal fifty to sixty hours of regular work. And we had to do much of the due diligence work after general working hours, so we wouldn't bring unwanted attention or raise any suspicion.

I was responsible for gathering all master service agreements (MSAs) for all active clients, as well as individual statements of work (SOWs) and purchase orders for all active engagements. As head of revenue, it was also my responsibility to pull the entire sales pipeline and backlog of work.

Given our significant footprint of Microsoft revenue, it was imperative that we forecast accurately, which meant all potential new business or renewals at the MS fiscal year (July) must be documented. It was like herding cats, pressuring the entire sales team to get their updates into Salesforce, only to get continuous pushback. I'm sure they suspected something was up, as I became relentless on inputting data into the system.

John continued to gather all his employee data with the

help of Sarah, and Steve helped add color to the engagement description document. It was a tremendous amount of work, detailing specific deliverables for the company's 135 active projects, which included technology stacks, methodologies, implementations, and form of engagement.

Other components of due diligence were primarily spread out amongst Chad and Kristin covering Society finance and tax, while John and Sarah drove anything IT, people, or legal. By mid-May, we were making great progress on delivering much of the data requested by EY's corporate development team, with only a few outstanding requirements. Everyone worked around the clock—gathering and documenting requested data, answering follow-up questions from the folks at EY, and blocking and tackling everyday business.

We were on track to hit the due diligence target date of June 13, but we still had much to accomplish.

By the beginning of June, we brought Frank, Felix, and Charley—three of our managing directors—into the Seahawk tent. The risk of word getting out grew with each additional person in the know. Like Steve and Sarah, they all took the news of the pending acquisition well, offering both gratitude and support to get the deal over the goal line.

As due diligence was wrapping up, the pressure was mounting exponentially for the founders, as we were entering a new phase of the acquisition process. Up to this point, it was mostly about gathering information for documents requested by EY, as well as ensuring we executed on day-to-day activity.

It was also a time of serious negotiations between EY and Society over the final purchase and sales agreement. John and Chad ham-and-egged the discussions with a good-cop bad-cop strategy. Chad played hardball on some sticky points of negotiation, while John came in with a gentler approach.

With the help of our legal counsel as well as other members of our executive team, we wrapped up due diligence by the second week of June. Major milestone achieved. Now the real fun began: working through all the final details of the definitive agreement, bringing additional core Society team members into the Seahawk tent, finalizing the communication plan, working through an integration plan, and managing multiple other workstreams necessary to closing the deal. Despite our excitement at all the progress, it seemed our work was just beginning.

The final piece of the overall package was the partnership agreements that the four of us would enter should we decide to move forward. We wanted to know exactly what we were committing to, so we asked to review. But EY wasn't willing to just "send over" the document electronically. No, the contents of their partnership agreement were so secret, so draconian in nature, our attorney had to literally fly down to one of the EY offices and review a printed hard copy, in person. From my understanding, he couldn't even write anything down and was forced to take mental notes of the more important components.

On Friday June 16, 2016, Josiah, John, Chad, and I sat in the boardroom of the law offices of Cairncross to make one final pass of the purchase and sale agreement, as well to review our head attorney, Bob's, perspective on the partnership agreement. The mood was lively but still very serious, as our outside legal counsel walked us through each line item, carefully outlining risks and benefits. The exercise took hours and required ample caffeine and sugar to keep our attention.

After reviewing the entire document, Bob distributed the two-inch thick agreement for us to each individually sign. We each knew that there was no turning back. We were officially committed to being acquired by EY.

The Storm

In order for the acquisition to close, we had to satisfy several conditions ranging from client assignments to employee acceptance and transition. To perform these tasks effectively, we divided the responsibilities—with John taking on any employee workstreams, Chad covering any communications, and me doing all client and business assignments. Josiah supported by continuing to drive business development and employee morale and culture—which was critical, especially in those times of change.

Remember I mentioned EY's classification of audit and advisory clients? Channel one versus channel two? This is where things got really interesting. After analyzing all the revenue sources, we determined that nearly 30 percent of our revenue came from channel one clients, with the rest coming from channel two.

This meant that for us to satisfy what EY called *Independence*, it would be imperative for us to terminate all services to channel one clients by date of close. That's right; I'll say it again. We had to tell each client who was currently being audited by EY that we could no longer engage with them. Essentially, we had to fire them, and ensure we had executed termination letters for each and every one of them—twenty-three companies to be exact! There was no debate here. This wasn't a point of negotiation. This was a critical component that must be addressed, otherwise the deal would not happen.

To make matters worse, we were still operating under the dome of silence, with the majority of our employees unaware of the pending acquisition. To say we were stressed is an understatement.

I took point on coordinating all the communication, as well as collecting status updates on the daily. I also joined many of the client calls to explain the following:

> *Society Consulting is confidentially in contract to be acquired by Ernst & Young, with an expected close date of July 15, 2016. Therefore, as of this date, Society will not be able to continue its contractual relationship with [channel one client name here]. We will be sending over a termination consent to your legal counsel which needs to be executed by the end of June.*

As you can imagine, the response was nothing less than a shitstorm. A couple of clients understood and executed the required documents with little pushback, recognizing and respecting the legal implications. Most were pissed off, and I completely understood. There we were, working on business-critical analytics and big data projects for companies like AT&T, Verizon, and Salesforce, and out of nowhere, we tell them, "Sorry, but we've got to wrap our work up, effective in a few weeks."

One of those clients, USAA Insurance, had just gotten started with our project only months earlier. This one really stung, as we'd put so much effort into developing the relationship, and suddenly had to wind it all back. They understood but were not very pleased, to say the least.

Some clients even made calls to their own executives, claiming our work was imperative to the business, and that they should fire EY as their auditor. It was a welcome gesture that showed our clients appreciated our work. But that obviously didn't go anywhere. Given the very nature of changing audit vendors, acts of God might not even impact those changes. The bottom line was we were tasked with firing 30 percent of our revenue in hopes of satisfying all EY's expectations and successfully closing the transaction.

For us as founders, this was the equivalent of lighting a fuse to a bomb that could seriously impact our ability to survive. The sheer amount of risk of letting go of a substantial percentage of revenue, while retaining almost 100 percent of our operational costs, was downright scary. What if the deal didn't go through for any reason? It's not like we could go back to the clients we fired and say, "Sorry, things changed again, and we would like to reengage with you." That turn of events would mean downsizing. It would mean a hit to our reputation and culture. We would be seriously fucked. Once we started informing our channel one clients of the pending termination consents, our dependence on closing the deal was essential—lighter meet fuse.

To add to the madness, channel one clients weren't the only necessary targets for termination. Any business that was even *associated with* EY as an auditor was impacted—including vendors and partners, or anyone else we had a formal business relationship with. And since most of our partnership agreements had termination clauses with thirty, sixty, or ninety days of notice, it became critical to get all the termination consents executed, so we could close by mid-July. This was painful, as we had worked with many of these partners for quite some time.

For example, Society had a formal partnership with Tealium, a developer of customer data platforms and marketing software. We would bring them into client discussions, and vice versa—very typical of normal professional services and software vendor partnerships.

But Tealium was funded by a venture capital firm that was audited by EY. This created potential conflict of interest, and therefore Tealium was deemed a channel one issue. It didn't matter that EY didn't audit Tealium directly, but two degrees of separation was still enough for the partner to be considered too risky, and therefore they must be terminated.

Another example was Wells Fargo, with which we had a contractual relationship for a single copy machine we leased for general office use. Wells Fargo was a channel one EY client, so we had to navigate an excruciating process of identifying what part of Wells Fargo the copy machine was associated with, who was responsible for managing the contracts, and whether it was a capital or operating lease. I thank my lucky stars that John ran point on this one, given that copy machines fell under his facilities domain; but this cost him the addition of a few more grey hairs. It was a clusterfuck, and the whole copy machine debacle almost derailed the entire acquisition —I shit you not. Poor John suffered through multiple, painful conversations just trying to get in touch with the right person.

Due to the risk management of EY, we had to cross every t and dot every i. No exceptions, even for a stupid copy machine. After days of toiling, eventually we got clarification, and EY signed off on the copy machine line item. Overall, we had to terminate over twenty formal client relationships and close to twenty other business relationships.

For the remaining clients that were classified as channel two, we took a different yet equally painful approach of amending each individual MSA and assigning them to EY. For this process, we had to reach out to all twenty-four active clients and request the following:

> Society Consulting is confidentially in contract to be acquired by Ernst & Young, with an expected close date of July 15, 2016. Therefore, as of this date, we require the current master services agreement and all current purchase and work orders with [channel two client name here] to be assigned to EY. We

will be sending over an assignment consent to your legal counsel which needs to be executed by the end of June.

This process was made even more taxing by the fact that every account was different, based on the legal terms and conditions of each MSA and SOW. Sometimes EY wanted to amend with just minor changes to the language. Other times they had significant redlines and edits. As you can imagine, this required us to set up calls with every internal legal counsel representative, along with our outside legal counsel, EY's internal legal counsel, and EY's external legal counsel—a firm called Pillsbury Winthrop Shaw Pittman LLP.

For starters, just getting the attention of some general counsel representative for a client was a painful exercise. It's not like amending MSAs or SOWs—let alone accommodating the acquisition of some vendor—was at the top of their priority list. But there we were, stalking each of them, doing anything we could to get their attention. When we were successful in nailing them down, it was still an absolute cluster to get all parties involved and coordinated to a specific time and date. The whole herding cats metaphor couldn't describe the situation more accurately. And even when we got all the required parties on a call, we still had to negotiate the details of the language changes—which proved difficult depending on the temperament of the internal counsel.

I learned in short time that some attorneys have serious god complexes, and they do not like to be told what to do. I mean, I get it; they're looking out for the best interest of their employer or client. But some seemed to posture and pump out their chests metaphorically as if sending some message. Sometimes I had to circumvent the process by reaching out directly to their legal counsel, to smooth over some roadblocks and ease the tension.

Some lawyer-on-lawyer discussions went nowhere, arguing over the simplest of details. I found that just being nice to them, interjecting with questions about what it would take to compromise on language, would settle some nerves and calm the tension in the air. At times, semantics in the language, simple words here and there, seem to make all the difference in what I considered a very subjective approval. But what the fuck did I know? I was no attorney.

To make matters even more complicated, we also had several business relationships that required assignment to EY, along with some amended contracts. These entailed services like our power, internet, janitorial, and various other providers, which were imperative to our day-to-day running of the business. Nonetheless, we faced the very same obstacles in contacting the correct legal representative in each company, coordinating all the required legal representatives with EY and Society, and agreeing on all the changes required to satisfy both parties.

One of the most compelling aspects of the entire acquisition process was that EY had a ton of resources at its disposal. It was such a large organization, with at the time over 230,000 employees spread out all over the world. Several were involved in our due diligence, negotiation, closing, and eventual onboarding. Some folks were specifically tasked with onboarding our employees. Others focused on the direct admit program for the four founders as principals. And some handled the closing process itself.

If it weren't for the assistance of a couple EY senior managers during the closing process, I'm confident we wouldn't have hit the target date. Ankur and Tim were critical players throughout that process, helping us navigate the mysterious and unchartered landscape of EY. Also, a gal named Elizabeth helped us on the daily, addressing questions, clarifications, and general follow-ups.

We held multiple daily status calls where reviewed a "close tracker" spreadsheet of all the moving pieces. Imagine reviewing all the assigned client contracts, assigned business relationships, amended contracts, terminated client contracts, terminated business relationships, Society employee offer acceptances, subcontractors, documented exceptions, and new business opportunities—more than 250 individual line items that, if completed to EY's satisfaction, would eventually lead us to a final closing. Ankur even came onsite during the entire closing period, which meant absence from his family for weeks on end.

By the third week of June, we were all being pulled in different directions. The closing conditions and punch list were top of mind for the founders, but we still needed to operate the business effectively. Many of the core operations team members from my sales team were tapped to help run down any random executed contracts, and Sarah Bingham and the human resources team were busy working with John on employee mapping.

This was also when we officially announced the pending acquisition to the entire company. Chad ran point on all communication and did an exceptional job with preemptive FAQs addressing the many questions or concerns any employee might have. We needed to handle the announcement with extreme care, as we were contractually bound to keep the news confidential. This meant that no one beyond our employees (and their spouses/significant others) could share any details associated with the acquisition. No social media. No informing their clients. Once the deal was officially closed, it was free reign, but until then, mum's the word.

As we approached late June, signs of fatigue began to surface amongst the founders. Probably the most significant was Chad communicating to us that if the deal didn't go through, he would likely leave Society. This brought on a whole new level of stress to the rest of us, as we weren't in agreement with his rationale.

You see, Chad had serious street cred when it came to leadership in the big data and analytics space, and the demand for his talent was undeniably high. He could walk down the street and get several offers from major brands like Amazon, Google, and Facebook—offers that would guarantee a healthy seven-figure salary and tons of stock. This was the reasoning that led him to the pragmatic idea that if he could make more money on a guaranteed basis down the street, why stick around a small consulting firm where the chances of selling were marginal?

This created a significant strife amongst us, as we were still very bullish on the idea that we would close and everything would work out wonderfully. But Chad transparently defended his practical options of working for a different employer, giving us yet another thing to worry about. The tensions ran high, making it even harder to focus on all the details of the closing conditions and general operations. John, Josiah, and I were all in lockstep over the transaction—a goal we had planned from the very get-go. But Chad hadn't been with us at the original company formation, and his buy-in and sheer confidence were fading.

We also believed a contributing factor was another voice pressuring Chad to leave for greener pastures. This person apparently didn't have any confidence in our ability to close, nor did they feel the effort would be fruitful enough for Chad, given his lower percentage of ownership. We also felt an undercurrent of animosity, since this person believed the three of us wouldn't have accomplished jackshit if it weren't for Chad.

This may be true to a certain point, but it was a short-sighted perspective in my mind, and likely in the others'. The three of us had built a $10 million company in three years without Chad. Yes, his experience helped supercharge our organization to new levels. But on the flip side, Chad could not have done it himself; it was a team effort, where all four of us individually shined, and our individual moments raised the tides and therefore ships for all.

With respect to ownership, we always treated Chad with parity. As owners, we all earned the same annual distribution. The only difference was our individual equity, which might have triggered some resentment. It was an ugly situation, especially during an already stressful time. John tried to reason with Chad. Josiah and I did as well. The only idea we could get him to embrace was to do everything he could to get this transaction over the goal line, and he would be rewarded accordingly—proving the effort was in fact worth it.

Ankur and Tim of EY were also doing their best trying to manage all the madness of the transaction. We were slowly picking off each line item on the punch list for closing, but our efforts felt futile. You would think that getting a simple signature for a termination or assignment consent would be easy once you got it in front of the right person. But each request revealed a series of obstacles prolonging the timelines and complicating the process. Just when we thought we'd nailed down an agreement with a client to execute the consent, we were thrown a curveball that required an additional meeting or person to sign-off—one step forward, and two steps back. This kept happening, and the emotional tax it created grew daily.

Given that our book of business with Microsoft was a

significant component of the transaction, it was imperative we managed the transition to EY with the utmost attention to detail. The biggest piece of the closing conditions for Microsoft entailed amending the Society-Microsoft MSA to match the language of the EY-Microsoft MSA. From here, every single statement of work must be assigned to EY, also with new terms that were up to their corporate legal standards. We did our best to assure each client within Microsoft that this was a great thing, that the delivery would be seamless, and that by being a part of EY, we would have extensive resources behind us to up-level our offerings. In the end, all they cared about was ensuring the acquisition wouldn't fuck up our ability to service their needs.

With regard to the Microsoft amendments and assignments, various representatives needed to be involved in some way at different times. First, we had to identify the specific person within Microsoft to whom we could explain the change and what we required legally to continue our working relationship. Then, we had to get the appropriate representation from EY, EY's outside legal counsel, EY's corporate development team, Society's outside legal counsel, and Society itself (which was me) all on a call with Microsoft and their necessary representation to discuss and negotiate the details of the language changes.

I recall trying to get ten different people scheduled for a call, and this was just the very first call! It took at least three more meetings, again with a different permutation of representation, to hash out and agree on all the changes.

This entire process took weeks to navigate but felt like an eternity. Eventually, Microsoft's legal team signed off, and we checked off the box for the entire book of business there on the closing conditions list—a huge milestone.

Since the four founders were coming into EY as principals, one of the required processes to navigate was their direct admit program, specifically created for outside individuals coming into the firm at the partner or principal level. This involved a series of meetings with various people ranging from HR, finance and accounting, sectors and markets, Independence, and others.

It also entailed documentation. A shit ton of documentation.

The four of us sat in front of our computers reviewing the required files. The laundry list was daunting to say the least.

First, there was your somewhat standard yet highly detailed chronological resume. It was funny, as I hadn't produced an actual resume in years. Then we had to share any documents that might restrict us in any way—any employment agreements or contracts with terms and conditions we might still be subject to. Additionally, we needed to provide income statements, proof of compensation, W-2s and K-1s, bonuses, and any 401(k) documents.

Luckily, a lot of the necessary documents were nicely filed away due to our finance department and CPA's organization. But we continued to be surprised by exactly how far and granular EY needed to investigate.

For anyone to qualify for partnership at EY (and I can only assume the same goes for other major accounting/assurance firms), they needed to disclose all their personal and immediate family business relationships, financial holdings and bank accounts, business interests, loans, mortgages, and insurance. A group within EY would then scrutinize every single detail and verify whether any of them explicitly represented what could be perceived as a conflict of interest. If it did, there were specific directions on how to remedy, actions that must be handled as soon as possible.

For example, if Geico was your insurance carrier for your home and auto, and EY happened to be Geico's auditor, you would be required to change insurance carriers. There was no debate on the matter.

The takeaway is this: Every single aspect of your life that could be conceived as a potential conflict would need to be disclosed and evaluated for action. Many times, there wasn't anything to do. But it seemed that most of the time, there was. Dump a stock or mutual fund. Change insurance companies or your primary banking relationship. Sell your interest in a business venture.

We even had to disclose all our immediate family interests. My wife, Sherry, had her own consulting firm that provided leadership development and executive coaching to several clients nationally. As part of the independence process, we had to disclose every client she was working with, as well as all the business relationships associated with her company—her bank, insurance company, business partners, etc.

Lucky for Sherry and me, all our business relationships and financial investments satisfied the requirements of EY's independence and risk management organization. But some of the founders had to engage in tasks like rolling over investment vehicles into allowable IRAs and liquidating certain stocks in their respective portfolios.

Independence was also a major obstacle that every other transitioning Society employee had to navigate. Overall, they experienced less scrutiny than the founders, but it was painful, nonetheless. Mortgages, car loans, student loans, insurance policies, brokerage accounts, savings accounts, and family estates were all investigated. Many found it frustrating to have to disclose personal financial statements, assets, and liabilities.

I Want to Punch the Punch list

Pressure continued to mount as we rolled into early July, as there were still quite a few outstanding items on the punch list. Day after day, Ankur and Tim helped keep us motivated and organized on all the tasks in motion. Each item was carefully examined in our daily punch list meeting. It took an hour to cover them all—every line item specifically highlighted in red, yellow, and green. It felt like we were spinning a bunch of plates, and the effort to keep them all going was overwhelming.

I specifically recall a time when I got super punchy with Josiah, as I had just pulled an all-nighter with John the night before. Josiah was traveling and doing everything he could to get in front of clients and execute his assignments, amendments, and terms—but it was taking longer than I'd anticipated, as we hadn't made any progress on several fronts. On a call the next day, I got a little overzealous in my tone.

"Hey man, JB and I are working around the clock here trying to get shit done, and I need you to step up with some resolution," I stated emphatically. "It feels like there's no urgency for you, while the rest of us are busting our assess here in the office."

Josiah calmly stood his ground and said, "PJ, I know you guys are working around the clock, and I appreciate all you're doing. But know that just because I'm not there in the office with you doesn't mean I'm not working. I'm doing everything I can to get in front of these clients and execute the necessary contracts."

I sat down in my chair and took a deep breath. I felt terrible. My accusation was uncalled for. I'd let this whole process get way too much into my head. I'd just wanted to get his attention and let him know exactly how much pressure I was feeling, and how much this whole process meant to me.

"Dude, I'm sorry I snapped. I'm just overwhelmed right now, and this punch list is driving me crazy," I responded.

In typical Josiah fashion, he responded with understanding and encouragement. "PJ, you're doing an awesome job getting shit knocked off the list, and we're making progress. Keep doing what you're doing, and together we'll get this deal over the goal line."

The second week of July brought a new injection of energy into the company, as we hosted Society Days, our annual all-hands meeting, over three days. All employees flew in, giving the office an even livelier feel. It also offered a nice distraction, amidst social events like happy hours and dinners, and on the final day, we hosted a block party in the parking lot complete with food trucks, a DJ, and fun activities for all. The timing was also welcomed, as many employees had questions concerning the pending acquisition. We used the opportunity to bring in various leaders from EY to participate and hold a townhall-style chat to address their myriad of concerns. Gary Angel, Saj, and Julianne Woo were a few principals that attended, and their presence reassured the audience.

By the third week of July, the four founders were all running on fumes. We were exhausted. We were frustrated. And even though we were also starting to see lots of progress, we weren't getting much feedback from the leaders within EY's legal and corporate development teams as to what exactly it would take to finish the deal. Did we need to cross off every single item on the list? Would 95 percent be considered enough? Any information would have helped give us context to our progress, but it never came. We felt lost without a map on all fronts.

Getting Over the Goal Line

One evening, John sat down with me and Josiah to share an idea he'd come up with to make closing more equitable. He proposed that we sweeten the deal for Chad by each offering up $250,000 from our own individual stakes at closing. At first, I was pissed.

"What the fuck?" I said indignantly. "Why should we give up $750,000 collectively to Chad, when he knew what he was signing up for when we put this deal together? It's not like he's going to walk away with peanuts compared to us, and now we must kowtow to him with more of our own dollars?"

Personally, I despised the idea of anyone holding leverage over us, especially this late in the game. I stopped to let it all sink in and fell back in my chair.

Josiah's reaction was a little less brusque than mine, but I could tell he was annoyed.

John explained how the gesture would buy us some goodwill with Chad, and how it could alleviate some of his malcontent. In the grand scheme of things, $250,000 wouldn't compromise the fact that each of us would be millionaires once the deal closed. With that in mind, why not throw Chad a bone, as the benefits far exceeded the cost?

We sat there in silence, and I looked over at Josiah. He looked back with a half grin as if to tell me he didn't have the energy to fight this one, and that John made some very good points. Perhaps we were just too tired to argue the point any further. The two of us acquiesced to John's idea and decided it would not be a topic of conversation in the future.

Early in the evening on July 22, I got a knock at my office door. The other founders had left for the day, but I'd stuck around to finish up some of the punch list reporting. It was Mandy, one of my business development managers, and she was visibly unhappy. Her offer from EY was underwhelming and frustrating due to the mapping based on her role within the organization. Mandy shared her concerns regarding the salary, lack of variable compensation or significant bonus structure, and limitations to her ability to grow.

At first, I felt a little defensive, as I was stressed already based on all the closing conditions I was managing. I settled down and took a deep breath of my own. Then I listened intently. I could tell she was angry but was doing her best to hide it, resulting in a flood of tears running down her face. She tried to keep her composure, but her emotions won. Her reaction was justified in my mind. Mandy was a go-getter who was making great strides as a business development leader. She aspired to greatness, and in her mind, the details of her EY offer would prevent her from accomplishing her goals. I handed her a box of tissues, and she accepted them in embarrassment. She took a deep breath and sat down in a swivel chair next to my desk.

"Mandy, I completely understand where you're coming from and don't necessarily disagree with your rationale. EY treats business development differently than we do, but the bright side is you get a guarantee on your compensation. I know it's capped, and that you won't have the unlimited commission potential you have here. But do yourself and me this favor, and give me one year. One year to integrate into EY, lean in, learn their ways, and do the job. One year to understand what options you have within the organization. And if that year goes by and you still aren't satisfied with how things are progressing, let's talk. With lots of unknowns right now, we'd be selling ourselves short if we made rash decisions off assumptions. Plus, after one year, the worst position you'll be in is you'll have a global brand name on your resume, which I believe holds significant street cred. Please trust me on this."

By this time, Mandy had settled and let out a smile. We talked for a little while longer, and she left my office saying, "Thanks for understanding, and I'll think about what you said over the weekend."

I would come to learn in time from Mandy that this specific encounter, her emotional discourse so to speak, was a pivotal moment in her career that she shared on the regular to various up-and-coming employees at Ernst & Young. She could have easily reacted differently, as there was very little I could do to change the fate of her new offer. Mandy could have stuck to her guns, said "fuck you" to the system, and walked on to apparent greener pastures. But she didn't. Instead, she trusted me and my word, and in a short time, found herself on an epic professional trajectory toward partnership that even she wasn't anticipating.

As we rolled into the fourth week of July, we began to see some hope that the deal would close, but still had a few significant items to get over the goal line. The four of us were all operating in the redline, and the combination of the transaction details, complications with Chad, and running the business meant little sleep and plenty of tension—a house of cards that could come crashing down with the slightest misstep. Eventually, EY came to us with a targeted close date—July 26. This meant the world to us, as we now had a specific date we could leverage in our desperate attempt to close out the punch list.

I finally wrangled all the appropriate people for Disney, along with the proper representatives from EY, Pillsbury, Society, and Cairncross. After a few separate meetings and lots of back-and-forth emails, we received the final sign-off for contractual assignment. Salesforce came down to the wire as well, but we eventually received the termination agreement, fully executed.

The last items on the list were Providence and Redbox; they had been extremely taxing to navigate. Amending the two assigned SOWs was like pulling teeth, and at the pace we were going, we weren't going to hit the close date. So we got creative and requested that we add an amendment to the asset purchase agreement that essentially pulled Redbox and Providence aside from any EY liability. This indemnification was exactly what was needed as we drew up the amendment, received input from all legal representatives, and fully executed it with signatures.

Hearing that we'd satisfied all EY's closing criteria felt almost anticlimactic. We had been sprinting so hard and for so long, once emails started flying around that stated we were going to close, it didn't even feel real. I was sure something would come up that would necessitate more meetings, more calls, and more documentation.

But this time, it didn't happen. Everyone had been working hard to get the final documents over the goal line, and with our emotions completely drained, we received an email from Dwight at Cairncross confirming the wire transfers had been received by our banks.

At 2:40 in the afternoon on July 26, 2016, Chad sent the following congratulatory email to the entire employee base, announcing the amazing milestone of officially being acquired by EY:

> *Congratulations, team, the transaction with EY has officially closed! This is an amazing milestone for the company and the start of a very exciting new chapter in our history. Starting tomorrow (7/27) we will be known as EY-Society, and you will*

all be onboarded as EY employees per the schedules shared in your onboarding emails.

On behalf of myself, John, Josiah, and PJ, I want to say how grateful we are for the trust you have put in us during this transaction and the upcoming transition. We can't wait to get started on all the opportunities we will have at EY, and the most exciting thing is we get to continue to work with the best people in the business—all of you!

As usual, please wait until EY makes a public announcement (we will share the press release after it comes out) before you post on social or communicate beyond a need-to-know basis.

Congratulations, and thanks again.
Chad

It was official. Tomorrow, we would be EY-Society, the next chapter in a life that felt so much longer than our eight years of existence. No more Job Mob, Pentad, or Society. It was a new world, a new moniker, and we had so much to look forward to.

That afternoon at 4:30, the four founders jumped on a call with Derek, Tim, and Jason of EY's corporate development team, along with their outside counsel, and Bryce and Bob from Cairncross, and congratulated each other on the closing of Project Seahawk. We thanked everyone for their participation.

I still can't believe we were able to coordinate all the resources—with all the moving pieces, secrecy, and legal and financial hurdles—in such a relatively short time frame. The sheer amount of work expended by everyone was enormous. The final two days prior to closing, I had received and sent more than 350 emails—and those were specific to the acquisition itself. That doesn't account for the countless meetings and phone calls during the process, let alone the level of effort by everyone to get through the initial courtship, letter of intent, and eventual due diligence. The undertaking was huge. It was monumental. And despite all the learnings throughout the process, I doubt we could do it again in the same fashion.

The win felt momentous, a point in life where all the hard work, strife, and fortune came together harmoniously. This was *our* equivalent to winning the Super Bowl, Ryder Cup, or World Series.

That evening, John, Josiah, Chad, and I made our way to John Howie Steak Restaurant to celebrate the closing of the deal. We sat in the bar and enjoyed a ridiculous feast comprised of cocktails, oysters on the half shell, A5 Wagyu steaks, sashimi crudo, and all the side fixings imaginable. There might have been a couple of bottles of cult California cabernets thrown in for good measure. We rejoiced in the milestone by sharing some of our outstanding memories from our eight-year journey together.

As I walked back from dinner to my residence only a few blocks away, my heart began racing as I thought of the magnitude of that day. It was surreal. I stood out on the street, in front of my condo building, and took it all in. Was it the wine? The food-coma from all the extravagant cuisine? Sure, I had a strong buzz from all the libations, but that was in my head and stomach. I also felt energy coming from my heart. It felt heavy, but not from sadness. I felt happiness. I felt relief. I felt gratitude. All these emotions filled my heart and left me dazed and confused. I pulled out my phone and logged into my online banking app. I checked the balance. *Holy shit*, I thought. This wasn't a dream.

I tried to collect my thoughts but struggled. All I could think of was whether I was beyond happy because of my newfound fortune, or out of tremendous relief that the process was finally over. We'd started the process months ago and getting the call that Ernst & Young was satisfied with all the punch list items—all attorneys signed off on the deal, and the wire transfers complete—meant the risk was finally over. I also felt scared, as I would find myself in a whole new world. It was often referred to as *new money*. And with it came a new level of responsibility that I was ill-prepared for.

I made my way through the lobby doors of my condo building and said a quick hello to Ricky, the front desk attendant. He looked up and gave me a smile.

"Good evening, Mr. Ohashi," he responded professionally.

Around the corner was the bank of elevators, and just as I pushed the up button, I heard Jesse behind me, as he also lived in the same building. He excitedly yet cautiously asked, "Is it closed?"

I turned around, and for a split second, tried to respond with an emphatic "yes!" But I couldn't speak. I just stood there for a moment, trying to get some words out, but I was unsuccessful. My eyes filled up with tears, and I broke down crying uncontrollably.

Jesse looked at me and knew the answer. A huge grin appeared on his face, expressing a sense of pride and understanding. He walked over to me and gave me the biggest and longest hug.

"Bro, I'm so proud and happy for you. You deserve this."

I still couldn't respond. After a minute, I gathered my composure and collected my thoughts. By then, my elevator had come and gone. "Thanks, man, that means a lot to me," I finally replied.

We talked for a couple of minutes, but he could tell my head was still swirling from all the emotional weight I was trying to manage.

Running into Jesse that evening will forever be near and dear to my heart. He'd been my roommate, my business partner, my teammate, my direct competitor, my boss, and my mentor, but most important of all, he'd been my friend. A friend who saw me in one of the most emotionally taxing moments of my life. A friend who was undoubtedly responsible for where I ended up. We shared a moment that was filled with absolute gratitude and happiness, but also complete, utter vulnerability in its purest form—a shared moment only he could have understood.

Chapter 14

#WeAreEY-Society

I'm sitting in my car, my eyes glossed over with tears of sadness, relief, anxiety, and a tinge of anger as I gaze vacantly into the dark, dank concrete wall in front of me. I pause before hitting the start button and let out a long, exaggerated sigh. Mixed emotions swirl around in my head, as I said my final goodbyes to many fellow colleagues just minutes prior. Some I'd worked with for years. Others I'd just begun to know. There were lots of hugs and a few tears of their own. All of my personal items sit in a small cardboard box in the trunk of my Mercedes AMG GTC—an EY-branded coffee tumbler, some files, my separation contract, a picture of me and my wife from our honeymoon in Bora Bora, Pepe's water bowl—all that remains from more than ten years of building a company and eventually selling it. The box is a metaphor, a symbol of change, finality, fear, and excitement. I will miss this, I think to myself. But it's all for the best. I rev the engine and immediately focus my attention on the burble and crackle from the powerful twin-turbo V8. I smile. Nothing like the sound of a combustion engine, I think to myself. It never disappoints. I drive out of the underground parking garage, glancing in my rearview mirror at the office building. This will be the last time I leave work at EY.

I can imagine that anyone who sells their company has a similar experience, both in process and emotion. Common denominators of relatable feelings tug at our heartstrings. Automated processes supersede the once-scrappy maneuvering of the past. This entity—essentially a child you've raised from a newborn and poured every ounce of your heart into—becomes a soulless object of transaction. No one cares how personal it was to you. No one pays attention to the details of how you got there, the emotional currency you invested over the years, or the relationships you developed. The number of hours you invested. The sacrifices you made. The company becomes nothing more than a transaction filled with attorneys, negotiation, and documentation. The process takes over, very robotic in nature, leading down a prescribed path of legal, financial, and operational steps.

It's futile to try to hold onto the personal connection. You must let go and accept the fact that it's no longer your baby. It's now someone else's responsibility to look out for —even though you know that they probably won't put in the same level of love and care you did.

Beyond the process, there's an emotional tsunami that hits from all directions. The feeling of accomplishment once the transaction closes: momentary relief, pride, distinction. You're now part of an elite group of professionals who all wear this badge of honor. After all, it's every entrepreneur's dream to have a proper exit, right? An acquisition. An IPO. A recapitalization of some form. But the less obvious feelings that come are undeniable. Perhaps some inadequacy. Feelings of momentary regret. *Did I do the right thing? Was this a mistake? Should I have stayed the course?*

These questions swirl around the minds of all entrepreneurs to some degree. Other emotions include excitement for the future—the anticipation of a new venture with unknown challenges, new relationships, and plenty of learning. There's also fear of the unknown. All these feelings and thoughts plagued me at one point or another post-acquisition.

And then there are the emotions associated with finding your newfound wealth. Gratitude. Vanity. Guilt. Even trepidation. These pull you in all directions as dreams and goals turn into reality.

I've heard people say that if they win the lottery, they won't allow money to change them. I truly believe they idealistically want this, and in some rare cases, they live by this intention. But new money inevitably changes everything around them, and I was no different. Choices. Options. Lifestyle. Attitudes. Even relationships. Some come out of the woodwork for what they think they're entitled to. Others present a façade of happiness for you, but you learn that underneath that thin layer resides resentment and animosity. These folks are the exception, as most people in my life were generally happy for me.

Integration

Even though Ernst & Young had years of experience acquiring companies of all shapes and sizes, and even more sheer resources at their disposal, our integration was fraught with oversights and mistakes from the very get-go. It didn't matter how many eyes were on each aspect of the acquisition, something was inevitably mishandled or missed altogether. Employee mapping, client and account management, and internal processes were just a few of our issues from day one.

From one day to the next, life as I knew it changed significantly. In all honesty, I was so caught up in the actual acquisition process—knocking out every single punch list item, and doing my best to keep an eye on the target of closing the deal—so when the deal actually closed, I was ill-prepared. Looking back, everything about the business changed, and nothing changed. We were Society on a Tuesday and EY-Society the very next day. All our emails were now EY. The Society website pushed all traffic to an Ernst & Young splash page announcing the acquisition. Our paychecks and benefits. Even all our computers with special VPNs and top-notch security were EY's. We were living in a new world.

And some things didn't change. We were still in the same office. The same familiar faces roamed the halls. The same clients. Our mission remained around helping our clients compete on customer experience. And we did our very best to hold onto our fun, scrappy, and dynamic culture we had worked so hard to build.

In fact, many of the folks at EY made a point of supporting our ability to influence their culture. They recognized that EY was stuck in the past and lacked a modern culture driven by digital mindsets and next-generation attitudes. The tail wagged the dog, so to speak, and we were excited to take on this challenge.

The first few months post-acquisition were filled with countless flights to many of the EY offices around the country. Chicago. Portland. New York. Atlanta. San Francisco. Boston. Cleveland. We met with other partners and principals who led various geographic, industry vertical, and competencies that would benefit from our data analytics services. We shared the breadth of our offerings, the specific talent and leadership we had in place, and the past successes of our work. We learned about the inner workings of the massive company, from operations, client engagements, sales and workflow processes, to continued compliance that ensured our individual financial and legal independence.

My first impression can only be described as a honeymoon phase. I was drinking out of the proverbial firehose, trying my best to absorb information about the firm while remembering as many names, faces, and respective responsibilities as possible. My head was spinning. There was so much excitement in the air, like the first day of grade school. The hype was building as internal EY leadership showcased their newest acquisition.

Everyone was welcoming and excited to learn more about data analytics and what we offered. And we were all filled with curiosity, wondering, *What cool experiences await us now that we're a part of this global behemoth?* We had lots of questions to answer: *What services are complementary to theirs? What clients would benefit from our services? How can we quickly integrate into existing projects, thus upleveling the value proposition for all?* Our employees expected so much growth and opportunities for success.

However, the honeymoon was short-lived to say the least. Within six months, I found myself frustrated at the lack of understanding and follow-through of many of the groups we had just met. Promises of introductions never came. Brainstormed ideas never came to light. It became hard to tell whether all the evangelizing of *who we are and why it's important to your clients* was actually getting through. It's as if we were the shiny new object for everyone to momentarily admire and pay proper respects to, but as soon as we left, it was back to business as usual with little to no follow-up.

I can imagine there were various reasons shit just didn't materialize as expected. First, many of the EY leaders we met didn't fully grasp some of the concepts associated with big data and analytics. The business use cases were lost on them—something we took for granted, as we'd been swimming in these waters for years. These ideas were engrained into our brains over many years of conversations, meetings, and presentations. Even basic concepts like marketing automation across digital customer touchpoints, analytical insights into consumer behavior, and big data processing weren't exactly comprehended. Beyond all the leaders in our specific competency and a few closely associated practices, they just didn't get it.

I'm not specifically calling out anyone at EY for the lack of immediate impact or implying fault. There really wasn't any. I can imagine it happens to most companies that go through an acquisition. You can plan all you want, strategize about synergies, clients, technology, and opportunities, but until the actual deal goes through, countless factors can prevent that anticipated smooth transition.

I also think that people were just busy. Taking time out of their day to meet with us took lots of commitment and valuable hours, resulting in opportunity cost to other business-critical duties. With no shortage of distractions, it became apparent that managing the interruptions was top priority for any executive director, partner, or principal at the firm.

Oversight of very specific methodologies was also a significant fuckup. Gross margin is the lifeblood for any company in consulting (or any business, for that matter), but the legacy methods for calculating gross margin differed significantly from EY. No one ever pointed this out prior to the acquisition, and we found ourselves in some complicated conversations, trying to explain why the numbers suddenly went down when plugged into EY's calculator. We managed through it as best we could, and luckily, the leaders pushed blame on the folks responsible for our transition. We didn't know, but it was a valuable learning experience for all.

As monumental of a year 2016 turned out to be, it ended on a personal note of heartbreak. My friend and adopted Grandmother Mary Ellen passed away due to complications after a fall. She was ninety-three years old.

Finding a Rhythm of Business

Over time, things seemed to settle down, as everyone fell into EY's cadence of operations. Josiah began working with leaders in the retail space and connected to their client, Nike. The company was hellbent on leveraging their data more effectively for customer connection as well as supply chain, given the ever-increasing shift to online sales. The team welcomed Josiah, as he brought a combination of executive presence, practical industry knowledge, and talent for building trust with clients. He quickly began leading numerous multi-million-dollar engagements with the global shoe manufacturer, thus representing a nice win for our practice and EY in general.

Chad also found a rhythm, as he partnered with various other EY leaders and spearheaded a campaign to promote our data analytics prowess. A roadshow, he called it—bouncing around from office to office, explaining the intricacies of big data, analytics, and customer experience. Chad eventually got involved in a project that fell near and dear to our hearts: golf. EY partnered with the PGA and Ryder Cup to help with data analytics and visualization for the 2018 event in France—including strategy and execution of real-time data crunching for both TV viewers and supporting commentators. For us data and golf geeks, the project was right up Chad's alley. I looked on from afar with envy as he had multiple meetings with Jim Furyk, the captain of the US team and former US Open champion.

Despite John's primary toolkit being filled with more operational versus sales or analytics skill sets, he fell into a role that would define his overall contribution to EY. One of the first major projects that John spearheaded post-acquisition was the search for new office space. He worked with a team within EY to identify, plan, design, and eventually build out a new location for our EY-Society headquarters. It appeared that everything related to the new office fell on John's plate—representing a significant effort. He quarterbacked budget meetings, negotiation with the brokers, design concepts, procurement of furniture, technology infrastructure, and our eventual move-in. This required constant communication, deft timing, and little margin for error.

We identified a new office high-rise in downtown Seattle, and EY was going to be one of the first tenants. This would be the next step in maturity for us as part of a larger firm.

It was sad saying goodbye to our Bellevue location, as it had provided us with so many memorable experiences—be it the buildout of the downstairs, company parties and barbecues in the parking lot, or ad hoc happy hours. The place had seen a change from Pentad, a new CEO, tremendous growth in revenue and employee count, a refined go-to-market, and lots of successful delivered projects.

One of the primary distinctions of the new EY-Society office was the build-out of our own innovation space called Wavespace. The branding represented various offices around the world and involved dedicated space for everything ranging from thinktank initiatives, innovative prototyping of technology, and the experimentation of new ideas for clients and partners. The space was meant to be flexible, where EY could showcase its latest solutions—be it robotics and automation, generative AI, or blockchain.

John jumped in and quickly partnered up with Woody in running operations for all the Wavespace offices around the country. This was the perfect role for John, as his experience with anything *business operations* made him a valuable asset. His newfound position became a confluence of legal, logistics, infrastructure, finance and budgeting, and people management—very complementary to Woody's role as the primary evangelist for Wavespace.

I, on the other hand, continued to struggle with the integration and felt pulled in various directions. First, the Microsoft account I had helped manage at Society, as well as the transition to EY, became fraught with issues. I entered many intense conversations, doing my best to understand and resolve problems, despite my short tenure with the firm. As a newbie, all the lingo, processes, calculations, and specific people involved were lost on me.

Second, I was pulled into meetings where they expected me to be the subject matter expert given my principal status within the analytics group. This I was not, and I never claimed to be. But that didn't matter much to some, as they involved me in client discussions that I had no business representing. I'd bullshit my way through, waxing as best I could about data platforms this or optimization that. I kept it high-level, offering up perspective and opinions about data analytics just one level lower than conjectural. But as soon as the conversation went deeper into the technology, architecture, or workflows, it became obvious I had hit my threshold.

As I've stated, I'm a sales guy who just happened to sell digital analytics consulting services. I'm about sales excellence, reporting, business development strategies, variable compensation programs, account management, and marketing. And as a partner within the firm, those were useful good skills.

Unfortunately for me, I lacked the other necessary components that made Josiah, John, and Chad successful in their own right—including depth in operations or a competency. I had functioned as a utility player, and when I stepped into the realm of a global consulting firm with more than 200,000 employees, all my professional shortcomings became evident.

When I wasn't focused on Microsoft account strategies or developing new relationships at a client's organization, I often engaged in evangelism of our services. This was an imperative job all the partners took on to some degree. I boarded planes to New York; Boston; Miami; Washington, DC; San Jose; Atlanta; and other cities to spread the analytics gospel and educate employees and their clients on the value of our services. The level of spending on airfare, hotels, and food and entertainment by the firm was downright surprising.

Back in the Society days, as an owner, we scrutinized travel expenditures, as they could easily get out of hand. But at EY, all I had to do was hit up my administrative assistant who supported me (as well as John and Josiah) and let her know I needed a flight to somewhere, a hotel to stay at, and boom, she would turn it into fruition. No one ever questioned the cost. As long as it was justified by some account code or business development activity, it passed through without a second thought.

I was amazed at the level of latitude the partners of EY were afforded. Mind-boggling amounts of money were spent on what I can now say was unreasonable. On multiple occasions, I flew across the country to support an account for a one-hour meeting, with my portion sometimes relatively small. But the account leaders felt it was important, and they spared no expense or inconvenience to flaunt the comprehensive services the firm provided.

In another circumstance, I was asked to fly from Seattle to Boston to participate and present in a global innovation summit held for EY leaders. I can imagine that Chad and Josiah were either too busy or came up with excuses not to attend, so I had to represent. At the venue, I was led to a large conference room where about forty EY leaders were sitting around tables in a horseshoe formation.

The only available chair happened to be between Mark Weinberger and Carmine Di Sibio. Mark, at the time, was the EY global chairman and CEO, and Carmine was slated to be his successor, which materialized just a couple of years later. *How the fuck does a small-time entrepreneur like me find myself in a room full of heavy hitters?* Imposter syndrome kicked in as doubt and inadequacy became persistent. I was perplexed, nervous with excitement, trying to figure out how I could make the best of the moment.

The meeting began, and one after another, leaders stood in front of the audience and presented their spiels. Blockchain. Supply chain management. Artificial intelligence. Even quantum computing. Then it was my turn.

I made my way to the front of the room, connected my laptop to the projector, and paused. *Don't fuck this up*, I thought to myself. Everyone was listening attentively as I began my presentation. I talked for about fifteen minutes, sharing pretty much everything I knew about big data, analytics, and its business application. I gave examples of our engagements. I connected it to the content of other presenters in supply chain and AI.

Then there were questions. Lots of them. One after another, they came at me from all directions. I took this as a good thing, as it clarified certain areas I might have glossed over. After my time was up and everyone seemed satisfied with my answers, I grabbed my computer and walked back to my seat.

As I sat down, I wondered if my performance had helped solidify any outstanding questions about our acquisition. *Are the leaders satisfied that their money was put to good use? Or is there confusion, or even worse, disappointment: who are these Society guys, and what are we doing wasting our money on them? Do I even belong here?* I could feel my heart beating and beads of sweat running down my brow.

A second later, Mark leaned over to me and said, "Nice work. I see lots of potential here and am excited about Society joining the team." I smiled ear to ear and expressed my gratitude for the opportunity. This wouldn't be the last time I presented in front of such a distinguished audience, but it would certainly be the most memorable.

Another duty that I spent a little time on was ensuring a smooth transition for the many employees who came over with the acquisition. Many were also experiencing ambiguity and disorientation given the unfamiliar landscape. When I was in the office, I'd make a point to walk around at least once per day, checking on all the EY-Society employees to see how things were going and if I could help them in any way. I can say with confidence that John and Josiah did the same.

While at Society, we'd pretty much had a handle on how employees were feeling at any given time, given our close proximity. But at EY, everyone was spread out, going their separate ways into the vast universe of the firm, working with new clients and engagements. So it was critical for me to ensure that people were getting the proper air cover they needed to be successful. And as a partner, I could wield my title to get shit done.

But as time went on, I felt far too much distance between me and the others. I wasn't working very closely with John, Josiah, or Chad, as they were all off doing their own things within the firm. My day-to-day consisted of client meetings, account strategy sessions, and some form of training to ensure I was keeping up with my continued professional credits or CPE. I was bored and uninspired. I lacked motivation. Everything I touched had lackluster results, thus adding to my growing lack of confidence. This weighed on me considerably.

Perhaps the most significant event was the inevitable announcement one year after the acquisition that we would be changing EY-Society to just plain EY. Our legacy was completely consumed by the firm, like light in a black hole. It was the end of an era. We knew this would happen in time, but when it did, it meant things were never going to be the same.

By the second year at EY, I began to recognize that I wasn't happy. My options basically led down two distinct paths, neither of which I was thrilled about. One path was to stay the course, remain in the analytics competency, and focus on a specific account. This seemed to be a viable option for Josiah, as he was kicking ass with Nike and a couple of other accounts. For me, though, this option brought consternation, as I knew my ability to lead analytics engagements had its limitations. Further, I had been working with Microsoft for so long, I was starting to feel fatigue from all the changing processes, continuous hoops we needed to jump through, and constant pressure to reduce bill rates. Perhaps all the work leading up to the acquisition had burned me out. Even after twelve months, I still hadn't fully recovered.

The other path was to look for a new role within the central business services group (CBS), where I would no longer be tied to an account or competency. Instead, my role would consist of sales reporting, training, and business development strategies. Although appealing to my strengths, it felt like a complete step back. It would mean walking away from my team, my former company, my other cofounders. Plus, the likelihood of actually finding a position in CBS was trivial, given there were only so many partner-level positions within the group. Disappointment and insecurity crept into my mind. I needed to find something fast. I reached out to leaders in CBS but found very little opportunity there. Desperation started to reveal itself.

The Beginning of the End

Some time later, I received a call from one of my Microsoft clients sharing news that they were about to release an RFP for outsourcing major components supporting the Bing Advertising team. I knew we had a strong baseline of knowledge to work off of. A week later, the detailed RFP landed in my inbox. I quickly acknowledged our willingness to participate, which prompted a flurry of account meetings.

Microsoft's ask was far from simple; the vendor must have a wide array of skills ranging from big data platform engineering, segmentation of target audience, email execution, and analytics and reporting. The scope was essentially broken down into three key areas. The first was the data infrastructure, which included a current technology stack held together with duct tape and bailing wire. This required a completely new system to be engineered, migrated, and brought into production. The second entailed building out a combined on-shore and off-shore team for all the campaign execution, namely email. And the final area was the analytics, reporting, and closed-loop automation for continuous optimization of their targeting.

EY was positioned nicely for a massive project like this, so I jumped all in.

I rallied the appropriate team, with the help of a few leaders, and created what would turn into three months of tireless effort. We established a war room where we strategized technical solutions, workflows, team structure, timelines, skill sets, and pricing. We hashed out tasks for each of the dozen or so team members. The group was elite—the very best of the best, the Green Berets of the RFP world, the SAS of consulting. Barry had pricing. Frank and Mandy had analytics and automation. Tom and Jill researched current processes and technology gaps in the system. Norm owned all the data engineering. We brought in project management specialists, content and graphic design experts, and other team members as needed. The sheer number of resources we threw at the RFP was staggering.

For weeks, we burned the candle at both ends, toiling over every detail. I could tell burnout was imminent. Some were living out of hotel rooms and away from their families. Twelve-hour days took their toll. Tempers were starting to show, as various leaders would, out of nowhere, derail a decision that had already been made, thus creating even more work.

We scrutinized words and phrases to the point of contention—holding senseless debates over the simple wording of a graphic. One evening, we were engaged in an exhaustive discussion on whether we use the word *must* or *should* in a particular sentence, when the chip on my shoulder emerged, and I found my alpha voice and shut down the bickering.

"What do you think we should use, PJ," asked one of the leaders in the room. "Should or must?"

I promptly and angerly replied, "I think it's a fucking

waste of time that we've been arguing over must or should for the past thirty minutes."

An awkward silence followed as everyone around the conference table stared down at their laptops.

I'm certain I could have been gentler with my wording, but at the time, I just didn't care. The team was in the redline and starting to lose focus. Something needed to be done. We were already bringing in lunches, snacks, and dinners for the team, but it wasn't enough.

Two days later, I hired a massage therapist to set up shop in one of the smaller conference rooms. Each team member graciously stepped away from the madness for thirty minutes of bliss. Just a half hour escaping from the constant discussion brought a chance to decompress both mentally and physically. It worked, as each team member came back fully recharged.

After weeks of war room activity, side strategy meetings, and fine tuning of our proposal, it was complete. The result was a one-hundred-page PowerPoint presentation that encompassed every detail we could muster. It was a fucking masterpiece. A Rembrandt of proposals. A document worthy of the Smithsonian. Anyone and everyone would say, "Yes, where do I sign?" after reading the proposal. Sure, its hyperbole, but we couldn't have been prouder. Even if you didn't know a thing about databases, analytics, or marketing campaigns, this proposal would have inspired you; it was just that good.

The proposal walked the client through a series of solutions addressing many of their current pain points, as well as others we knew would find their way to the surface in time. We shared out-of-the-box solutions that our competitors were incapable of providing. We included a comprehensive playbook and methodology for not only standing up and operating the various pieces of the program, but also seamlessly transitioning the current work without any negative impact to the business. I submitted the proposal and took the next day off to catch my breath. I felt relief. Pride. Accomplishment. Then fear.

Then came the waiting. In typical fashion, Microsoft's procurement team didn't disclose any information and policed any communication we had with the actual client. They wanted no competitive edge for any one vendor, thus creating an even playing field for all. Our client contacts remained stoic, not sharing any insights into the process, which way they were leaning, anything. The waiting was painful and brought out the worst of my imagination. Guilt. Failure. Disappointment. Tons of resources wasted. Another shot against my ego.

After a couple of weeks, we got the call. Microsoft asked if we could come in and meet with them to discuss solutions face-to-face. We knew it was the subsequent step in the process, but it felt like a huge win for us and a personal relief knowing we were still in consideration. With three weeks to prepare, the real work began.

We assembled a smaller team consisting of Frank, Matt, Mandy, Norm, Barry, Mike, and myself, and set up the war room once again. A couple of EY executives familiar with the account popped in on occasion to share their thoughts and check on the preparation. Over the next couple of weeks, we fine-tuned our messaging, delivery, and general content.

Mike, EY's global Microsoft account manager, played a key role in coaching us through our content and delivery style, even down to the words we chose. I didn't recognize my blind spots when giving presentations until Mike pointed out a few. Body language. Intonation. Affirmative versus negative speech. Energy levels. It blew me away. But with plenty of handholding by Mike and lots of rehearsal pitches, the team found a new confidence. We were ready.

Game day came, and Frank, Mandy, Matt, and I made our way to the designated Microsoft office to meet with a few stakeholders and representatives from their procurement group. The rest of the team stayed back at the EY office and planned to call into the conference line, just in case something came up where we needed backup. We were greeted by Brad—our primary contact in the Search Advertising Group—exchanged some pleasantries to ease the obvious tension in the air, and found our seats.

After thanking the client for the opportunity to present, I jumped into the presentation with an outline of the major components of our pitch. I started with a seriously cheesy line like, "Come on a journey with us as we explore the art of the possible." Really? Luckily, the audience saw the levity in my approach and kept listening intently. I continued with my spiel and then handed the baton to Mandy, who dove into the email, analytics, and reporting section with spectacular delivery.

The audience held onto her every word, interjecting clarifying questions when needed, only to have Mandy dive even deeper into the material to their apparent satisfaction. Then Frank jumped in to share his prowess in the technology portion of the pitch. He waxed poetic about data management platforms, marketing and analytics tools, and big data processing. More questions came our way as the Microsoft stakeholders tested our understanding of automation and how it could be implemented into their ecosystem.

Frank didn't hesitate as he jumped up to the whiteboard and started scribbling diagrams, boxes, arrows, and workflows that outlined the use of artificial intelligence for continuous improvement of their marketing campaigns.

Then Matt jumped in to put the final touches on the presentation. He shared a comprehensive methodology to manage all the moving pieces of the business, escalation points, best practices, and talent. This wrapper brought all the components together, creating a blueprint on how to take the client's business to new heights.

I closed the meeting with, "You have a billion-dollar business today. Let's work together to make it ten." I looked around the room. All I saw were smiles. This was a good thing.

"Well, I'm ready to buy," exclaimed Brad, breaking the momentary silence and catching us all off guard. His look of satisfaction couldn't have been more welcoming. We all shook hands, reiterated our gratitude for being there, and went on our way.

When we made it back to the office, I was spent emotionally and physically. We joined with the EY team that had been on the phone to do a quick postmortem. A lot of compliments were exchanged amongst the team, along with a "nailed it" from one of the business development managers. We talked about some things that perhaps we missed as well as the prominent highlights. I reiterated Brad's "well, I'm ready to buy" comment as a significant buy-sign.

All the hours we'd put into the original proposal, along with preparations for the oral presentations, seemed worth it now. The late nights, laboring over every microscopic detail in the content, role-playing and mock presentations, stress—all worth it.

I also felt that perhaps there was a successful future for me at the firm. All my stress about how I didn't belong or how my skill sets didn't align with our group seemed to disappear for a bit. Maybe a win like this could set me on the right path.

Now all we had to do was wait.

We got the bad news a couple of weeks later, and it landed like a gut punch from Mike Tyson. Microsoft made the unfortunate decision to go with another vendor, noting specifically that as much as they liked our proposal and presentation, our pricing was magnitudes higher than our competition. This made it a nonstarter. We had already tried to put our best pricing together in hopes of a longer-term commitment from Microsoft. But even our best couldn't compete with companies offering rock-bottom prices to win the business. I pleaded with Brad, telling him that I thought he was making a mistake. Sure, they would save a few dollars in the short-term, but inevitably the solutions from the other vendors would come up well short of success. We might cost more, but our strategy and execution would make it worth it. Unfortunately, it didn't work. He, along with his higher-ups, had made up their minds.

The days and weeks after the announcement that we lost the deal became a time of personal reflection for me. *What am I even doing here?* I asked myself. *I'm losing deals, disappointing the people around me, and costing the firm a shit-ton of money.* I wore my apparent frustrations on my chest, so I did everything I could to avoid the office. I'd find excuses to travel. I'd take longer lunches. I'd hit the gym midday. Anything to evade interactions with my colleagues. People started to notice.

I found myself in a quandary. I knew my heart wasn't into it like it had been back in the day. Too many things had changed, leading me down a path of bitterness and frustration. I had failed on so many fronts in such little time—closing deals, leading successful projects, generating new business relationships—all examples of my shortcomings. I took a mental scorecard of all my successes post-acquisition and found the win column virtually empty. This weighed on me heavily but wasn't enough reason to simply jump ship. Significant, seven-figure retention bonuses were waiting for me at the end of my third year—too substantial to walk away from.

On the other hand, I still loved the people I worked with. The office EY created was vibrant, and given it was in the heart of downtown Seattle, it offered plenty of access to shopping, restaurants, and sporting events. Plus, the exposure to the latest and greatest the firm had to offer was intriguing. I was surrounded by so many talented professionals to learn from, which could lead to something beyond analytics. The opportunities were endless. And being a partner with the firm brought status, respect, and to a certain degree, power. It led me to mistakenly believe that for the time being, I was untouchable.

That came to fruition on a random day in October of 2018 when Greg Jenko, one of our competency leaders, called me into a small conference room for a talk. Before I walked into the room, I knew this was it. *This can't be good.* A familiar feeling settled into my stomach, very reminiscent of the multiple times in my career I was let go or asked to leave. It's a combination of a fight-or-flight adrenaline rush, utter humiliation, and indignation—thrown together in a shit sandwich just waiting for you to take a bite. I sat down and heard Saj's voice on the phone, apparently working in a remote office. The two were well-prepared.

"PJ, thanks for taking the time to talk," began Greg. "We would like to offer you an opportunity to move on from the firm on your terms. It has become apparent it's not the best fit given your skill set, and perhaps we can work together on separating our relationship amicably."

I nodded in agreement but continued to stay silent. Saj continued. "PJ, I really appreciate everything you've done for the firm, the team you built, and your contributions to the cause, but I think things have run their course."

"I understand," I reluctantly said with a sinking feeling in my stomach. In a flash, I mentally drifted back to Boeing, Endeavor, and MDI—when I was asked to leave my post. I deserved it then, and I deserved it now. Feelings of failure and disappointment with a tinge of sorrow and regret tugged at my heart.

We talked for a few more minutes, as Greg and Saj presented me with details of a generous severance package. Today would be my last day in the office, but I would technically be employed till the end of the year. In addition, they gave me six months' distributions and guaranteed my third retention bonus.

The two of them couldn't have been more professional, as I know it's never easy to let someone go. But the compassion they displayed and flexibility to work with me on every detail was so appreciated. They gave me the opportunity to make any announcement I felt appropriate and in whatever timeframe of my choosing.

The conversation could have gone in a completely different direction based on my response. I could have played hardball and basically called their bluff on letting me go. It would have been awkward, putting the two of them on the defensive. But it wasn't in me. I knew deep down it was the right thing, and serendipitously, the firm knew it as well. A small shot against my fragile ego, but the right thing for all parties involved.

Greg and I shook hands, and I shared my gratitude with Saj.

I immediately found a private conference room and called Sherry. "Today's the day," I announced. "Greg and Saj gave me my walking papers, and today is my last day. It's a great package, and I'm grateful I can go out with some dignity."

"Well, it's what you ultimately wanted, right?" she asked, knowing that it had been on my mind for a while. "We're going to be just fine. Come home, and we'll talk about it."

I walked back to my desk to gather my belongings as well as my thoughts. I didn't want to cause a commotion or make a big deal of it. In time, word would get out to everyone of the real reason I left, but for now all I cared about were the people closest to me. I shared the news with Sarah and Barry. I made my way around the entire office, sharing the news with a select few others that I was moving on. Hugs. Handshakes. A few tears. I gathered my personal items, thanked Belinda, my admin, for all her support, and made my way to the elevator. As bittersweet as the feeling was, I knew the stars couldn't have aligned more perfectly.

Getting Closure

A couple of years after leaving EY, I ran into a neighbor whose vacation home was just a block away from where I moved. Sherry and I were out walking Pepe when we struck up a conversation. He introduced himself as Steve, and after some light get-to-know-you conversation, I asked him what he did for a living.

"I work at Microsoft and run advertising for search," Steve replied. I immediately took notice. I asked him if his last name happened to be of a particular Steve that I knew to be the ultimate decision-maker in the RFP that I'd lost years prior while at EY. *Bing? Search advertising? Holy fucking shit. I know this guy.*

"Yes, how did you know?"

I paused for a few seconds trying to decide how to

answer. What I really wanted to tell him was: *Thanks. Thank you for NOT awarding EY the business. Thank you for giving it to someone else. If we had won the project, I would have been obligated to stay there and manage it. I still may have been walked out the door in the mid-term, but I certainly would have been committed to oversee the initial components of the engagement. Most importantly, thank you for inadvertently and unknowingly helping me along in my retirement.*

It's a small world, and at that moment, it seemed even smaller.

"My company used to do some analytics for Microsoft back in the day," I responded, not bringing up any additional color.

Maybe one of these days I'll get the chance to properly thank Steve.

Epilogue

If I haven't made it clear, my parents played a monumental role in giving me the tools to find success and happiness in life. Therefore, it's only appropriate for me to give credence to them in the sincerest of ways. I know for certain I wasn't an easy child to raise, many times letting my short temper and defiant attitude get the better of me. They, of all people, probably recognized the chip on my shoulder well before I ever did.

Throughout my life, I have bounced from one end of the spectrum to the other, either acknowledging my parents for all their wisdom, or convincing myself they knew very little about the world I lived in.

As a youth, my parents were the primary reference point for all things in the universe. What they shared with me was not only taken as truth, but I developed an undeniable feeling that their principles were all that mattered. Theirs was the one and only voice I heard, guiding me on the daily, creating the foundation for morality, ethics, and general life principles.

As I grew older, I fell into a phase, probably like most

adolescents, of questioning everything. I tested the boundaries of discipline, searched for holes in their values and perspective, and convinced myself that the real truth lived somewhere else.

I held on to that belief for quite some time, rolling my eyes internally as my mother revealed some form of worldly advice, usually given in an unsolicited manner. "Just make sure you do the right thing," she'd share without specific context. "PJ, all you have is the family name, so don't do anything to tarnish it." These were platitudes I heard my entire life, eventually leading me to question their significance.

What does that have to do with solving the myriad of business problems I face on the daily? I thought. *What the fuck does she know about the business world after all?*

I would even question my father's abilities with regard to business, the world of finance, and aspiration in life. He didn't impart any sort of wisdom through one-liner sayings, yet I found myself judging his character simply based on how far he made it professionally. By my early thirties, I had far out-earned him salary-wise and was convinced I knew much more than he ever did based on my own professional endeavors. The deals I negotiated and closed. The size of my network. The titles I carried.

It wasn't until around the time I became an entrepreneur that I realized I got the whole fucking thing wrong. I'm not quite sure if it was simply a lack of appreciation, but my misaligned credit of their influence in my life is an unpardonable sin.

Sure, the experiences of both my parents didn't mirror my own. But in time, I came to realize all the goodness they shared, despite my history of scoffing at my mother's lectures or devaluing my father's accomplishments.

All my mother's dogma around being a good person,

positively contributing to society, and honoring our family name became recognized assets for me in starting a business. I both consciously and subconsciously brought those values to the office every single day, attributing them to a myriad of business scenarios ranging from our company culture, how we specifically and compassionately handled employee situations, to servicing our clients with the utmost integrity.

I look back and hope my mother would be proud of me and my business partners for how we handled various situations. Although I certainly made my share of mistakes over the years, I tried my very best to always "do the right thing."

She further helped shape my identity as a professional sales executive through uncompromising principles rooted in our Japanese heritage. Honor was always top of mind, and disgrace was to be avoided at all costs. I tried my very best to uphold that ideology and applied it to every business meeting, email, phone call, and relationship. Little did I realize at the time, but it was my mother's voice that guided me throughout my entire career.

My father's influence on me also cannot be overstated. His professional achievements in his career and eventual leap into entrepreneurship helped pave the way for me to follow years later.

My father became an entrepreneur when he was seventy-one years old, and even though he didn't plan on building an empire, his success was reflected in the quality of relationships he developed and maintained over the years. He was an old-school businessman who focused on providing the highest level of service imaginable. My father's methods were undeniably extraordinary. The loyalty of clients for over forty years. Handshake deals. A constant stream of referral business. Hand-delivering orders. Minimal mark-ups on pricing. No marketing. No website. Just the purest form of integrity, trust, and sincerity. Everyone in the business knew of my father, and his reputation preceded him throughout the years.

Beyond his professional network existed a collection of values that I will forever carry with me. First, my father's work ethic was unquestionably amazing. Any blind spots or weaknesses he may have held over the years were conquered by his ability to simply work his fucking ass off. He applied this to all aspects of his life, reflected in his scrappy, straight-hustle attitude.

A value that my parents both exuded through everyday actions was their undying desire and need to take care of those around them. As far back as I can remember, this tenet was accomplished through charitable donations to various nonprofits, dropping everything to assist a friend or family member, or provide a stranger with a helping hand.

Since I was a youth, my mother would drag me kicking and screaming to the strawberry farms in Auburn, where I undoubtedly consumed more berries than I picked. I'd glance up to look at her, only to find her in the next row, as she'd already picked through ours. She was a berry-picking machine, filling five large, wooden carriers to one of mine. We packed up the car—with the trunk and backseat filled with boxes and bowls of freshly picked strawberries—and made the rounds, generously delivering our bounty to friends and relatives all over Seattle.

This was just normal life for them; you share what you have with others. And their generosity didn't stop with just those they knew. My parents took on what they would call random acts of kindness to strangers. They would pay for someone's bill at a restaurant without them knowing. My dad once picked up a hitchhiker and took him to coffee before dropping him off at his work. Example after example made a serious impression on me to continue paying it forward to those around me.

The many principles and values instilled by my parents over my years on this planet made the basis upon which I built my life. From that, I have learned to take all the goodness and wisdom and mix them in a giant Cuisinart along with a bunch of my own ingredients.

Which brings us back to my personal recipe of life that, for better or worse, has helped me overcome obstacles, learn from my mistakes, and find purpose. Artificially created discomfort. Controlled anger. Self-preservation. Continued effort to manage my dysfunctional relationship with money. Loyalty to my loved ones or those who can't fight for themselves. All elements contributing to a product of positive motivation and ambition.

Now I'm retired and writing this book. And after that, I'm sure I'll find something else to focus my attention on. Maybe it's a second book. A new business. A new foreign language. Some new form of me fucking around. The opportunities are countless.

What is certain is my continued reliance on the chip on my shoulder.

I believe having a chip is the universal commonality amongst all people who desire more. You see it in all walks of life, be it business, sports, or any other life endeavor. It's what pushes people to persevere after failing. They fall, get back up, learn from their mistakes, and push forward. In my opinion, when harnessed appropriately, the chip has the power to transform oneself and those around them.

Jesse has one. Ryan has one. Josiah and John do as well. Even my wife, Sherry, has one. It's the source of their own fuel and drive that distinguishes them from just raw talent and knowledge. It's the edge that I believe all entrepreneurs have. A differentiator. Something that cannot be taught but must be found. It's innate. Buried deep within one's soul. A source of motivation derived from the emotions of past experiences. Each of these people in my life has learned to harness its power and put it to good use.

This chip is what drives Ryan to build companies. It's what compels John to pedal his bike across the continental United States. It's what motivates Josiah to provide open-handedly for his family and friends. It's what prompts Jesse to invest in new ventures. It's what motivates Sherry to optimize a balance of health, work, and play. It's the common denominator we all share in life—and regardless of how it's directed, it will always be my source of inspiration.

So that begs the question: Where does the chip on your shoulder take you?

Acknowledgments

Mixing Business with Pleasure

John D. Rockefeller was quoted as saying, "A friendship founded on business is better than a business founded on friendship." Others take it further by saying, "Don't mix business and pleasure," or put more plainly, "Never go into business with your friends." In most cases, I imagine this rings true. It potentially opens the door for unpleasant and difficult circumstances, confrontation, and discussions—many times leading to the end of one, or in worst-case scenarios, both relationships.

Bonobos cofounder Andy Dunn takes it further by writing in his book, *Burn Rate*, "A friendship that expands into a business partnership becomes riddled with obligations. Obligations to employees, customers, and shareholders. It is an intertwining of financial interests and personal reputations. It can be a battle over who makes decisions, who gets the credit, and who takes the blame. It is, in short, a recipe for the evisceration of a friendship. It's not that you might lose your friend when you go into business. It's that by definition you do."

There's truth to John's and Andy's perspectives on mixing friendships and business. I know several professionals who are no longer friends with their once thriving business partners. And there are countless other examples out there, wherein personal greed and ego somehow overshadow professional behavior and ethics. Sometimes it's deliberate and intentional. Other times, it happens at a glacial pace, almost by accident. To be clear, going into business with your friends *is* a risky proposition, and unless all the right boxes are properly checked, one should simply walk away.

But in spirit, I don't necessarily agree with this premise that it's impossible, or bound to bring destruction. To me, this isn't a universal rule that everyone should follow. In fact, I think it's kind of bullshit. Bullshit because I believe, under the right circumstances—meaning the right friends with similar values, trust, communication, and life goals—the journey can be gratifying beyond expectations. Bullshit because the process has the potential to take both relationships to new heights. Knowing your successes positively impact someone you care about is so rewarding. Maybe I'm the anomaly. An outlier of sorts. An exception to the rule. But fuck the rule, as far as I'm concerned.

I say fuck the rule not because I want to be provocative or contrarian. It's because it's too easy to *not* venture down that road. It's easier not to have complicated, difficult, and even awkward discussions. It's easier to make decisions unilaterally without having to think about the implications for others. It's easier to retain all the notoriety, profit, and credit to oneself. And when has anything great ever happened that was easy?

But it's indeed difficult to balance all the necessary layers of trust, communication, vision, and values when going into business with friends. It's difficult to always agree that the friendship comes first, and the business second, especially when people change over time, the business evolves, and the stakes increase. It's not easy making decisions collectively—considering perspectives that don't align with yours—or sacrificing for the greater good.

But when you really dig deep into the relationships you value the most in life, none of them ever come easy. It's a challenge of epic proportions. And the more partners you have, the more complex the equation becomes. You can liken it to a marriage. Actually, it's exactly like a marriage. You become legally bound to one another, and the same values that make up a healthy marriage are exactly the same with business partnerships.

I certainly have experienced the trials of mixing friendship and business, and despite the highs and lows of the various business lifecycles, I remain steadfast that the journey was more gratifying with my friends than if I had done it alone.

Seriously, what can be more rewarding than going to work daily with people you care about while helping them (and having them help you) achieve professional goals and a living for their (and your) families?

OK, THE REAL ACKNOWLEDGMENTS

I cannot stress enough the importance of my respective connections and histories with Josiah, Jesse, John, Ryan, and Chad as they relate to my professional life. Each person came to me unexpectedly, but with profound significance and purpose. At any given time in our relationship, I would play the role of a colleague, subordinate, best friend, roommate, mentee, confidant, life coach, and teammate. In time, I would learn to fully appreciate each and every interaction—including each granular detail to every conversation—as some form of universal fate destined specifically for me.

As you have read throughout this book, our interactions over the years were not always pleasant. There was drama. There was conflict. Exchanges that brought out the very worst of our natures, many of which we're not proud of. But those interactions had to happen, as they all made us all better in the long term.

What started out as a disparate group of friends evolved into a unique, thriving business partnership. All of us were responsible for each other's success and failures. I acknowledge what they did for me, the sacrifices they made, the learnings they brought, and the love they shared. Each of them, in some form or another over the years, helped break me down and build me back up as a more gracious, resilient, and secure individual.

Josiah

I'd like to start out by first describing Josiah—in a bit more detail than you've already seen in this book. Picture a half-Black, half-White forty-something guy with a clean-shaven head and model-like face. Six feet of height with an athletic build, mix in an extroverted disposition and infectious laugh, and you undeniably get someone who stands out from the crowd. That's Josiah.

And if you were to either spend any significant time with the guy, or ask someone who has, you're very likely to reach a similar answer. To put it plainly, he's an amazing human being who has touched the hearts of many. He's a family man. A friend's man. An individual who goes out of his way to take care of those around him. Words that come to mind are generous, tenacious, charismatic, and loyal. I emphasize generous, as anyone in Josiah's life has been a recipient of his benevolence. His passion for life experiences is equaled by few, and his desire to share those experiences with others is even more paramount. He'll make you laugh through his quick-witted jokes or pop-culture references. At any given point, he may very well start dancing by busting out the robot or running man or unexpectedly shouting at the top of his lungs "Whooo!" in an effort to lighten the mood.

I cherish every second I get to spend with him, regardless of if we're on the golf course, sharing a wonderful meal and bottle of wine, or just sitting around discussing politics. He is the proverbial "brother from another mother" and someone I respect and love beyond limits.

Jesse

Jesse has always been a mentor to me in ways I never realized until writing this book. Even back in the day, I admired his work ethic, passion for taking care of others around him, and uncanny ability to acquire and retain any sort of information. Jesse is well-read, a sponge for anything historical, and more times than not, the smartest person in the room. He's influenced me in all aspects of my life including career choices, relationships, and as much as I hate to admit it, even playing basketball. Jesse inspires others around him to be better. He, like Josiah, loves to take care of those closest to him. Be it work or play, friends or family, Jesse wants you to come along for the ride.

He also has his own set of demons, and he'd be the first to admit that. Insecurities, pride, and a short temper have haunted him over the years. But his scrappy nature and big-picture view on life overshadow any liabilities, allowing him to conquer pretty much anything he chooses. I've seen him at the top of his game, and I've seen him at his worst.

The first year of our venture posed a very difficult time in my life, particularly due to my divorce, and Jesse was there by my side providing relentless support. A place to stay. A bed to sleep in. Food to eat. An ear to listen. Navigating those emotionally taxing weeks and months would have been damn near impossible if it weren't for my friend.

Jesse and I have run through the gauntlet of life together in so many ways, yet through thick and thin, our friendship not only remains unscathed but stronger than ever.

Ryan

Two words embody Ryan's ethos: resonate and elevate. He is a modern-day Renaissance man, if there even is such a thing. Not only is he good at everything he does, but he also constantly takes on new challenges as if his life weren't busy enough. Ryan epitomizes the semi-cliché idea of *work hard and play hard.* He's built a small empire of companies in technology and real estate, taught courses at University of Washington's School of Business, helped raised a wonderful daughter, and even recorded three albums as lead vocalist and guitarist in his band, Iris Drive. He commits to health and fitness by running half-marathons and completing century bike rides monthly, and he participates in various charitable causes. Ryan's tenacity toward business was recognized through a nomination for the *Puget Sound Business Journal*'s prestigious "40 Under 40" award.

Some of his harshest critics would say that his ambition sometimes gets the best of him. That there's a way to be both nice and victorious. That drive, sacrifice, and success aren't mutually exclusive. But in his defense, I don't know a soul who has climbed to the top of the business world without leaving some kind of collateral damage along the way. Regardless of any obstacles, his life trajectory continues to soar upward like a rocket ship, without the slightest sign of slowing down.

I relish in anticipation what Ryan will accomplish both professionally and personally. Maybe someday, he'll learn how to bottle his spirit and share it with the world.

JOHN

There are so many things I could say about John; it's actually difficult to know where to start. One of his most likeable aspects is his humility. He exudes confidence but never arrogance. He asks a lot of questions and listens with full attention and presence. He's naturally curious, and ferociously competitive. I've never met someone with more determination and perseverance. In fact, nobody comes close in my opinion.

Shortly after meeting him, I learned that John is a world-class endurance competitor whose resume from his athletic endeavors would eventually rank him as one of the *fittest people in tech* by one publication. Countless Ironman and Ultraman races, mountaineering explorations, and multiple bike rides across the continental United States put him in a category few can claim. John's ability to mentally conquer any physical challenge is unmatched.

One story that best describes John's willingness to make sacrifices and test the limits of his pain threshold was his preparation for the Race Across America, or RAAM. The RAAM is a grueling, single-stage bicycle race across the entire continental United States, starting in Oceanside, California, and ending in Annapolis, Maryland. Many claim it to be the most demanding endurance event in the world—over three thousand miles of desert, mountain ranges, and prairies—exposure to any and all weather conditions Mother Nature could throw at you.

To properly prepare for the event, John would subject himself to a training regimen so punishing that I can only describe it as sadistic. He would work a full day at the office, go home and spend time with his family over dinner, then proceed to jump on his bike and ride from his home in Seattle to the Canadian border and back, a distance over two-hundred miles. John would then ride back to the office, shower, and work another full day with zero sleep.

Intensity and focus are two attributes that define John's influence on others around him. This made it extremely difficult for *any* of us to complain, as we all knew in the back of our heads that John was putting in way more effort at any given time.

John is a well-rounded human who tries his very best to balance his professional and personal life with precision. He would say that he's a husband and father first, and all his business and competitive endeavors are a distant second.

I trust John with my life and look forward to sharing many more life experiences.

Chad

Without any hesitation, I can say we would never have achieved what we did without Chad. His contribution to Pentad first and subsequently Society Consulting was paramount to our overall success and eventual acquisition. Timing was everything, and all his experience, skills, and knowledge helped propel the company forward and make everyone around him better.

In all honesty, Chad had a very tough job coming into our company, but he did his very best to navigate all that stood in his way.

First, he wasn't officially with us from the beginning, so breaking into the bond of John, Josiah, and myself was dauntingly challenging. It's not like we did anything specifically to hold him at an arm's distance. The situation just was what it was. I can only liken it to the replacements coming in to lead the 101st Airborne months after the initial company jumped into Normandy on D-Day. Chad was forced to learn how the three of us worked together, earn the respect of the existing employees, and effectively establish himself as our new CEO.

Second, Chad took care to not disrupt the culture we had firmly established. This required kid gloves and a delicate touch, balancing what made us a fun and exciting company, while upleveling the maturity and sophistication of our service offerings. This was not an easy task, and certainly a high-wire balancing act I wouldn't have wanted to take on. But he navigated the challenge deftly, carefully applying the correct pressure in the right places, and leaving much of the goodness alone to organically flourish.

Over time, Chad established himself as our CEO by formulating a mission, strategy, and vision that ultimately brought a new gear for us to operate within. He was the supercharger to our engine, the adrenaline shot to our pulse, a lightning bolt to our atmosphere. For all he has done, I will forever be grateful.

Chase

It wasn't until recently, perhaps only five or so years, that Chase Jarvis entered my life, and I can honestly say, I couldn't be more grateful to call him a friend. In such a short time, I've learned so much from him, found inspiration in his gospel around creativity and entrepreneurship, all of which was a major contributing factor to writing this book. In fact, Chase pulled the original Society Consulting story out of me during a nine-hour drive from Bandon Dunes, inspiring me to take the first step in putting it down on paper.

For those that don't know Chase, look him up. You'll thank me later as you quickly realize the genius in his multiple books he's authored, the professional photography, the quality of the content of his podcast, and overall talent as an entrepreneur and advocate for all things creative. He is someone everyone should follow.

I look forward to any time spent with him, be it on the golf course, or discussing politics over a nice bottle of red wine.

A Great Number of People

I hope it doesn't come across disingenuous or ungracious to give credit to everyone who, at one point or another, came into my life and positively contributed to where I am today. Nothing would be more appropriate than to name each person individually, tell the story of their role, and pay proper respects with sincere gratitude. But in the spirit of brevity, I'm lumping them all together as best I can.

First off, thank you to all The Job Mob, Pentad, and Society Consulting employees. Each and every one of you took a chance on us, trusting our mission and competency to provide you with professional challenges, a culture you could be proud of, and a livelihood for you and your families. Over the eight years we were in business, we hired over four hundred people, each of whom contributed to our success. Whether you were in finance, operations, sales, recruiting, or project delivery, your contributions were appreciated.

The Society executive team members need a special

shout-out. Not only did you each contribute to the success of the company, but you also provided exceptional leadership through thick and thin. Further, by being the leaders we could trust in running the day-to-day operations, you gave me and the other founders confidence to focus our efforts on creating a better company. So, let me express my thanks to Steve, Dennis, Sarah, Kristin, Frank, Ilya, Amanda, Charley, Felix, and Tanja.

Two writing coaches, Marcia Zina Mager and Jocelyn Carbonara, were instrumental in helping me navigate the many highs and lows of writing this book. They brought perspective to the table, along with detailed feedback on the various drafts, and over the past year, gave me the confidence required to put my story out there.

Two other professionals, George Stevens and Jenny Lisk, helped walk me through the complicated waters of cover design and publishing. Their respective knowledge of the industry helped propel this project over the goal line.

Although he is no longer with us, I must extend gratitude to my dog, Pepe. He came to work with me every single day and witnessed the evolution of the business. When we found our new office space post-acquisition, we specifically negotiated with the building managers to allow dogs. Pepe was a true confidant whose unconditional love was felt by everyone.

And most importantly, my loving and supportive wife, Sherry, deserves the medal of honor for being by my side for the past thirteen years. She is the inspiration behind many of my personal endeavors, including this book. One day, perhaps she will find the inspiration to tell her own story—something that is unquestionably more interesting than mine. Her hunger for living a healthy and adventurous life has inspired me to no end and has, without doubt, made me a better human being. I love her dearly and look forward to what the future holds for us.

Sherry has had a front-row seat to all the highs and lows of the business and has been my personal counsel since the beginning. So, maybe I did find my coach after all.

About the Author

PJ Ohashi is a retired (for the time being) entrepreneur, active investor, forever student of life, and travel adventure-seeker. Previously, he was a cofounder and senior vice president of revenue at Society Consulting, a data and analytics professional services firm, where he helped lead sales operations, marketing, and partnerships. PJ helped grow Society to multiple offices across the country and more than 250 employees before selling it to a global consulting firm.

PJ is a living paradox, embodying a confluence of conflicting ideologies associated with humanism, collectivism, individualism, and materialism. He doesn't identify first as Japanese American, yet his family crest and last name are tattooed on his arm. His love for gangster rap music clashes with his adoration for humanity. And PJ's life philosophy—described as *discomfort equating to positive growth*—is undermined by his habit of accepting complacency. This contradiction provides a constant struggle but also a purpose.

PJ and his wife, Sherry, split their time between living in the Pacific Northwest and Southern California and exploring foreign lands. You can usually find him having a complete meltdown on the golf course, enjoying family and friends, playing competitive pickleball, gushing over a bottle of cabernet sauvignon, or fine-tuning his culinary exploits. Connect with PJ to discuss business, engage in political and social discourse, or have a friendly debate on old-world versus new-world wines.

[in] linkedin.com/in/pjohashi

Milton Keynes UK
Ingram Content Group UK Ltd.
UKHW041132151024
449742UK00016B/150/J